Fidel's Ethics of Violence

Fidel's Ethics of Violence

The Moral Dimension of the Political Thought of Fidel Castro

DAYAN JAYATILLEKA

Pluto Press

LONDON • ANN ARBOR, MI

First published 2007 by Pluto Press
345 Archway Road, London N6 5AA
and 839 Greene Street, Ann Arbor, MI 48106

www.plutobooks.com

Copyright © Dayan Jayatilleka 2007

The right of Dayan Jayatilleka to be identified as the author of this work has been
asserted by him in accordance with the Copyright, Designs and Patents Act 1988.

British Library Cataloguing in Publication Data
A catalogue record for this book is available from the British Library

Hardback
ISBN-13   978 0 7453 2697 9
ISBN-10   0 7453 2697 8

Paperback
ISBN-13   978 0 7453 2696 2
ISBN-10   0 7453 2696 X

Library of Congress Cataloging in Publication Data applied for

10   9   8   7   6   5   4   3   2   1

Designed and produced for Pluto Press by
Chase Publishing Services Ltd, Fortescue, Sidmouth, EX10 9QG, England
Typeset from disk by Stanford DTP Services, Northampton, England
Printed and bound in the European Union by
CPI Antony Rowe, Chippenham and Eastbourne, England

Contents

This book is dedicated to the memory of my parents, Mervyn and Lakshmi de Silva. Journalist, editor and broadcaster, Mervyn wrote and talked of Fidel and Che, introducing them into my life. He was at Che's press conference in Colombo in 1959 and took me, still a primary schoolboy, for lunch at the Harbour room of Colombo's Hotel Taprobane, with Armando Bayo, Cuba's ambassador to Ceylon, 1960–65. Bayo was the son of the legendary General Alberto Bayo, veteran of the Spanish Civil War, who trained Fidel, Che, Raul and the Granma expeditionaries in Mexico. While he turned fifty my father witnessed Fidel Castro taking over the chairmanship of the Non-Aligned Movement at the sixth summit in Havana in 1979 and featured Fidel on the cover of his magazine, the *Lanka Guardian*, that month. After his death in 1999 I discovered that Mervyn still had in an old briefcase the personalised invitation to the conference, signed Fidel Castro Ruz.

Acknowledgments

My warm thanks to Roger van Zwanenberg, Chairman and Commissioning Editor of Pluto Press, who responded positively and promptly to my proposal for this book.

I would also like to thank Professor John Kane of the Department of Politics and Public Policy of Griffith University, Brisbane, for his encouragement, critique and constructive suggestions, and Dr Jeffrey Minson, formerly of the Department of Arts, Media and Culture of Griffith University and presently with the University of California-San Diego, for his continuous engagement and close critical scrutiny. Back in Colombo, Sri Lanka, Professor Nira Wickramasingha and Ms T Gunasekara read through an initial (proto) draft and made revisions.

Without the dedication, support, effort and active contribution of my wife, Sanja de Silva Jayatilleka, an impassioned extended polemical essay may never have made it into this book. She helped give it structure and shape, transforming it qualitatively, just as she did my life.

Preface

A little over half a century ago, a brilliant, passionate, Jesuit-educated young lawyer-politician led a group of rebels on an attack on the Moncada army garrison in the Oriente province in Cuba. The aim was to seize the weapons, distribute them and trigger an uprising in the province, which would then become generalised throughout the country. The goal was to topple the military junta of Batista, which was supported by the United States.

The attack failed, the rebels were arrested, tortured, murdered. Thanks to luck, the integrity of a military officer and the intervention of an archbishop, a few survived. That should have been the end of the story, like that of so many rebellions in Latin America. Yet it was not. Brought to trial in what was presumed to be an open-and-shut case, the young rebel leader conducted his own defence and made an oration that ranks in the annals of the finest emancipation literature in human history.

Itemising and denouncing the unjust structures of his society, drawing on the literature of human freedom and injustice (including the Bible), and unfailingly dignified and fair to his judges, he concluded with a phrase that has become part of the consciousness of modern humankind: 'Condemn me if you must. History will absolve me!'

It is by his deportment in defeat and by turning a material defeat and disaster into a moral victory that Fidel Castro entered History. Revolutionary Cuba was born six years later. Cuba has remained revolutionary, anti-imperialist and socialist despite the longest-running economic embargo in known history, and despite the collapse of its ally, the Soviet Union, more than a decade and a half ago. It has remained defiant despite being located on the doorstep of the mightiest power the world has ever known, and despite the active hostility of that power. The survival of Revolutionary Cuba issues from the specificity of Cuban socialism   and that specificity derives not only from the history and culture of the Cuban people, but also from the specific theory and practice of Fidel Castro.

The global scenario today is polarised between the sole superpower and terrorism of Islamic provenance. Might there not be, however, a third way of being as represented by Fidel Castro? The most visible resistance to unipolar hegemony and interventionism by the US (and/or Israel) tends to take the form of terrorism and suicide bombing. This book argues that Castro provides an alternative ethic of resistance and rebellion, one in which violence in the cause of liberation consciously eschews the targeting of non-combatants.

The present global polarisation is commonly represented as the struggle of the forces of anti-modernity and parochialism against those of modernity and reason. There is a need for an ideal and ideology of resistance and rebellion, which springs from the wellsprings of modernity and universalism but stands for an alternative modernity. Castro's ethic, I suggest, is such an ideology and he constitutes such an example of modernity, reason and militancy, not in the interests of the status quo but of progressive change. The study teases out the values that Castro stands for, thereby setting forth an alternative way of being for the rebel, including the violent rebel. However, Castro's ideas and example are relevant not only for rebels. The *Fidelista* ethic of violence, in which the moral high ground is permanently retained, is of relevance both to resistance/liberation movements and to states. It is hoped that the study would contribute to the setting out of a moral and ethical third way and sketch the contours of a different kind of hero: modernist, rational, internationalist; fighting full-scale wars when necessary, but never resorting to targeting of non-combatants, physical torture and execution of captives.

The study is marked with what may appear as a surfeit of quotation and quotations of excessive length. This, however, is necessitated by its character. Firstly, it is an inquiry into Fidel Castro's political thought, and therefore cannot but rest upon his words. Secondly, it makes a radical and original claim about his thought and strategy, and therefore seeks to prove that contention through extensive recourse to his words. By drawing directly upon his words I attempt to demonstrate that these ideas were not occasional, fleeting references and that the themes in question were crucial to his ideology. Apart from those quotes from Castro, secondary sources are also given, sometimes at some length, in order to set evaluations of his political and military practice against his ideas and to assess whether or not there has been a unity of theory and practice.

A rebel asked Castro what should be done with the prisoners, and Fidel replied, 'Treat them humanely; don't insult them. And remember that the life of an unarmed man must be sacred for you.'

Tad Szulc, *Fidel: A Critical Portrait*, p. 256

'We must have our feet solidly on the ground, without ever sacrificing the greatest reality of principles.' – Fidel Castro

Tad Szulc, *Fidel: A Critical Portrait*, p. 318

Part I
Background

Introduction

'Suddenly Latin America has grabbed the world's attention', opines *The Economist* (London), in its issue of 20 May 2006, behind a cover story entitled *The Battle for Latin America's Soul*. According to *Newsweek*, the central symbol in the drama of a resurgent Latin America is Fidel Castro: 'Fidel has more fans in the region than he's had in years... The symbol that has benefited most from the new perspective is ... the left's reigning lion in winter, Fidel Castro... Castro has experienced a remarkable resurgence.'[1] Jorge Castaneda, former Foreign Minister of Mexico and critic of Fidel Castro, points out that the Latin American left did not undergo the same process of decomposition and conversion to (British) New Labour-ism that the European left did, for two reasons: 'the collapse of the Soviet Union did not bring about the collapse of its Latin American equivalent, Cuba' and 'the left's close ties to and emotional dependency on Fidel Castro'.[2] The *Chicago Tribune* in a story on 8 August 2006 confirms that 'The guidance and support of Cuba's Fidel Castro and Venezuela's Hugo Chavez have helped the political left make a remarkable resurgence in Latin America.'[3]

Fidel Castro was an influential presence in the defining struggles and themes of the twentieth century – capitalism and socialism, imperialism and national liberation, reform and revolution – a presence that will be shown to cast an illuminating retrospective light on these struggles and themes, and that age. He has also shaped the landscape of the present. The Cuban leader's 80th birthday, his renewed significance in Latin America, and his illness, perhaps presaging the passing of his era, render relevant a re-evaluation of *Fidelismo*.

Fidel Castro is listed in *The Routledge Dictionary of Twentieth Century Political Thinkers*, the editors of which define those included as 'important thinkers from the early years of the century to the contemporary period... [whose] ideas have influenced political thought and activity in the twentieth century'.[4]

Although it straddles the intersection of political thought and political theory, the present study is primarily located in the domain of the history of ideas, of political ideas and thought, and must be evaluated as such. While it may prove pertinent to issues of political

3

philosophy, it does not belong in that domain. Leo Strauss delineates the realm of political thought thus:

> By political thought we understand the reflection on, or the exposition of, political ideas... All political philosophy is political thought but not all political thought is political philosophy.[5]

This is not a study of the totality and evolution of Fidel Castro's political thought. It does not purport to be his intellectual biography. It is a study of the moral and ethical dimension of the political thought of Castro, with an ethic of violence located at its vital centre. As such it focuses on two ideas, the one within the other. It explores the moral and ethical aspect of Fidel Castro's political thought and strategy, and examines as a crucial constituent component of that moral and ethical aspect Castro's idea of the correct and incorrect use of violence. More generally, it hopes to shed light on the issue of the good and bad use of violence, using as prism and principal illustrative case, the political, strategic and diplomatic thought and practice of Fidel Castro, both as revolutionary insurgent and leader of a state, as rebel and ruler.

The study undertaken here argues that Fidel Castro, near-universally regarded as a charismatic leader, was also one who made a contribution to Marxism and political thought in general, and that his main contribution to revolutionary Marxism was the introduction of an explicitly moral and ethical dimension. This in turn has enabled him to occupy the moral high ground (specifically in relation to his main foe, the USA) and has helped him survive the collapse of communism with no diminution of his stature and prestige. The study also suggests that the moral and ethical dimension issues from a combination of Marxism and Christianity.

Further, I attempt to show that the Castro doctrine of armed struggle is based upon the conscious cultivation of a moral asymmetry between the enemy and the liberation fighter, a moral superiority that is cultivated not by abstinence from violence as in the case of Gandhi, nor by the limited and tactical use of violence as in the case of Mandela, but by conscious restraint in conduct, methods and targeting within the practice of armed rebellion, liberation war and revolution. Though it does not derive from the corpus of just war theory, Castro's is a variant of just war thinking, one that applies to a field of violent political action wider than that of (conventional) war. For veteran Cuban revolutionary Ulises Estrada, a key actor in Cuba's internationalist missions in Latin America and Africa and an

Kain,
Marx &
Ethics,
1988,
The Transc
endence of
Morality'
p.176

important organiser of Che Guevara's Bolivian expedition, Cuba's 'declaration was like a new call to just war against colonial and imperialist domination in Latin America and the Caribbean'.[6] Castro's thinking is governed by and seeks to achieve a moral superiority that does not rest on culturally specific and circumscribed notions (such as those that inform Islamic militants) or claims of self-evident (actually, self-referential) systemic superiority, but on universal values of humanitarian conduct in warfare.

The study suggests that Fidel Castro's ideological discourse and practice represents a synthesis of phenomena regarded as antithetical. In an essay on Machiavelli,[7] Sir Isaiah Berlin argued that Machiavelli's great merit was in making explicit that there were two distinct paradigms, that of Christianity and that of Rome; that of morality and theology on the one hand, and that of politics on the other. One was not intrinsically superior to the other and each was valid within its own force field. However, the two were separate, incompatible, and if one wished to succeed in the political domain one had to abandon the theological–ethical outlook. The political practice and relative success of Fidel Castro shows that the distinction is not necessarily a Great Wall, and that a synthesis is possible. Castro effected such a synthesis. While he was a Savonarola in his moral denunciations, exhortations and efforts at reform, he was no 'prophet unarmed' as was Savonarola, Machiavelli's principal illustration of the dangers of being such. He combined Savonarola's moral idealism with the realism that Machiavelli commended to the new prince.

It could equally be said that Castro combined the grasp of power and the military virtuosity that Machiavelli urged upon a new prince in a new principality with the moral virtues of the classical Roman humanists such as Cicero and Seneca, whose morality Machiavelli had rejected and was regarded by the Realist tradition as having superseded. Cicero argued that while there may appear to be ethical decisions that are inexpedient and expedient decisions that are unethical, this dichotomy is illusory, for in the last instance only that which is moral and ethical, only that which is virtuous, proves truly in consonance with expediency.[8] Machiavelli argued the contrary, either brushing aside the notion of a morality higher than expediency or stating that the highest value should be that which is expedient for reasons of state and the considerations of power; he went on to provide examples of political disasters wreaked by an excess of moral scruple. However, Castro was far closer in his discourse to Cicero and the classical Roman humanist–moralists, and to Renaissance notions of *virtu* recommended to Christian princes by some of Machiavelli's contemporaries than to much of Machiavelli's 'new morality'. Castro retained the tough-mindedness of Machiavelli and did not permit an excess of scruple or procrastination to erode his and the revolution's grasp of power – errors that cost progressive leaders from Arbenz through Lumumba, Nkrumah and Sukarno to Salvador Allende, the Sandinistas (in 1990) and Mikhail Gorbachev their power. Thus he forged a synthesis between Machiavelli's Realism and classical Roman moral humanism.[9]

Leo Strauss also identified an antithesis in values, pertinent to political philosophy. For him, the contending paradigms were Athens and Jerusalem; reason and prophetic revelation, as it were. Though each made valid claims, one could not adhere to both models – tragically, modern man had to choose. The present study of Fidel Castro suggests that such tragic choice is not inevitable in that he represented a synthesis of Reason and the denunciatory moral and ethical stance of the Old Testament prophets.[10]

To change the historical metaphor to that of the French Revolution, Castro was a Jacobin, not a Girondin, and was an avowed admirer of Robespierre, but far more sparing and surgical in his use of violent measures in general and capital punishment in particular.

The search for a synthesis of types, representing values, was central to the philosophy of Nietzsche. His celebration of the Homeric hero, his ambivalence towards Socrates, his discovery of the Dionysian and the dualism of Apollonian and Dionysian, his assertion of a synthesis between the Apollonian and Dionysian as the source of Greek dramatic achievement, and his final call, in *The Will to Power*, for 'a Caesar with the soul of Christ', illustrate this fevered search for synthesis of types and values in the creation of a new mentality and mode of being.[11]

While the political thought of Marxists, revolutionaries and Third World political figures have been amply studied in their own right, hitherto they have not been considered as having contributed to political theory and the philosophy of politics in general. That has been unconsciously regarded the preserve of mainstream, that is, liberal to conservative, white, First World figures. This exclusion is the result of a paradoxical combination: prejudice on the part of the privileged, the establishment or ruling elites, and the claim of radical difference, demarcation, discontinuity and departure on the part of revolutionaries and socialists. Now however, in the twenty-first century and after the collapse of the socialist system, the matter can be viewed in a more distant and dispassionate manner, and the contributions, if any, to political theory as such of these rebels can be evaluated. It is the claim of this study that Fidel Castro, a revolutionary, Marxist and Third World political figure, has made a contribution to the understanding of one of the larger problems of politics, one that properly belongs in the province of political theory and philosophy: the question of violence, political power and morality.

EXAMINING THE EXCEPTION

'Cuba: Exception or Vanguard?' was the title of an essay by Che Guevara.[12] It argued against the notion of a Cuban uniqueness, and posited instead the thesis that despite the important specificities of the Cuban experience (not least the personality of its leader) it would be the vanguard of a revolutionary process throughout Latin America. For decades, this appeared a probability or at least a possibility, as guerrilla movements sprang up throughout the continent. However, in cooler retrospect at the beginning of a new century and millennium, it is clear that the Cuban Revolution was indeed an exception.

It is so in two dimensions, distinct but interlinked. It is an exception in that it has survived the downfall of socialism as a global challenger to capitalism. It has survived despite the retrenchment of the Marxist challenge (though not the Marxist critique) as theory and movement to capitalism. It has done so while avoiding the Scylla and Charybdis to which communist regimes have fallen victim: though it has embarked on an economic 'opening' Cuba has not converted to capitalism in its economic doctrine, internal model and ethos, as have China and Vietnam. Nor has it gone into deep involution like North Korea. It retains its socialist identity and spirit, sees itself as an alternative to capitalism and as superior to it, and is proudly assertive in international affairs.

The second dimension of Cuba's exceptionality is its performance as a revolution and a revolutionary state. It has never wittingly engaged in lethal violence against unarmed civilians in its own country or in its extensive military involvements beyond its shores. It has not engaged in internal executions without due process, murders within its own ranks. It has not killed ideological or political competitors and rivals within the anti-systemic space. It alone is an example of a revolution that had *a Jacobin phase or character but did not practise a*

Great Terror. 'Encirclement' is the standard justification for paranoid violence within and by revolutions. Even while it practised and advocated armed revolution, even as it faced a tight encirclement (the longest-recorded embargo in history) and destabilisation plots by the US, the Cubans adhered to certain parameters in their use of armed violence, on their soil, in their recommendations to other movements and in their numerous 'internationalist missions' in far corners of the world.

This morality and ethic of the Cuban Revolution – instilled by Fidel Castro and a motif of his thinking – mark it out as exceptional, which may indeed explain at least in part its survival beyond the collapse of global socialism. In the history of communist rule it is arguably the only case of sustained moral and ethical hegemony, fleetingly commented upon and commended by Antonio Gramsci.

Why study this exception? Carl Schmitt cites Soren Kierkegaard's identification of the methodological importance, indeed imperative, of precisely *the exception*:

> The exception explains the general and itself. And if one wants to study the general correctly, one only needs to look around for a true exception. It reveals everything more clearly than does the general. Endless talk about the general becomes boring; there are exceptions. If they cannot be explained, the general cannot also be explained. The difficulty is usually not noticed because the general is not thought about with passion but with a comfortable superficiality. The exception, on the other hand, thinks the general with intense passion.[13]

Castro is the exception in the history of socialism, in liberation struggles and more generally in the practice of political violence. Applying the methodological point made by Kierkegaard and Schmitt, the study of Castro's ideas and practice helps one understand – and is perhaps the best way to understand – the socialist experience of the last century, the problem of violence and liberation, and the ethics of violence in politics.

THE ETHICAL VACUUM IN CASTRO STUDIES

The existing literature on Fidel Castro falls into two or three categories: biographies and histories or international relations studies of the Cuban Revolution and its policies. Despite the often excellent quality of many of those studies, hardly any pertain to his political thought and philosophy. Sheldon B. Liss has the only book-length study of the social and political thought of Fidel Castro, and that too, as its title reveals, conflates the social with the political, and is thereby unable to grasp the specificity of his political thought, with its distinctive ethics.[14] The other study is a pamphlet by Marta Harnecker and pertains to Castro's strategy.[15] Theodore Draper's study of 'Castroism'[16] analyses it not as political idea but as a political and economic system, while Loree Wilkerson's monograph researches the ideology of the Cuban Revolution and Fidel's political programme as it evolved in the first three years in power.[17]

A significant exception to these limitations is Donald E. Rice's book on a single important aspect of the discourse of Castro, namely, the latter's recourse to Jose Marti as an authorising and legitimating figure. This work, which takes Castro's rhetoric as worthy of analytical research and relies on his speeches and interviews as raw material, acts as something of a precursor of the present study.[18]

What seems to me to be singularly missing from the existing literature's treatment of the Cuban revolutionary process is any investigation of the possibility that so dogged a survival and exceptional a performance as Castro's might be informed by a body of general ideas that it might be feasible to abstract from his achievement in political leadership. The assumption seems to be that Castro's personal moral contribution to Castroism is adequately captured by conventional references to his charismatic personality. Nor, *ipso facto*, does the literature seek to identify what distinguishes Castro's moral and political thought from the better-known versions of Marxism-Leninism.

These omissions are perhaps not surprising. Though Fidel Castro was the undisputed leader of the Cuban Revolution, he never projected his leadership as residing in the realm of theory and ideology. This was in contrast to the examples of Lenin and Mao. The communist tradition, echoing that of the Church, has always sought to frame its choices and leaders in clear doctrinal terms. The leaders of the Cuban Revolution chose to do otherwise, partly to avoid a cult of the personality, partly to maintain a high degree of strategic and tactical flexibility and evolve their own ideological synthesis. As a consequence, Che Guevara's famous theorisation of the Cuban Revolution[19] and of Castro's leadership notwithstanding, there has been no sustained conceptualisation of his political ideas. This is the lacuna in studies of the specificity of the Cuban revolutionary struggle that this book will attempt to address.

Having said that, this study of Castro's moral dimension is not without precursors. Che's characterisation of Castro's leadership qualities bears repetition in this study since it is a comprehensive yet compressed account of Castro as political and moral personality by a close colleague and observer known for his intellectual brilliance and sharpness of comment, for example:

Various features of his life and character make him stand out far above his compañeros and followers. Fidel is a person of such tremendous personality that he would attain leadership in whatever movement he participated ... added to which are his personal gifts of audacity, strength, courage, and an extraordinary determination always to discern the will of the people – his ability to assimilate knowledge and experience in order to understand a situation in its entirety without losing sight of the details, his unbounded faith in the future, and the breadth of his vision to foresee events and anticipate them in action, always seeing farther and more accurately than his compañeros ... his capacity to unite, resisting the divisions that weaken; ... his faith in the future and with his capacity to foresee it, Fidel Castro has done more than anyone else in Cuba to create from nothing the present formidable apparatus of the Cuban Revolution.[20]

Che's essay appeared while Castro's ideas were still in evolution, and in any event his own relationship with Fidel as a peer would not have permitted him to subject Fidel's thought to systematic analysis.

Che's identification of the distinctive contribution of the Cuban Revolution blazed the trail for Regis Debray's subsequent theorisation of 'Fidelismo' or 'Castroism' in his essays 'Castroism: The Long March in Latin America' (in *Strategy for Revolution*) and 'Revolution in the Revolution?'[21] According to Che's conceptualisation, the essential lessons and distinctive contribution of the Cuban Revolution were that a popular army, essentially a guerrilla force, could win a military victory over a conventional army; it was not necessary to wait for all the conditions to mature to initiate guerrilla war – the launch of the armed struggle in the presence of a sufficient minimum of factors could itself create those conditions; the countryside is the main arena of battle. Regis Debray focused on one additional set of ideas as the acme of *Fidelismo*: the negation of the notion of a Marxist-Leninist political party (essentially urban-based) that gives leadership to the guerrilla army (essentially rural-based); the abolition of the distinction between the party and the army; the merger of the two in a unitary politico-military vanguard organisation, and the renunciation of the idea of a prolonged period of peaceful preparation and mass work before the outbreak of guerrilla action. Thus Castro's contribution was seen to be located in the realm of the theory and practice of guerrilla war and more generally, the military-strategic and organisational, that is, in *the realm of the problems of armed revolutionary struggle*.

Where scholars have focused on the Cuban Revolution's stress on moral over material incentives, the main stress has been on the writings and praxis of Che Guevara. Despite these references to the moral factor, this latter interpretation tended to the reduction of the specific contribution of the Cuban Revolution to *the realm of the socio-economic*. These twin displacements, then, to the *military* and *socio-economic* spheres, completely overlooked the essentially political contribution of what was an essentially political process – a revolution – and by an essentially political leader, Castro. The focus on 'model' – either or both military and socio-economic (moral over material incentives) – obscured the contribution of leadership in the realm of political ideas and thought.

There were two exceptions from within the Cuban leadership. A small but significant one was the identification, albeit undeveloped, by Che Guevara in a little-known essay penned in the aftermath of the Cuban missile crisis, that the most important impact of the Cuban Revolution was in the moral dimension:

Its [Cuba's] increased importance now is due not only to its opening a door to America. The force of its strategic military and political position, the power of its moral influence, the 'moral projectiles' are weapons of such demoralizing strength that *this element alone has become the most important in determining the value of Cuba*.[22] (My italics)

The second exception of seminal importance is a reference by the late Armando Hart, a member of the July 26th Movement and the generation that made the revolution, Cuba's Minister of Culture and a reputed intellectual and Marxist theoretician. His suggestive identification of what he terms 'the ethical or moral plane', 'the ethical-moral note' and the 'strategic and moral level' was made in the concrete context of Castro's remarks on Christianity in the dialogue with Brazilian cleric Frei Betto but has a broader validity.

In his preface to the book *Fidel on Religion*, Hart writes (with, some might argue, a degree of exaggeration) of the 'two most important historic wellsprings of man's thinking and emotions – Christianity and Marxism'. He comments on Fidel's ideas as expressed in the volume and underscores the ethical–moral aspect:

This isn't however a unity conceived of only on the plane of a tactic of struggle. It isn't just a happenstance or a political alliance. It is of course by definition, but the tie that is established here on the ethical or moral plane concerning man's role – whether he be Christian or communist – in defence of the poor has the nature of a lasting, permanent, strategic alliance. It is a proposition with a solid moral, political and social basis. This, in itself, is a tremendous achievement in the history of human thought. The ethical-moral note appears in these lines.... Thus a deep exchange of ideas – not only at the tactical and political but also at the strategic and moral level – has been initiated.[23]

The present study argues that the Cuban synthesis brings together the moral-ethical element, humanism, dialogue with Christianity and other religions as sources of the moral-ethical, socialism and a militant commitment to anti-imperialism and rebellion. Castro cuts across the usual divide within socialist theory and practice – and indeed political theory and practice as such – between 'hard' and 'soft', 'open' and 'closed', moderate and militant, realist and idealist.

The study further argues that over the long duration, Castro's most abiding and distinctive idea has not been in military, organisational or socio-economic realms, but rather in that of political thought, addressing the core problems of morality, ethics, power and violence. The political thought of Fidel Castro grapples with the crucial problem of means and ends and their proportionality.

1
The Ethics of Violence

This chapter introduces the question of violence and pacifism as modes of resolving conflict; criticises that dichotomy; and suggests a third way or synthesis, namely, *the correct use of violence*. It charts the limits of relevance of 'really existing' just war theory. It discusses the lacunae in radical and Marxian thought. It locates Fidel Castro's ideas on violence against the backdrop of the perspectives on violence both in just war theory and the discourse of armed rebellion, and suggests that the gaps in these traditions are filled by Castro. It concludes with reference to the debate between Albert Camus and Jean-Paul Sartre as a discussion relevant and proximate to an evaluation of Castro's specific contribution.

THE QUESTION OF VIOLENCE

One of humanity's oldest-recorded political thinkers, Kautilya (also known as Chanakya) unambiguously defined in the *Arthashastra* the central problem of philosophy as the good and bad use of force: 'One should study philosophy because… above all it teaches one the distinction between good and bad use of force.'[1]

There are two axes of demarcation within political practice involving resistance, rebellion or rulership: one between violent and non-violent perspectives of struggle, and the other between differing perspectives of violent struggle. In philosophical terms the division is tripartite: between those who say violence is wrong, those who say it is right if it serves a just cause or end, and those who believe that while a just cause and end are necessary conditions, the means adopted too must be ethical.

As long as there is a perception of injustice and oppression, there is the likelihood (some would argue, possibility) of its antipode: resistance, rebellion, revolt. But what will be the spirit of such rebellion, the sensibility of the rebels and revolutionists? In a demarcation that translates into the same as that set out here, Gail M. Presbey, a Fanon scholar, argues that there are three main perspectives on violence, exemplified by Gandhi, Fanon and Mandela. Gandhi was opposed to violence, Fanon stood for the liberating violence of the oppressed, while Mandela coupled non-violence with the limited use of violence.[2] However, while Mandela may be presented as treading the middle path, in the study undertaken here it is Castro who is identified as effecting the synthesis between the contradictory perspectives of the *non*-use and the *unlimited* use of violence in the cause of resistance and emancipation.

The argument underlying the first perspective, that of pacifism/ Gandhianism, is fairly simple, which does not mean it is invalid. It is that violent means cannot but entail moral corruption, and that the risk, both spiritual and strategic, outweighs the possible gains. Violence is morally wrong because the taking of life is wrong and would corrupt the soul while brutalising society. It is also strategically unwise because it may set off an avalanche of violent repression that would either bury the struggle or necessitate an escalation of counter-violence, triggering an endless 'inflationary' spiral. The non-violent option is also strategic: the calculus is that the tangible material and often overwhelming superiority of the oppressor in weaponry and wealth cannot be challenged by those very means and on that very terrain, but can be matched and defeated only by moral means, which by definition have to be the antithesis of the oppressor's chosen means. In this reckoning there is an explicit or implicit identification of the moral and the non-violent. A second consideration is that victory gained by violent liberation struggle would be Pyrrhic because the society and economy inherited by the victorious struggle would have been devastated through violence. Mandela is the most prominent advocate of this neo-Gandhian variant.[3]

The other line of demarcation runs through a more complex, contested terrain of perspectives. These perspectives fall within an overall outlook that may or may not *advocate* the use of violence, but accepts the use of violence as a legitimate or inevitable (and in that sense legitimate) means of struggle. This outlook and approach accepts, in the words of anti-fascist martyr and Protestant theologian Dietrich Bonhoeffer, the burden of *guilt* inherent in that choice.[4]

Within liberation literature, only Mao Ze Dong touched upon these themes. In his 'Rules of Discipline and Points of Attention for the Peoples Liberation Army',[5] he set out a protocol that included the non-harming of prisoners. In his 'On the Correct Handling of Contradictions Among the People',[6] written in 1957 as a revaluation of Stalin, he elaborated his distinction between antagonistic and non-antagonistic contradictions, where he had classified as antagonistic those contradictions that involved irreconcilable conflicts of interests and thus could not but be resolved by violence, and as non-antagonistic those that did not and therefore could and should be resolved non-violently. In this essay, Mao argued that violence should be deployed against the enemy and enemy classes but not against competitors, that is, members of the Communist party or social classes including the 'national bourgeoisie' that formed 'the people'. Stalin, he said, made the cardinal error of confusing these categories and deploying violence to resolve non-antagonistic contradictions. Mao's ideas on the right and wrong use of violence were never a recurrent theme or major motif of his thought, unlike that of Castro. Its credibility was vitiated by Mao's resort to or permitting of precisely the categories of violence he deplored during the Cultural Revolution. Castro would, for his part and by contrast, observe these distinctions, though there is no evidence that his ideas and practice derived from a reading of Mao.

JUST WAR THEORY – THE LIMITS OF RELEVANCE

The issue of the right and wrong use of violence is central to the doctrine of 'just war' of Saints Ambrose, Augustine and Aquinas. However, this doctrine and its developments deal mainly with the deployment of violence by existing powers, religious establishments and states. The doctrine does not primarily pertain to the resort to war by non-state/anti-state forces or by explicitly anti-status quo-ist states.[7] The just war tradition is preoccupied with the right use of violence by established states, by statecraft, as James Turner Johnson emphasises.[8] Indeed, one of the three principal criteria of a just war was that it should be waged by the rightful authority, the sovereign, and one of the criteria of a just outcome was stability.[9]

From its inception, the *problematique* or interrelated set of concerns of this tradition was Western, in the sense of the global North or First World, and status quo-ist. Even in its modern mutations at the hands of Michael Walzer and Michael Ignatieff, and notwithstanding tangential treatment of the conduct of insurgent movements by these two writers, just war discourse not only remains concerned with the dilemmas, ethical and policy, of liberal democratic Western states and publics, but is written from that worldview and perspective. The treatment of guerrilla movements is almost a detour.[10] Extensive as the literature on the ethics of violence is, particularly the corpus of writing on just war, there is little evidence, if any, that it has had an impact on those leaders who actually wage war or decide to do so. This may be because such leaders tend to be influenced by the writings of, or about, others who have been actors in history, while most of the writers on the ethics of violence/just war have not actually confronted the dilemmas involved in the use or non-use of violence, and are therefore seen to have little to offer. This attitude is most pronounced among leaders of anti-state/anti-establishment struggles, coming as they do from a tradition that is dismissive of purely academic contemplation and privileges practice instead. Of the modern writers, two who, by contrast, have had authentic experience with violent political practice, and whose writings are reflections arising from that lived experience, are Bonhoeffer and Camus.

Just war theory had little in common with and no attraction for, and therefore no possibility of influencing the thinking and conduct of armed insurgents, who were left with the task of evolving such doctrines out of their own experience. Most did not. Given the remoteness of just war theory from the doctrines and practice of rebels and revolutionaries, and the lack of evidence of any influence of the former upon the latter, the present study of Fidel Castro does not engage with this body of work. That is not the universe from which Castro or this study comes, and it is not the backdrop against which it must be located.

That backdrop is the intersection of Marxism and the anti-imperialist rebellions of the global South. In his landmark text 'The Second Declaration of Havana', Castro identifies and demarcates the common historical experience within which his thinking was formed and must be contextualised:

What is Cuba's history but that of Latin America? What is the history of Latin America but the history of Asia, Africa, and Oceania? And what is the history of all these peoples but the history of the cruellest exploitation of the world by imperialism?[11]

Jon P. Gunnemann confirms the different origins and mental universes of just war theory and Marxian radicalism respectively, arguing that they refer to two different types of revolution. The former posits a pre-existing moral community, which the revolution is striving to restore by overthrowing the authority that undermined that community by usurping power. The latter is a revolution that makes no such assumption, bases itself on social contradictions and strives to establish a just order of a new type. Just war theory assumes a moral community and a social contract, while Marxism assumes a society riven with sharp contradictions and strives to generate radical transformation, not restoration.

It would seem that the obvious starting point for an inquiry into the ethics of revolution would therefore be this tradition of natural law and the just war. But a reading of the literature on revolution and particularly the literature of the Marxist tradition (which is the revolutionary literature of the modern world) shows that any attempt to apply the categories of the just war tradition would involve a fundamental distortion of what the Marxists mean by revolution. Natural law assumes a fundamental structure to the world and human society, an overarching 'ideal' human community... In contrast the Marxist tradition makes no claim for the prior existence of a moral community, nor does it justify the revolutionary impulse with an appeal to an immutable moral structure. This reflects not merely a different moral viewpoint but also a very different conception of what revolution achieves. In effect, the Marxist maintains that a revolution brings into being a mode of human existence that has no precedent. The revolution is not for the purpose restoring justice in the face of a contemptible violation of God's law, but rather to change fundamentally the relations people have with each other.[12]

Among modern political leaders, Mao was the most identified with the theme of violence, in that revolutionary violence bulked large in his doctrine 'all political power flows from the barrel of a gun'. Castro, however, is quite distinctive among modern political practitioners for his repeated reference to the right and wrong use of violence, as well as his combination of the practice and justification of anti-establishment armed violence with a doctrine of its right and wrong use. His ideas on the subject are therefore more likely to have an influence on the minds and policies of contemporary and future leaders and cadres of armed rebellions/resistance movements.

While just war theory contributed little or nothing to Castro, Castro may have something to contribute to just war theory and tradition. Indeed, in an atypical reference to insurgent movements, Walzer mentions the treatment of prisoners by Castro's forces (an episode sourced in an article in the *US Marine Corps Gazette*, and significantly entitled 'How Castro Won'). Walzer cites Mao's rules of attention as regards the treatment of prisoners, but qualifies it with another quote from Mao, which seems to justify the disposal of prisoners if the liberation army could not cope with them. Castro's rebel army is the sole insurgent movement cited by Walzer, which goes uncriticised. Yet Walzer does not develop this into a line of inquiry.[13] It is fair to say that Castro was the only leader of an armed revolutionary movement and state to stress the distinctions between the right and wrong use of violence. He was the only practitioner to evolve something akin to a just war theory within the anti-establishment space, or to independently apply what amounted to just war theory. In doing so he has arguably made a contribution to just war theory by being the only one outside the Western liberal tradition to grapple with its concerns. Yet, insofar as the established canon of just war theory was not an explicit source of inspiration or reference in his thinking and actions, it lies outside the field of this present inquiry.

The conceptual situation identified in this chapter, in which just war theory has not recognised and encompassed anti-systemic movements, and anti-systemic movements have not developed a just war theory, leads to an undifferentiated response on the part of both states and movements.

Today the two central phenomena are on the one hand that of the sole superpower, the USA, and on the other, that of terrorism. The US tends to view all armed resistance against its policies, interests and allies as terrorist and responds to it as such, while resistance movements consider terrorism as a legitimate and in some cases the only possible form of asymmetric warfare.

How then does Kautilya's idea of the correct and incorrect use of force apply to armed anti-systemic leaderships/movements, and how is it applied (consciously or not) by such leaderships? Is it possible to differentiate between the correct and incorrect use of violence by armed movements, revolutionary and national liberation, in the post-war period and more especially the period of contemporary history in the global South (the so-called Third World or Tricontinental areas)?

This study deploys a fourfold identification of 'the bad use' of violence: (a) terrorism, understood as the deliberate targeting of unarmed, non-combatant civilians; (b) the torture and arbitrary execution of prisoners; (c) internal killings, that is, executions within the organisation; and (d) the use of lethal violence against political competitors within the broad anti-systemic movement/space. The correct use of violence is understood to be the avoidance of these target categories within the theory and practice of violence, not necessarily limiting the use of violence to a means of secondary importance, as a tactic (as did Mandela).[14] Castro opted for sustained organised armed violence, war, as a politico-military strategy for the achievement of the cause and objectives he represented.

The study will argue that Castro illustrates the correct or good use of violence, which in turn leads to the accretion of moral and ethical hegemony in the Gramscian sense:

Here we are dealing with a subaltern group, which is prevented by this theory from ever becoming dominant, or from developing beyond the economic-corporate stage and rising to the phase of ethical-political hegemony in civil society, and of domination in the State. ... Though hegemony is ethical-political, it must also be economic, must necessarily be based on the decisive function exercised by the leading group in the decisive nucleus of economic activity. ... An analysis of the balance of forces – at all levels – can only culminate in the sphere of hegemony and ethico-political relations. [1933–34; first version, 1930–32][15]

Castro shows that one may arrive at what Nietzsche termed, in *Beyond Good and Evil*, 'a *typology* of morals' (emphasis in original) within the space of politico-military resistance and rebellion; a typology that has Castro at one corner and Bin Laden at the other. This point is taken up in the concluding chapter.

Unfortunately, within the radical and Marxian tradition in which Castro must be situated, there is for the most part a silence concerning the correct use of violence. The assumption tends to be that the violence of the oppressor is so endemic and the cause of liberation and the end of a better social order so intrinsically just that no further criteria except strategic and tactical ones, that is, no further moral criteria, are needed for the use of violence. Paul Hollander identifies the lacuna in question in the following way:

The single most important factor that enables the individual to retain radical leftist (or other radical) beliefs is the capacity to dissociate ends from means... Such a capacity rests on what Arthur Koestler called 'the doctrine of unshakeable foundations' – the overwhelming, superior moral importance attributed to the ends....[16]

Though it is perhaps deserved, this rightist reproach against the left-radical tradition is not entirely supported by the facts. As we will shortly see, this tradition does contain hints and assertions at the margins that constitute an embryonic attitude towards the right and wrong use of violence. Castro's contribution was to independently develop these into an ethic.

MARXISM, RADICALISM AND THE USE OF VIOLENCE[17]

Violent rebellions are age-old, the best known being that of Spartacus. The uses of violence in slave and serf uprisings were philosophically unproblematic to Marxists. The use of violence by the oppressing class was so ubiquitous that the killing of feudal families and retainers by rebellious peasants was regarded as a natural and justifiable response. Yet Marx and Engels tended to disdain the wars waged against capitalism or colonialism by social forces they regarded as pre-capitalist and therefore reactionary. There was considerable clarity in their minds about the recourse to violence. In the aftermath of the crushing of the democratic upsurge of 1848, Marx had both envisaged and championed a violent insurrectionary strategy, of which his militant address to the Communist League in 1850 is the best evidence. It is well known that in their advanced years, Marx and Engels had envisaged the possibility of a peaceful path in certain Western societies, while simultaneously applauding the outbreak of violence against the Tsarist autocracy in Russia. The Russian revolutionists they applauded were terrorists, but not in the current sense. Indeed, as Camus dramatised in his play *The Just* and noted in *The Rebel*, the use of violence by the Russian terrorists up to the early twentieth century was surgical, scrupulous in its avoidance of civilian targets.

In his last essay in 1895, Engels advocated a gradualist strategy, taking as his model the undermining and eventual takeover of the Roman Empire by the persecuted Christians. Yet this was in no way a conversion to pacifism by Engels, nicknamed 'the General' by Marx for his intense interest in military affairs (the 'military-diplomatic' was the largest single subject category in the collected writings of Engels).

The correspondence of Marx and Engels, as well as their writings on Britain, contains a complex duality, which was never elaborated into a perspective. This complex comment concerns a specific instance of the use of violence by a movement and in a cause that Marx and Engels enthusiastically endorsed: that of the Fenians, of Irish national liberation. The Fenians exploded a bomb outside a prison in Clerkenwell, London, in a botched attempt to liberate some Irish prisoners, which caused the death of several English civilians and injured 120 others. Marx's and Engels's responses were unambiguous in their condemnation.

That negative response had several strands woven into it. One was class: the English victims had been of working-class origin. The second was strategic: the project of winning support from among the English working class for Irish independence was jeopardised by the civilian nature of the casualties.

The last exploit of the Fenians in Clerkenwell was a very stupid thing. The London masses, who have shown great sympathy for Ireland, will be made wild by it and driven into the arms of the government party. One cannot expect the London proletarians to allow themselves to be blown up in honour of the Fenian emissaries... [18]

However, there was a third dimension to Marx's and Engels's response to political violence, a moral-ethical dimension that does not derive automatically from their strategic response but, together with the latter, forms a complex whole. This moral-ethical dimension is more explicitly articulated by Engels than by Marx. Consider Engels's vehement comment that:

The stupid affair in Clerkenwell was obviously the work of a few specialised fanatics; it is the misfortune of all conspiracies that they lead to such stupidities... and then a few asses come and instigate such nonsense. Moreover these cannibals are generally the greatest cowards, like this Allen, whose seems to have already turned Queen's evidence, and then the idea of liberating Ireland by setting a London tailor's shop on fire![19]

The present study will show that the sensibility of Castro and Guevara seems closest to that of Engels, with his relish for military matters and actual participation in them, and his condemnatory views on terror. In a little-known letter to Marx dated 4 September 1870, Engels makes a markedly critical characterisation of the Jacobins' Great Terror:

Terror implies mostly useless cruelties perpetrated by frightened people in order to reassure themselves. I am convinced that the blame for the Reign of Terror in 1793 lies almost exclusively with the bourgeois frightened out of their wits and demeaning themselves like patriots, with the small philistines quaking with fear and the mob of the underworld who know how to coin profit from terror. [20]

This passage not only adjudges the Great Terror as blameworthy, it also implicitly yet clearly indicts terror in general as a product of cowardice. Both indictments are *moral*. While this dovetails with Marx's and Engels's critique of the Fenian use of terrorism, it contrasts not only with the upholding of the Jacobins as a model by the Marxist tradition, which reckons its lineage from them, but also with Marx's and Engels's own enthusiasm for the Russian terrorists.

The implicit distinction observed by Marx and Engels then, is between (a) what would later be known as individual terrorism, that is, surgical tyrannicide, when directed against entrenched absolutism (Tsarist Russia) on the one hand, and (b) the targeting of non-combatant civilians (by the Irish nationalists), as well as (c) the practice of mass terrorism, which arises after the seizure of power (and was the case in almost all socialist societies apart from Cuba, as I shall argue in Chapter 2).

Marx's and Engels's endorsement or lack of criticism of the Russian terrorists seemingly contrasts with their relentless condemnation of Bakunin and the Anarchists. The distinction is consistent: though the Anarchists targeted Russian autocracy as well as rulers in general, they – certainly the sinister Nechaev – did not balk at the murder of non-combatants, while the Russian terrorism of their correspondent Vera Zasulich's generation (the 1870s) eschewed the killing of uninvolved civilians. In short, then, this attitude suggests an embryonic doctrine of the good and bad use of violence within the thinking and strategy of Marx and Engels (that is, of classical Marxism).

For Lenin too there was a right and a wrong use of violence. If violence was against the oppressor, it was a just war, irrespective of who initiated it. In the era of imperialism, violent uprisings even by nations and social forces that Marx would have termed reactionary were accorded warrant in Lenin's thinking, insofar as they were blows against the imperialist world system. The strategy of 'individual terrorism' as practised by the Narodniks and their successors the Socialist Revolutionaries (SRs) was wrong because it was strategically erroneous: you could not overthrow the system by eliminating hated or representative individuals. The Leninist doctrine did not place moral-ethical constraints on the use of violence.

It often goes little noticed that Lenin made his revolution less than half a century after the defeat of the Paris Commune, with its hideous reprisals against civilians (conducted by Thiers). The Bolsheviks were determined that the same thing would not happen to them. Their revolution, which contained the hopes and strivings for social emancipation of the ages, would not go down to defeat owing to a lack of resolve and tough-mindedness. Marx and Engels, who initially cautioned against the Paris uprising, had later identified a lack of ruthless purposiveness as one of the causes of the Parisians' defeat:

If they are defeated only their 'good nature' will be to blame. They ought to have marched at once on Versailles after the withdrawal first of Vinoy and of the reactionary section of the Paris National Guard. They missed their opportunity because of moral scruples. They did not want to start a civil war, as if that mischievous dwarf Thiers had not already started the civil war with his attempt to disarm Paris! Second mistake: The Central Committee surrendered its power too soon to make way for the Commune. Again a too 'honourable' scrupulosity![21]

However, it is not usually noted that Marx's strictures on the excessive moral scruple of the Communards refers to their lack of *decisiveness in strategy and tactics*, and not their behaviour in warfare, their deployment of violence. Tragically Marx's strictures were taken, not least by Lenin, to be an urging of greater ruthlessness in the use of violence.[22]

Following the defeat of the Paris Commune, Lenin was sworn to a doctrine of necessity to defend the revolution. The Russian Revolution also took place against the backdrop of and as a result of World War I, which with its unprecedented mass carnage had totally undermined world capitalism's moral credibility, certainly on the issue of violence.

Lenin deployed violence against his rivals on the left only in *retaliation* for the return of the SRs to their individual terrorist roots, this time against Bolshevik power. The very notion of using lethal violence *within* the Bolshevik party would have been unthinkable for Lenin, as evidenced by his suggestion that Stalin be removed from the office of general secretary because of the personal quality of rudeness!

It was in the post-Lenin period that the question of the correct and incorrect use of violence within armed revolution manifested itself. This was not a matter of personality, but because a new phenomenon had arisen. Until then the vanguard party stood at the head of the mass uprising, and the arming of the party would neither be total nor permanent, but limited to special units and to a climactic phase of the revolutionary process. But now, for the first time, the vanguard party would be armed almost from its inception and the revolution would proceed via a protracted civil war. This was identified as a specific feature of the Chinese Revolution: in China, the armed revolution is fighting the armed counterrevolution, said Stalin.

A party engaged in warfare had to elaborate regulatory guidelines for the conduct of war. There are three main wellsprings of the moral question in revolutionary theory and practice: Gramsci, Mao, and the most famous figures of the Cuban Revolution, Castro and Che Guevara. Of these, Gramsci's references are not explicitly on the use of organised armed violence, while the latter sources speak explicitly to this issue. This is not to say, however, that the insight of Gramsci, who focused on the dual aspects of force and consent (the Machiavellian metaphor of the Centaur), is not rich in relevance to the question of the correct and incorrect use of force. It is a gentle irony that Gramsci, the man who, within the Marxist tradition, did most to rehabilitate Machiavelli intellectually, is also most renowned within Marxist theory for having brought back the moral-ethical dimension. The irony resides in the fact that Machiavelli had to liberate Florentine political practice and political thought in general from the moral-ethical dimension in its religious form (which was the ideological expression of the dominance of the Catholic Church).

In the domain of political thought and philosophy, three sons of Rousseau, as it were, have dealt with the practice of violence: Sorel, Sartre and Fanon. While these thinkers applauded the liberating effects of violence – and here they were following a hint given by Marx, who had spoken of a violent revolution as the only means for the proletariat 'to rid itself of the muck of ages' – they did not stipulate restraints, still less an explicitly moral and ethical regulatory framework for the use of violence.

Sorel argues that violence is necessary not only for the regeneration of a class or nation but for the purpose of scission, of severing the links between the decadent and spiritually healthy worlds. His views lay a heavy stress on the moral factor, but the Sorelian use of moral tends to be a composite of *morale* and puritanical private morality (and sexual norms). Though he does not advocate the use of violence against innocents and indeed shuns the unrestrained use of violence, his extensive use of the category violence is not accompanied, let alone matched, by a code governing its use and non-use.

Sorel had a keener intuitive sense than others of the importance of the moral dimension in and on socialism, and aspects of the present study, especially Chapter 2, could be said to bear him out:

Socialism is a moral question in the sense that it brings to the world a new manner of judging all human acts and, to employ a celebrated expression of Nietzsche, a new evaluation of all values. It is in this way that socialism must be compared with Christianity in the first centuries... It stands before the bourgeois world as an irreconcilable adversary, menacing it with a moral catastrophe even more than a material one. (Italics in original) [23]

However, there is no notion in Sorel of the negative impact on *morale* of the excessive use of violence in the causes of emancipation and scission.[24]

As for Sartre, violence in the cause of liberation or issuing from the oppressed is justifiable, necessary and inevitable. The willingness to engage in violence that may be ethically ambiguous, the willingness to get one's hands dirty in the service of the right cause, on the side of the working people or the colonised, could even be a marker of a commendably tough-minded realism. ('Dirty Hands' was the title of one of Sartre's plays.) There are but two sides in the historical struggle between socialism and capitalist-imperialism, and public reproach of the violence of the oppressed would be to provide comfort to the class enemy.[25]

Raymond Aron identifies the weakness in Sartre's ethics of violence:

perhaps he felt that an ethics was excluded by contemporary society, that within the world of alienation, no ethics save the ethics of rebellion is possible... The ethics of Sartre has suddenly become a politics, but as this politics has rebellion as its expression, it suggests an ethics since it tends to extol revolutionary action as such. Only the reference to universality prevents this ethics-politics of rebellion from sliding into the fascist cult of violence.[26]

For his part Fanon 'systematised the treatment of revolutionary violence', writes Cedric Robinson:

He pursued its significations philosophically ('It is solely by risking life that freedom is obtained'), psychologically ('violence is a cleansing force'), historically ('the war of liberation introduces into each man's consciousness the ideas of a common cause, of a national destiny and of a collective history') and organisationally ('the practice of violence binds them together as a whole, since each individual forms a violent link in the great chain').[27]

Sartre's Preface to Fanon's *The Wretched of the Earth* 'expresses in an extreme form and in a philosophical language the humanization of man by violence', says Aron.[28] The issue of violence as it features in the thought of these figures, and the interconnections between them, especially Sartre and Fanon, has been the subject of extensive discussion and therefore does not warrant repetition here.[29] It may be observed, however, that none of these thinkers went beyond the understanding of the effect of dehumanisation of the violence of the oppressor on the oppressed and the effect of *humanisation* on the oppressed of the exercise of counter-violence, to an understanding of the effects of *dehumanisation* of violence on the oppressed (which the Gandhians and other pacifists understood), when used by them without limits. *There is no dialectical understanding of the violence of the oppressed, encompassing its contradictory aspects, both liberating and dehumanising.* This, however, was a concern of Camus, though his attempt to resolve the contradiction was unsatisfactory.

In one of Camus' best-known plays, *The Just* (also known as *The Just Assassins*) a leading character, Dora, a bomb-throwing revolutionary activist, asserts: 'even in destruction there is a right way and a wrong way – and there are limits'.[30] The 'ethics of rebellion' and the contradictions of violence in the name of justice for the oppressed were at the heart of Camus' *The Rebel* and his polemic with Sartre. *The Rebel* traced the successive upheavals in European thought that undermined and overthrew restraints and detonated the great revolutions, with their liberating promise and dictatorial outcomes. Sartre criticised Camus for the latter's criticism of the violence of the oppressed, which for Sartre was inevitable and beyond reproach because it issued precisely from the oppressed and the cause of progress; the correct side of History. For Camus, violence against the innocent, unrestrained violence, especially violent dictatorship, was morally reprehensible and should be condemned, whatever quarter it issued from and whichever cause it served. The present inquiry contends that it was Castro who resolved the contradiction.

Camus' conclusion was to opt for rebellion and reject revolution; in other words, he recommended a restriction and limitation of *the ends* for which violence would be the means. Castro (and Guevara) did not restrict the ends, the final goals, of violence; violence was in the service of both political revolution and total social change. Instead, they favoured practising restraint in the use of violence. Camus' great contribution – and one that makes him central to the present study – is his insistence (in the words of David Sprintzen) that 'moral limits must be drawn from within the moral framework articulated by the rebel's outrage. Ends must be balanced with means, since, as actions unfold in time, one tends to become the other.'[31]

2
Comparative Historical Perspective

What is the historic significance of the Cuban Revolution, the leadership of Fidel Castro and his guiding ideas? This evaluation of Castro's historical significance is not to be confused, as is usually the case, with the history of that revolution or the biography of its leader. The treatment offered here permits the location and assessment of Cuba's revolution through a critical assessment of the larger historical backdrop and the dynamics of that period of world history. It facilitates the comparative understanding of the significance of Castro's contribution by analysing the Cold War and the zenith and fall of global socialism (or 'historical communism', as Norberto Bobbio called it[1]); a generalised collapse that left Cuba as the sole survivor.

The chapter argues that the collapse of socialism had as one of its root causes the unrestrained nature of the violence deployed, which, by its internecine character and its magnitude, caused the internal weakening of socialism as a system, and its moral and ethical weakening as a cause and project. Given that the asymmetry of material strengths between capitalism and socialism was offset by moral conviction and a sense of moral superiority, the erosion of the moral factor resulted in the neutralisation of the moral challenge, and consequently contributed to the collapse of socialism.

The chapter concludes and the rest of the study argues that Fidel Castro's Cuba survived precisely because his ideology contained an explicit ethics of violence that constrained its use; his political practice was marked by an absence of internecine violence and its restrained use in the maintenance of state power and domestic authority. It was philosophically superior, in that it explicitly reintroduced morality and ethics into radical and liberationist discourse, synthesising the earlier 'utopian' or 'idealist' tradition with the subsequent 'scientific' and 'rational' Marxist tradition and its realist variant, Leninism.

These are the distinguishing features of Fidel Castro's ideology and his specific contribution to political thought and ideas. Scholars such as Richard Fagen[2] have identified 'the new man' as the distinguishing feature of the ideology of the Cuban Revolution, but this overlooks the fact that *all revolutions have sought precisely such a radical remoulding* (hence the phenomenon of Stakhanovism, and 'model' fighters during the Red Army's war against Nazi fascism). What these scholars do not discern is that nowhere except in Cuba, and more in Castro's political ideas than even in Che Guevara's (though it was manifestly present in Che's own practice), is the explicit idea of right and wrong, of ethics and morality, of a consciousness that entails conscience ('consciencia'), built into the notion of the New Man.

The chapter shows that an absence of internationalism and the clash of more narrowly defined and entrenched interests of state – or perceptions of such interests – contributed to the collapse of socialism. Internationalism has been a distinguishing feature of Castro's Cuba. While Comintern activists played seminal roles as organisers on many continents (for example, M. N. Roy, an Indian, organised the Mexican Communist party), the role of Soviets and Chinese as fighters was on the peripheries of their states or on the continents to which they belonged: Spain in the 1930s, Chinese volunteers in Korea in 1950. Furthermore this role was linked to the threat perception of those states. There was nothing that could compare with Cuba's role in Africa, given not only the much smaller size of Cuba but also the fact that it was a continent and an ocean away, and that no threat to the Cuban state emanated from a possible Moroccan victory over Algeria in 1963 or South African victory in Angola in 1975.

While 'proletarian internationalism' was always part of the new consciousness that Marxism strove to inculcate, it loomed far larger in the Castro–Guevara concept of the New Man. What this centrality demonstrates is that Castro's and Guevara's notion of internationalism was far less linked to national or regional concerns or state interests than was the case in the international policy of both the West and its rivals the USSR and China – or, more accurately, that state interests were far less conventionally perceived. In turn it leads to the understanding that internationalism, internationalist solidarity, was a *value* for Castro and Guevara. As Armando Hart, at the time Secretary of the Central Committee of the Cuban Communist Party and Cuba's Minister of Culture, informed a stonily indifferent audience at the 23rd Congress of the Communist party of the Soviet Union in 1966, 'Our borders are a moral concept'; and Castro, in a more definitive and radical statement made in Moscow, said, 'in my view internationalism is the most beautiful essence of Marxism-Leninism'.[3]

While scholars have remarked on the similarity between Communism and the history of the Church, organised religion has been far more successful because the horrendous violence of its temporal authorities does not detract in the minds of the faithful from the purity of the Almighty and/or the founding figures, and secondly because of the belief in an afterlife – neither advantage of which Communism had. However, there is a third realm in which religion has an appeal, source of durability and transmission: every religion almost by definition functions as moral compass; it contains an explicit code of good and bad, of right and wrong, which Marxian Communism eschewed in the name of science.

Marxism-Leninism did contain, in its heroic phase, a strong moral component, but that stressed altruism, self-sacrifice in the collective interest, and egalitarianism, and did not embody a notion of parameters or prescriptive limits especially in term of means and ends. This contained an in-built danger. The greater the self-sacrifice, the greater the sense of self-righteousness, and the self-justification of an unrestrained use of violence and repression. It is only when self-sacrifice is combined with an ethic of the right and wrong use of violence, when it is part of an overall concept of heroism that is marked by its circumscribed use of violence, that the antipodes of the moral horrors of excessive zeal (Stalin, Mao's Cultural Revolution) and the complete vacuum of moral-ethical motivation (the cynicism and pragmatism of the latter-day USSR, the crass consumerism of contemporary China) can be avoided. This has been Fidel Castro's singular achievement.

THE FALL OF GLOBAL SOCIALISM

Writing after the fall of the USSR, Zbigniew Brzezinski, former US Secretary of State and key political architect of that defeat, confirms the stakes and prospects in the latter half of the 1970s:

… Soviet momentum interacted with America's post-Vietnam fatigue and with widespread Western eagerness for détente to a degree that America seemed ready to settle the Cold War even on the basis of accepting strategic inferiority. President Nixon's brilliant coup in opening the US–Chinese relationship altered the geostrategic context, but it could not compensate for internal American dissension and demoralization. That condition prompted Secretary of State Henry Kissinger to diligently seek an accommodation modelled on the Peace of Westphalia: each side was to retain its geopolitical and ideological realms. It would be stabilized by a new emphasis on arms control, thereby slowing down the massive Soviet build-up but at the price of even accepting (in SALT1) Soviet strategic superiority. The Soviet global offensive continued unabated into the second half of the 1970s... For the first time during the entire Cold War the Soviet Union seemed to be genuinely preparing to dictate the outcome, both by encirclement and perhaps even on the central front...[4]

However, this moment of Soviet/communist ascendancy was to be short-lived. Brzezinski confirms the rapidity of the collapse of communism following a 'dramatic reversal' that occurred in the 'correlation of forces' dating roughly from 1979:

The moment seemed ripe for a historical turning point, but it did not occur. Instead the dramatic reversal only gradually took shape, mushroomed and eventually produced an outcome beyond the wildest expectations... The result was the final phase of the Cold War, roughly from 1979 until 1991. It was marked by the West's gradual recapture of the ideological initiative by the eruption of a philosophical and political crisis in the adversary's camp and by the final and decisive push by the United States in the arms race. This phase lasted slightly more than a decade. Its outcome was victory.[5]

Brzezinski's account of this historic reversal is interesting both for what it includes and for what it does not mention. He gives considerable salience to the dynamics of the contest, and to subjective factors. More importantly, there is, in his rendition, a total absence of the economic factor, that is, of the factor most commonly believed by both right and left to be the ultimate reason for the downfall of socialism. This absence of reference to the economic circumstances is justified by the fact that there was after all no dramatic boom in Western economies and/or a 'Great Depression' in the Soviet bloc in the years corresponding to or immediately preceding the decisive turnaround. All the factors mentioned by Brzezinski as characterising the final decade (1979–89) are intangibles, located in the realms of the 'superstructures': 'ideology', 'philosophy', 'politics'. The historical analysis is not related to static structures but fluid dynamics: 'recapture', 'ideological initiative', 'eruption of a philosophical and political crisis', 'decisive push'. Socialism was defeated in a struggle, a series of battles, a 'war', as a result of strategic failures, bad leadership 'Stalin's successors were second rate',[6] wrong decisions, matters of human volition. Thus, Brzezinski confirms that a potentially decisive shift occurred in the correlation of forces, in favour of socialism, in the 1970s, and continued into the second half of the 1970s, and that the reversal of this took place over a decade (1979–89), not earlier. Thus the issue hung in the balance. He also confirms that the crucial factors in the reversal of this balance and the defeat of socialism operated at the levels of conjuncture and contingency. Those factors were ideological and politico-philosophical.

Most histories locate the decisive moment in the radical inversion in the correlation of world forces after the decade of the 1970s, culminating in the almost vertical collapse of socialism, in the assumption of power by Reagan and Thatcher and the massive arms race imposed upon the Soviet bloc, which effectively bankrupted the latter. However the Reagan–Thatcher phenomenon *also* generated a wave of anti-US protest in the continent of Europe. Between June and November 1981, around 1.8 million people demonstrated across the continent against the deployment of Cruise and Pershing 11 missiles in Western Europe.[7] Therefore the return of the right was a mixed blessing for US global hegemony and could not be said to have been the decisive factor in causing the sharp reversal in the correlation of forces.

Paradoxically, this reversal took place in the Third World. The zone, which encompassed the wave of revolutions of the 1970s, proved to be the site of the weakest links in the chain of socialism. How, then, did Reagan succeed, precisely in the theatres of America's greatest defeats?

The answer, I want to suggest, is that something changed for the worse in these (largely) Third World theatres, within the revolutionary movement itself. The revolutionary victories had started to implode, their energies diverted and dissipated by internecine strife. The Reagan offensive in the Third World succeeded because it was against an enemy in the throes of self-destruction. The secret is that the global revolutionary moment of 1974–80 was swiftly followed by yet another conjuncture, a parenthetical, transitional and ultimately decisive conjuncture, which preceded that of the victorious Reaganite counter-offensive. That hidden conjuncture was that of the splitting up and unravelling from within of these revolutionary triumphs.

Che's 'Message to the Tricontinental' generates and sums up the *Geist* of the long revolutionary upswing of 1968–80. In a slogan that became legendary, Guevara identified the strategy needed to defeat imperialism: 'Create two, three, many Vietnams!'[8]

In 1972 Castro articulated the Third World communists' vision of imperialism's historical trajectory of retreat:

Vietnam is the most distant point to which the imperialists have gone to impose their domination, and it marks the turning point, the beginning of their definitive historical decline. They will have to get out of Vietnam and they will have to keep pulling back more and more, getting out of one place after another, until the day comes when imperialism ceases to exist.[9]

Between 1974 and 1980 Che's injunction had found itself adhered to. Yet the outcome in less than a decade was the total defeat of socialism. 'Two, three, many Vietnams' were created, but they, like the original Vietnamese victory itself, began to be thwarted, to be enmeshed in intra-socialist rivalry.

Socialism had long ago lost the mainsprings of its *élan vital* in the USSR and Eastern Europe. Its *élan vital* and *morale* sprang from victories in the Third World, just as the loss of America's spirit stemmed from its reversals in the Third World. With the spate of self-destructive strife, the morale and spirit of socialism in the Tricontinental World itself was depleted. Because the strife was internecine in nature it discredited the causes of socialism and the revolution. Whenever aggression emanated from the class enemy, revolutionaries could rally. Defeats in one place strengthened resolve and deepened radicalisation in another, but not so when the challenges came from fraternal or erstwhile fraternal quarters. Then, not just the spirit but the hopes and the rationale, the entire paradigm stood in jeopardy.

Since the struggle in the Third World was reckoned the decisive factor in the struggle between socialism and capitalism, the process of defeat precisely within that theatre decisively shifted the balance against socialism. Since internecine strife was the decisive reason for the internal weakening and disintegration of that wave of revolutions, it was the decisive factor in the global defeat of socialism.

The decisively negative role played by internecine conflict, especially violent fratricidal strife, also validates the innovative stress that Gramsci laid on the factor of moral-ethical 'hegemony'. Socialism lost because it lost the battle for moral-ethical hegemony. The defeat in the moral battle took place because of intra-socialist civil wars and fanatical left fundamentalism – Pol Potism being the prime example.

Fred Halliday[10] locates three major waves of anti-systemic struggle in the post-World War II period, of which 1974–80 was the third and last. Eric Hobsbawm notes 'the four great twentieth century waves of 1917–20, 1944–62, 1974–78 and 1989'.[11] Both scholars confirm the pattern of a revolutionary wave in the latter half of the decade of the 1970s. The momentum of the third revolutionary wave resulted in credible expectations that the last quarter of the century would see a further upswing, with socialism poised to prevail in the new century. However, every one of the major theatres of revolutionary victory in 1974–80 became the sites of internal explosions. All of the major revolutions were stopped in their tracks – disfigured, debilitated, discredited, by the phenomenon of internecine conflict. Thus the revolutionary conjuncture of 1974–80 ended by implosion.

These implosive conflicts fell into three broad types: (a) conflicts within the revolutionary vanguard (party, guerrilla army, regime); (b) conflicts within the broad revolutionary movement; and (c) conflicts between states with a revolutionary/radical anti-imperialist character. Each of these conflicts have been (unevenly) reported and commented on. However, they have not been viewed as being on a continuum, part of a single process or as links in a chain – even by a masterful scholar like Hobsbawm or by Halliday who mapped the wave of Third World revolutions. None of the major accounts or evaluations of the downfall of socialism comment on the collapse of the victorious revolutions, let alone identify this as a major reason for the fall, or even as constituting a context and catalyst.

When placed alongside each other, the splits within the major revolutions of 1974–80 add up to the picture of a single lateral fissure running across the world and through the ranks of the revolutionaries. This large fracture has not been noticed or commented upon by right or left, even though it weakened the third revolutionary wave internally to the point of utter vulnerability to the Reaganite roll-back during the Second Cold War. Using as a rough guide the table of revolutions listed by Halliday,[12] one is able to see the cracks emerging within each revolutionary site and eventually constituting the larger pattern of a global fissure and fracture.

Portugal witnessed the mildest version of the phenomenon of the abortion of the revolution through internecine conflict. The clash between Ethiopia and Somalia permitted the US to regain influence with the latter. Internecine conflict enabled the US to move beyond influence to activism/interventionism in Afghanistan and Grenada. Such internal strife also helped blunt the impact of the most massively popular revolution of the revolutionary conjuncture of 1974–80: Iran. The most striking instance of the debilitating and neutralising effect of fratricidal strife was precisely at the scene of the most dramatic triumph of the anti-systemic forces: Indo-China.

This exposition will endeavour to track the evolutionary dynamics of each of the revolutions in the sequence of their unfolding, demonstrating the unravelling of the preceding pattern of an upward moving revolutionary wave – the fate of the revolutions on the morning after.

THE RETURN OF THE EUROPEAN REVOLUTION: PORTUGAL

It was in Portugal after 1974 that the most seriously revolutionary prospect arose in the developed capitalist world.[13] According to Brzezinski, 'it initially appeared that the Portuguese Communists were destined to succeed'.[14]

The April 1974 revolution in Portugal, though it was a geographic exception, did not constitute an analytically inadmissible exception to the rule of the third wave of revolutions located in the Third World. This is because that revolution had its proximate cause in the radicalisation of segments of the Portuguese armed forces during their encounter with the liberation movements in Africa in the colonial wars. The Portuguese revolution was an illustration of the validity of the revolutionary grand strategy of undermining capitalism in the West through liberation struggles at the periphery, and a model of centre–periphery revolutionary reciprocity. The African liberation struggles radicalised the Portuguese officers who led the revolution, and those radicalised officers who were physically present during the transition of those countries to independence were sympathetic to and helped safeguard the most left-wing of the Angolan liberation movements, the MPLA.

The agency of the Portuguese Revolution resided in a convergence of senior officers who wanted to rid Portugal of the debilitating colonial burden, and younger officers grouped in the Armed Forces Movement (MFA) who stood for reform and democratisation of the armed forces and, in an interesting osmosis, had imbibed radical and leftist ideas from their guerrilla enemies. Rooted though it was in a Third World process, the Portuguese Revolution had a European provenance as well. It formed a part of the important collapse of three Southern European dictatorships: Portugal, Spain and Greece. It is in Portugal, however, that this 'crisis of the dictatorships' (as Nicos Poulantzas termed it) went furthest, perhaps because capitalist development was most backward there and the left was strongest, with a presence within the armed forces, unlike in the other two countries.

By 1975, the revolution took a left/radical turn, placing socialisation and property questions on the agenda. The US responded with alacrity, because for the first time since the Greek Civil War of 1947

the question of a left-led revolutionary seizure of power was on the
agenda in Europe, with clear strategic implications for NATO. The third
wave of revolutions, primarily a wave of Third World revolutions, was
now entering the hitherto sacrosanct 'central theatre', the Western
sphere of influence in the Yalta and Potsdam arrangements. This was
the sphere of 'sanitisation', where the Cold War commenced in the
form of the Truman doctrine of 1947 (enunciated in response to the
Greek revolutionary insurgency).

Meanwhile, on the Soviet side, the Portuguese process had its ripple
effects. The ruling CPSU (Communist Party of the Soviet Union) was
engaged in an ideological combat with the phenomenon of Euro-
communism. It was disadvantaged in this struggle because it was
defending a status quo gone stale and unimaginative. The Portuguese
Revolution handed sections of the CPSU a political weapon. While
some in the party were worried that the Portuguese communists
would 'adventuristically' trigger a US response that would adversely
affect Soviet interests, others upheld the Portuguese Communist
Party (PCP) as a model that constituted an alternative to the 'soft-
line' Euro-communists who were openly critical of 'really existing'
Soviet socialism. Euro-communism was seen as a strategic problem for
the USSR. In the Portuguese Communist party, the CPSU ideologues
found a rare asset. It was not only a party loyal to the USSR and hostile
to Euro-communism but also a party that had accrued great prestige
for its prolonged activism in the underground, and enunciated a line
that was militant, unlike most pro-Soviet parties, which were seen as
having long lost their revolutionary fibre. Most significantly, it was
a party that, in 1975, could credibly hold out the prospect of power
and thus an alternative path to that of Euro-communism. As Paul
M. Sweezy wrote at the time:

… its leadership tended to alternate between jail and exile in Moscow; its ideas
and style were in the nature of the case strongly Stalinist; and it never had the
opportunity or the temptation to follow along what may be called the 'national
reformist' road of the French and Italian CPs. Despite, or perhaps it was because
of, these characteristics, the Portuguese CP sank real roots in the working class
and was in a much better position than any of the other political movements to
spring into action when the iron grip of fascism was at last broken.[15]

Within the CPSU this was a time of greater global assertiveness (the
period of 'late Brezhnevism') and even a recrudescence of a pro-Stalin
sentiment. It was against this backcloth that the PCP was upheld as a
model. The most important ideological manifestation of this was an

article in August 1975 by the editor of the Soviet bloc's top theoretical journal, *World Marxist Review* (published in translation worldwide as *Problems of Peace and Socialism*), Dr Konstantin Zarodov, on the seventieth anniversary of Lenin's 1905 essay 'Two Tactics'. Zarodov used the occasion to justify the continued or renewed relevance of the model of the seizure of power, bypassing the question of 'arithmetical majorities'. In a significant gesture, he was congratulated by Brezhnev on the article that September.

The left radicalisation of the Portuguese Revolution in 1975 had considerable prospects. Unlike in 1947, when the Truman doctrine was enunciated, in 1975 the USA was on the strategic defensive, having just been defeated in Vietnam. The theatre balance in Europe had also changed, with the USSR far stronger than the immediately post-war USSR of 1947, and stronger than the West in terms of conventional forces – thus endowing it with a capacity to deter Western military intervention as in Greece. The standard instrument of the US in cases of counterrevolutionary intervention, namely the armed forces of the state in question, could not be used in Portugal since they were heavily influenced by radicalism, and were arguably the main vehicles of radicalisation. A coup equivalent to Indonesia in 1965 or Chile in 1973 was impossible. There was a tough-minded, cohesive Communist party and a number of *gauchiste* guerrillaist groups.

Thus the US was at a strategic impasse. Yet, the Portuguese Revolution was defeated within a year. This points to the existence of an internal factor at work, namely the fissiparation of the Portuguese left as a result of the rivalry of various tendencies. There was no unified or co-ordinated vanguard, nor an organisation whose leading role was acknowledged by the others on the left.

The Portuguese left contained four currents – the Social Democrats, the Communist party, the New Left revolutionaries, the Maoists; the last three were anti-systemic/revolutionary. The Social Democrats of Mario Soares were moderates and were finally part of Dr Kissinger's strategy to countervail the hard left. The latter, the potential vanguard of the second phase of the Portuguese Revolution, consisted in the main of three organisations: the Communist Party (PCP) of Alvaro Cunhal, the PRP-BR of Dr Isobel do Carmo, and the Maoist MRPP. A rare account of that period is contained in Michael Harsgor's 'Portugal in Revolution'.[16] Particularly worthy of note for our purposes is his profile of the PCP:

The power of the PCP was in its dedicated leadership – a rare group of stalwart revolutionaries who had outlived both Salazar's and Caetano's reigns. They had spent many years in prison, had resisted torture and privation, and in the process had lost not a few of their comrades, till they emerged through a kind of natural selection process as a unique hardcore of Communist Party functionaries. These men and women, generally of proletarian origin did not of course look on the PCP as one of the many parties allowed after April 25 to display normal political activity. For them the Party – with a capital P – was the one and only expression of historical necessity. A socialist revolution realised under PCP leadership was the only normal and necessary development; their own assuming of power was Portugal's manifest destiny. But for the time being the tactic adopted was to back the 'heroic MFA captains'...[17]

It was the competition, rivalry and hostility between PCP, radical left and Maoists that prevented the unification of the left fractions within the Portuguese armed forces, forestalled the creation of a single bloc of the radical social forces in the country, prevented the decisive revolutionary upsurge at a time the status quo was off balance and left room instead for an isolated adventurist putsch that scared the Social Democrats and sections of the armed forces into cracking down, ensuring the restabilisation of the endangered system:

... the PCP had been torn, in the years preceding the April coup, by a grave internal crisis. In 1963–4 it was split... All the armed groups which later took part in more or less coherent terrorist activity – the LUAR, the ARA, the Brigadas Revolucionarias (BR) – were the political offspring of that split.... Later in 1971, a Maoist group crystallised – bitterly anti-PCP – called the MRPP... At the beginning of the 1970s communist influence was on the decline among students and young workers (but grew among army officers, amidst whom the milicianos represented an older generation of students)... The leftwing radical revolt would influence PCP leaders after the April coup in a double sense. Cunhal and his friends would try by all means to turn the military power of the MFA against the leftwing radicals, thus shutting them up; and at the same time the PCP would attempt to outmanoeuvre its too-revolutionary enemies...While there was never the slightest criticism of MFA policy in any PCP declaration, its firepower was directed at its two main enemies: leftwing radicalism, and at the PCP's and the left radicals' common foe the Socialist Party.[18]

In mid-1975, a potentially revolutionary situation obtained in Portugal.

The prime minister had been unable to put an end to the gathering wave of strikes.... The whole fabric of Portuguese society, after some 50 years of

imposed stagnation 'looked like an active volcano' as a LUAR leaflet put it....
The government was paralysed.[19]

Most pertinently a powerful new instrumentality had been created
and headed by a charismatic leader, to further the revolutionary
process. Had the capacities of the PCP – the workers and the peasants
of the Alentejo region – been combined with the new instrumentality, the socialist outcome may have follwed. But there was no such
unification of the vanguard; indeed, there was bitter rivalry:

The MFA leadership... created on July 12, the 'Commando for Continental
Portugal', COPCON for short, which was to grow into a group of military
companies with some 5,000 men. It included picked volunteers, the best shots,
the best signals material (NATO stuff), the best light armour, and the strongest
(per capita) fire power of the entire army... The commanding officer, Otelo de
Carvalho... turned out to be the strongest man in the country...The COPCON
did not tarry in becoming, as its own officers readily admitted, 'a revolutionary
organ'. With Carvalho turning more and more to the extreme left, the COPCON
... took upon itself the task of public guardianship... In conflicts, disputes or acts
of violence with social or political undertones, the COPCON would always act
on behalf of 'the masses'. For many destitute Portuguese, COPCON appeared
as ... a new holy miracle-wonder. For a part of the radical left movement, it
was the 'motor of the political process', the 'nerve centre' the main link in the
MFA-Povo symbiosis ('popular masses'). The PCP was less enthusiastic. Carvalho
would loudly report and prevent acts of PCP members and sympathisers that
conflicted with public order as understood by COPCON. Otelo ... had stated
proudly that the men under his command would see that Portugal should not
become 'a satellite of imperialisms' with stress on the final 's', which meant that
in the COPCON commander's eyes the Soviet Union was no better than the
United States. He used to add that the country should neither be a 'bourgeois
democracy' nor a 'party dictatorship', another veiled allusion to the PCP.[20]

When Spinola's counterrevolutionary coup attempt (11 March
1975) was defeated by COPCON under the personal command of
Carvalho, the left held the initiative. Between March and November
1975, a situation in Portugal was akin to the dual-power situation in
Russia (February to October 1917). Though elections had indicated
the limits of hard-line left-wing support in the country, there was
a large and active critical mass of support for radical, pro-socialism
solutions. Nicos Poulantzas commented that

Up to the eve of November 25th, Lisbon saw the repeated demonstrations
of a gigantic scale, often involving between two and five hundred thousand

people, and with very advanced slogans. The experiments in 'popular power' also seemed to be making good progress, from factory and community councils to the 'Soldiers United Will Win' movement. 'Red' military units such as RALIS, the Military Police and even some parachute regiments, were in open rebellion against the government in its capital, fraternizing with the masses and so on.[21]

What was missing during the crucial period between 11 March and 25 November was a unification of the left, at least as an alliance or stable bloc. Such a convergence could not have guaranteed a victorious revolutionary attempt, but it may have considerably enhanced the social momentum to 'the acceleration of the revolutionary process before 25th November'.[22] However the fissure and fragmentation of that left meant that there was no cohesive political will, strategic direction and consequent unity of action. As Harsgor states: 'the two triumvirs Goncalves and Carvalho neutralised each other'. Unity of the revolutionary left took place as late as August 1975 and was a mere episode:

The PCP suddenly dropped the devastating criticism of the extreme left fringe, which only a few days previously had been described as 'objectively' helping the fascists. On August 20 Cunhal stated that a new line was in the offing. Five days later the FUR, 'United Revolutionary Front' was created: former enemies – orthodox communists, Trotskyists, anarchists, 'spontaneists' and revolutionary populists of the PRP-BR brand – merged. The FUR had the capacity to mobilize for street demonstrations in Lisbon at least 30,000 students, young workers, and unemployed, to which the disgruntled Goncalvists could add some 6000–7000 soldiers, sailors or deserters; the PCP could still count on some thousands of workers in Lisbon and of agricultural workers in Alentejo, who could be brought into the capital at a few hours notice. ... In the PCP tactic calculations the capital was the weakest link in Portuguese politics....[23]

But the spirit of sectarianism and 'left anarchism' was so strong that within weeks 'the FUR had noisily expelled the Communist party from its midst for reasons of "revolutionary tactics"; but the PCP front organization the MDP, stayed inside the FUR'.[24]

Poulantzas provides the most analytical summation of the salience of factional strife in that exceptional conjuncture:

The second reason for this defeat was the absence of an alliance between the organizations of the left... A popular unity of this kind at the organizational level was lacking in Portugal... the period in question displays a real ballet of successive establishments and breakdowns of organizational and conjunctural understandings, from the fluctuating relations between the Socialist and Communist Parties to the more heteroclite ties that united the Socialists and the MRPP, or the Communists and the front of far left organizations. The game is complicated still further when we take account of the relations between these organizations on the one hand, and the various fractions of the AFM (the COPCON, the 5th Division, the 'moderate' sectors etc) and the armed forces as a whole on the other hand. These factors not only prevented the co-ordination and unification of the mass movement, but in fact actually contributed to its division and disorientation.[25]

On 25 November 1975 one tendency among the revolutionaries made its move, in the form of a 'leftwing military uprising' (Poulantzas). But that was an adventurist putsch by the far left, unsupported by the PCP, and was put down by loyalist commandos. Its failure effectively put an end to the Portuguese Revolution.

Despite a powerful upswing of revolutionary struggle during 1918–23 and again in the 1930s (Spain), Portugal was probably the best real hope of socialist revolution in Europe after the Bolshevik Revolution of 1917. That original revolution had failed to extend its boundaries or be joined by others because the military apparatuses, and especially the officer corps, stayed largely loyal to the status quo. After World War II there were powerful communist-led anti-fascist liberation movements in Italy, France and Greece. However, the overall strategic balance did not realistically permit a thrust for power by these parties. In Greece the attempt was made, but its crushing by Anglo-American forces proves the point. According to Milovan Djilas, Stalin ruled out assistance to the Greek insurgents on the grounds that the Anglo-American alliance enjoyed an overwhelming preponderance of naval power in the theatre.[26]

May 1968 was the next wave, but spectacular as it was, the Communist parties were quiescent, the far left was unarmed and inexperienced in combat, the USA was not as much in retreat as it was in the 1970s, and above all, the military apparatuses were not fissured – producing a radical vanguard that was armed, trained and combat-experienced, as in the Portuguese case. In Europe in May 1968, the question of state power could not be seriously placed on the agenda because the state possessed the unquestioned monopoly of violence.

In 1975, the US could not adopt the same option as in Chile in 1973, precisely because of the MFA/COPCON phenomenon. Had it succeeded, the impact of a socialist revolution in Portugal on the already changed global 'correlation of forces' would have been quite considerable. As Paul Sweezy explained:

.... On a global scale it is a country which belongs to the developed capitalist camp not only by reason of its having had until recently a large colonial empire but, more important because of its socio-economic structure. And this fact gives it an importance in the present world political scene out of all proportion to its area or population. If a revolution should occur in Portugal, it would not be another Third World revolution but the first in a metropolitan capitalist country. And that would certainly be an event of very wide-reaching consequences and implications.[27]

But a prerequisite for such a revolution was a political equation that recognised the PCP as the 'main force' and the COPCON as the 'leading factor': a Carvalho–Cunhal duumvirate. The internecine conflict on the left was the greatest single factor that prevented that outcome. The failure of the Portuguese Revolution was a decisive defeat that turned back the global revolutionary high tide of the 1974–80 period.

ETHIOPIA: THE RED TERROR[28]

The phenomenon of internecine strife was present in non-lethal form in Portugal; it assumed a malignant, murderous manifestation in Ethiopia. As in Portugal, here the revolution (which overthrew the autocracy of Emperor Haille Selassie), was made by left-wing army officers. The Ethiopian junta, the Dergue ('Revolutionary Coordinating Council') later spun off a political party, COPWE (to co-ordinate the formation of a Marxist-Leninist working-class vanguard party).[29]

The Ethiopian Revolution was strategically important because of its latent strengths. It could have provided a model of radical activism for Third World military apparatuses, hitherto the mainstay of the social status quo, supported by the USA. It could have been an inspiration for Black Africa, since it was the first internal social revolution there, that is, not part of an anti-colonial or anti-apartheid national liberation struggle against an external/alien oppressor. The location of Ethiopia, on the Horn of Africa, and the pro-Soviet orientation of neighbouring Somalia, could have significantly changed the strategic balance in that theatre.

If these potentials had been realised, it would have meant, in the post-Vietnam context, a considerable enhancement of the global revolutionary momentum of the 1970s. However, the Ethiopian Revolution proceeded by way of bloody fratricidal strife within the ruling Dergue, culminating in the assumption of power by General Mengistu Haile Mariam; between the Dergue and radical left-wing groups of a civilian character – Meison (the All-Ethiopian Socialist Movement), the Waz (Labour) League and the Ethiopian Peoples' Revolutionary Party (EPRP), formed in 1972;[30] and finally between the Dergue and the (non-Eritrean) regionalist movements in Ethiopia – the Tigrean Peoples Liberation Front (TPLF) and the Oromo Liberation Front.[31] The inter-state war was the final factor that contributed to the weakening and discrediting of the revolution.[32]

Even when the three socialist-oriented protagonists were offered a formula constituting a way out of the conflict, they chose not to take it. They rejected Fidel Castro's 1977 compromise formula of a 'Red Sea Confederation' involving Ethiopia, Somalia and South Yemen, in which the Ogaden and Eritrea would be semi-autonomous entities. Thus, the Ethiopian Revolution was weakened and discredited by bloody strife between various left-wing actors.

KAMPUCHEA[33]

The implosion of the Indo-Chinese revolution proceeded by way of several contradictions and internecine conflicts. There were conflicts within the Khmer revolutionary ranks. The Pol Pot leadership carried out two bloody purges: against the Kampucheans, who fought in Vietnam's war against the French and were regrouped, in line with the 1954 Geneva agreement, in zones under North Vietnamese authority; and the 'soft-liners' within the Khmer Rouge, including suspected sympathisers of China's internal development line under Deng, and/or those potentially pro-Vietnam. There were also the contradictions between the Pol Pot regime and the Kampuchean people, between the Khmer Rouge and civilians of Vietnamese ethnic origin and between Kampuchea and Vietnam (plus Laos). Full-scale armed conflict of a protracted nature between China and Vietnam also contributed to the implosion.[34]

Wilfred Burchett[35] calls the Kampuchean tragedy 'one of the darkest events of our age':

The full dimensions of the horrors inflicted on the people of Cambodia by the Khmer Rouge will never be known. In the mass graves and death pits there are millions of anonymous skulls and skeletons that can never be counted or classified. ...Pol Pot set about exterminating not only Vietnamese, Chinese, Islamic Chams and other ethnic groups but also those of his own Khmer race.... The Khmer Rouge leadership transformed their entire country into one great concentration camp....The Khmer Rouge suppressed every form of religious worship. They turned Buddhist pagodas, Muslim mosques and Catholic churches into torture centres, pigsties, and warehouses, or else simply destroyed them.... Pol Pot and his gang destroyed all books and libraries, trampling every vestige of Cambodian culture and tradition...[36]

The internecine strife in Indo-China had several strategic implications for the third wave of revolutions (1974–80) and the overall 'correlation of forces' globally. The energies needed to consolidate the Vietnam victory and to rebuild were used to defend what had been gained against the Khmer Rouge and China. Revolutionary movements in Thailand, Burma and the Philippines would have received a fillip had the revolutionary states of Southeast Asia not become foes. Revolutions in Thailand and the Philippines would have had an especially deleterious effect on US strategic position in the vital Asia–Pacific region. Given this internecine strife the Indo-Chinese revolution's enormous 'demonstration/multiplier effects' ceased to function and began to operate in reverse. International solidarity was a conspicuous factor in the victory of the Vietnamese Revolution. The inter-socialist wars and mutual denunciations divided, disoriented and dissipated this powerful global solidarity movement. Vietnam's defensive intervention in Kampuchea was used as pretext by the US to orchestrate an economic embargo on that country. This economic embargo, added to the cost of the new wars (and the old wounds), aborted Vietnam's prospects of becoming a *socialist* Southeast Asian 'Tiger'. Finally, less than half a decade after its ignominious eviction from the region, the US was able to re-enter it, as part of a coalition with its ally ASEAN and its erstwhile foe China.

AFGHANISTAN: CADRE CONSUMPTION

In April 1978 in Afghanistan, a pro-Soviet Communist party effected a revolutionary seizure of power for the first time since the Sino-Soviet split.[37] Taking place on the doorstep of the staunch US ally Pakistan, it was a strategic setback for the West. Together with the Iranian Revolution that followed it, it disintegrated the old CENTO defence arrangement.

In a pre-capitalist, tribal society, the fundamental problems faced by the communists were the narrowness of their power base (their support was mainly urban) and the paucity of cadre. These structural problems were never overcome and indeed were exponentially enhanced by the dynamics within Afghan communism. The party had been split from the 1970s into two factions: the hard-line 'Khalq' (Masses) and the moderate 'Parcham' (Flag), which was closer to the Soviet line. This policy split also corresponded to long-running personality clash and a social differentiation. The Khalq was led by Noor Mohammed Taraki and was of a lower middle-class and provincial character, while the Parcham was headed by Babrak Karmal and was upper middle-class and urban in nature. The revolution was made in the main by the hard-line Khalqis, led by Noor Mohammed Taraki and Hafizullah Amin, with the latter playing a greater role in actual practice. Soon the power struggle erupted, replete with bloody purges. Amin was responsible for the murder of Parcham leaders. His ferocity made Taraki and Karmal seek a rapprochement through the intercession of Moscow. Fearing a coup, Amin turned his guns on his old leader Taraki.[38]

This debilitating fratricidal strife took place while the US and Pakistan were arming the tribal counterrevolutionary insurgents. The hard-line Khalqis engaged in social reforms that moved too far and too fast, causing a traditionalist backlash – which was militarily effective, since the actors involved were tribes with martial characteristics.

The USSR had two intersecting fears – a successful US–Pakistani inspired counterrevolution on its southern flank and a spill-over of Islamic influence across the border into the southern underbelly of the Soviet Union. Propelled by these apprehensions, the USSR made a pre-emptive intervention. The Red Army went in to shore up the besieged revolutionary regime, while that regime was simultaneously and coercively recomposed by the execution of Hafizullah Amin, whose bloodily sectarian political behaviour was seen to be narrowing revolutionary power, rendering it more vulnerable to counterrevolutionary overthrow. In his stead was placed Babrak Karmal whose Parcham tendency was seen as more capable of stabilising the situation by moderating the pace of reform and broad-basing the regime.

This calculation went wrong for three reasons: the Soviet intervention provided the justification for greater US, Pakistani and Iranian support for the insurgents; it earned widespread international condemnation as an act of superpower intervention against national sovereignty; and finally the bloody upheavals within the revolutionary ranks emboldened the Afghan insurgents to greater efforts.

The factional Parcham/Khalq split only took more subdued and subterranean forms. Years later, the Soviets substituted Najibullah for Karmal, in the hope that the former's religious credentials would stem the tide. But the 'infection' of sectarianism had travelled too far for too long, and proved fatal.

GRENADA: THE REVOLUTION ROLLED BACK[39]

It was in Grenada, in 1983, that the US was able to intervene militarily for the first time since Vietnam, pushing backward the revolutionary gains in the Caribbean and threatening those in Central America. The Grenadian Revolution's significance was twofold. It was the first ever revolution that had taken place in the English-speaking or 'Commonwealth' Caribbean, and it resulted in a pro-Cuban regime emerging in the Caribbean.

The split in Grenada was in the ranks of the revolutionary party, the New Jewel Movement, between the popular and flexible Maurice Bishop, and a hard-line faction of Marxist academic intellectuals led by Deputy Prime Minister Bernard Coard and his wife Phyllis, later backed by army commander Hudson Austin. The hardliners felt that Bishop was slowing down the revolution and pursuing too moderate a line on the economy, particularly with respect to foreign investment.[40] The split culminated in the murder of Maurice Bishop by Hudson Austin, swiftly followed by the US invasion of Grenada. This was the first projection of US ground troops in a combat role after Vietnam, and also the first under the Reagan administration (despite three years of belligerent hard right rhetoric). Once again, as in Vietnam/China/Kampuchea, and more importantly, the USSR–PRC, it took the factor of fratricidal strife to open the breach for the US to move in.

Fidel Castro tried to head off the disaster:

When they arrested Bishop I sent a message that the situation could create a serious problem in international public opinion and weaken the revolution inside the country. I asked those people to be understanding and generous. I feared that one of those radical elements might try to resolve the problem through violence.[41]

Castro judged the Grenadian case one of a revolution committing suicide: 'Our assessment of the situation was that the Coard grouping could not sustain itself after having killed Bishop. The revolution had committed suicide. But this did not justify intervention.'[42] One may discern the negative importance Castro ascribes the factor of self-destructive internal strife by his reading that 'suicide' was decisive in permitting a victorious US intervention, which would otherwise have been successfully resisted: 'And even Grenada, as tiny as it is and with a small population – if the revolutionary process there had not committed suicide, even Grenada would have struggles and would have been invincible.'[43]

IRAN: MULLAHS VS MARXISTS[44]

The significance of the revolutionary left in Iran is best captured by Val Moghadam and Ali Ashtiani,[45] who draw also on Ervand Abrahamian's study:[46]

With a base among university students and former political prisoners, the Left gained in stature and prestige as a result of its engagement in armed struggle against the Shah. Indeed, the moral and psychological impact of the urban guerrilla movement was an important factor in attracting large numbers of radicalised youth and intellectuals to the Fedayeen. As the revolution proceeded therefore, the Left emerged as a mass force, and, by 1979, represented a serious challenge to the Islamists. Its social base was principally among university and high school students, but included teachers, engineers, and some skilled workers. In addition, the Left was active among the national minorities, especially the Kurds and the Turkomans.[47]

But the massively popular Iranian Revolution was plagued by con-tradictions and violent conflicts among progressive forces. There was the conflict between Islamic and secular revolutionaries. The political competition between the radical left Fedayeen Khalq and the religious revolutionaries resulted in a bloody crackdown on the Fedayeen. There was also the conflict between the two main Islamic revolutionary tendencies: those who owed allegiance to the Mullahs (grouped mainly in the Revolutionary Guards) and those belonging to the Marxist-Islamic revolutionary organisation, the Mujahedin-e-Khalq. The Mujahedin were bloodily crushed. The conflict between the secular left organisations was rooted in the bitter rivalry between the radical left Fedayeen and the pro-Soviet Communists (the Tudeh party). The Tudeh supported the crackdown on the Fedayeen. In May 1983 the Tudeh party was violently suppressed by the regime. The conflict within the secular radical-left revolutionaries was manifested in the main by the Fedayeen split in 1980 into 'Majority' and 'Minority' factions. The former temporarily supported the Islamic regime, particularly at moments of greatest tension with the US, but was also suppressed by the regime. Finally, there was the war between Iran and Iraq.

Val Moghadam identified June 1980 as the watershed. The fissures in the Fedayeen commenced in 1979 and culminated in June 1980, with the split between the Majority and Minority:

The beginning of the end of the Iranian Left as a whole occurred at this time. The split had a devastating effect on four movements upon which the Left and notably the Fedayeen had considerable influence: the workers' councils, the students' councils, the Kurdish struggle for autonomy, and the National Union of Women. Each of these movements split and eventually disintegrated (with the exception of the Kurdish struggle).[48]

In 1979 Zbigniew Brzezinski had presented the panorama of vital US security interests and strategic arrangements coming asunder along what he designated an 'arc of crisis' or 'crescent of crisis' extending from the Horn of Africa through the Gulf to Afghanistan. However, this 'arc of crisis' for the US contained a hidden arc of crisis within it – violent conflict inside the ranks of the anti-imperialist forces. Nothing dramatised this more than the anti-imperialist Islamic revolutionary Iran placing itself objectively on the same side as the 'Great Satan', the USA, by supporting the pro-imperialist counterrevolutionary Afghan Islamic guerrillas against the anti-imperialist revolutionary Afghan regime! Thus the crescent of crisis for US strategic and economic (oil) interests disintegrated, as each revolution checked the other and deadlocked itself.

THE END BEGINS

Strategic consequences apart, it was in the domains of ethics, ideology and philosophy that the explosive chain reaction 'Vietnam/ Kampuchea/China' had its most devastating historic effect on the fate of socialism. As much as its defeat, its conduct during the Vietnam War had caused a colossal hollowing-out of the moral prestige and strength of the US. In the wake of each successive defeat in the 1974– 80 period, a fresh wave of evidence and testimony indicted the US morally for its installation and/or support of murderous, exploitative dictatorships. As World War II ended, the popularity of the US was at an all-time high. After Vietnam it was at an all-time low. This was a factor that caused the global correlation of forces to be adverse to the US and world capitalism in general. This changed with the testimony that emerged about the Khmer Rouge. The evidence of the carnage in Kampuchea, coupled with the phenomenon of wars between socialist states of similar origination, called into question and undermined the claims of moral superiority of socialism over capitalism, discrediting the entire socialist project and Marxism itself.

Thus the moral, and, indeed, the spiritual crisis of socialism, confronted in post-Vietnam War Indochina with its dark underside, preceded the collapse of socialism as system and movement. But it would take one more round for the inner moral/psychological crisis to become irreversible and fatal. If that round had culminated in victory, the psychological and moral-ethical crisis caused by the aftermath in Indochina could have been neutralised and reversed. But that round in Central America was also spiritually lost.

EL SALVADOR: ALMOST VIETNAM[49]

If a single occasion represented the peak of the revolutionary wave of 1974–80 it was the Sixth Non-Aligned Summit, in Havana (September 1979). The alliance of Cuba, Vietnam, Nicaragua and the newly liberated states of Black Africa held the moral high ground and the political initiative. In January 1979, Vietnamese forces had liberated the people of Kampuchea from Pol Pot. China's punitive incursion into Vietnam and the support that the US had given Pol Pot's Democratic Kampuchea were turned into bitter moral indictments.

The third wave of revolutions was so powerful that it retained momentum and initiative even after the carnage in Southeast Asia. That momentum was destroyed and, together with it, the correlation of forces that issued from the third wave of 1974–80, in Central America. In the rarest of accolades, Fidel Castro once said

The Salvadorans are the revolutionaries I admire most in the world for their courage, their endurance, their heroism, their intelligence. ...There is little we can teach them, because today everybody can learn from the Salvadorans. We ourselves have learned a lot: how a small country, with only 20,000 square kilometres, has been able to resist for almost eight years genocidal armies backed by the United States. We have learned military tactics. At the beginning we taught them; today we learn from them. Today we learn from their experience... their ability to disperse, their ability to regroup, their ability to resist have proven the infinite possibilities of a fighting people. So if at the beginning – in the early years – we were able to teach them, today they teach us and they can teach us about irregular warfare. I'm not going to say that they know more than we do about regular warfare.[50]

The United States was aware of the importance of El Salvador, as evidenced in the resources it spent on that country during the civil war. A RAND Corporation study noted:

The conflict there has been the most expensive American effort to save an ally from insurgency since Vietnam. El Salvador has absorbed… a total expenditure (approaching) $6 billion. Only five countries receive more American aid each year than El Salvador, a nation of 5.3 million people[51]

Had the Salvadoran Revolution succeeded, Nicaragua would have broken out of its US-imposed isolation and the guerrilla struggle in Guatemala would have received a decisive push forward. The US would either have had to retrench from its 'own backyard' or intervene militarily. Direct US military intervention in that region would have resulted in a war taking the whole of the Central American region as a single battlefield and the various Central American guerrilla struggles as a single process. Che Guevara's strategic dream of creating 'two, three, many Vietnams' in Latin America would have become a reality. However, when the Salvadoran Revolution was pushed on to the defensive, the revolutionary struggle in Guatemala lost momentum, and the US proceeded to invade Grenada and tightened its stranglehold on Nicaragua. Nicaragua and Cuba were isolated, vulnerable.

The last revolutionary victory was in Managua in 1979. The last real hopes of a Central American revolution would also die in Managua, on 6 and 12 April 1983, in clandestine hideouts, with a homicide and a suicide. Here the tragedy was far more personal. Yet its individual character was the microcosmic version of what happened in Indochina and in the other sites of recent revolutionary victories. This tragic episode was the murder of Salvadoran guerrilla leader Ana Maria, the suicide of topmost guerrilla leader Salvador Cayetano Carpio, and the revelation that it was Carpio who had given the signal that set off the chain reaction resulting in Ana Maria's murder.

The utterly decisive nature of the Carpio episode stemmed from three sources – the implications of a successful revolution in El Salvador; the prospects of such a revolution, given the exceptional nature of its vanguard and the array of international support it received; and the importance within the struggle of Carpio himself and of the organisation he led.

In the post-1968 period it is hard to identify any one personality (outside of the Vietnamese Communist leaders) who epitomised the combination of hard ideologies and radical philosophies better than Salvador Cayetano Carpio – and any political organisation that did so better than the one he founded, the FPL. In the words of two contemporary journalists, Carpio was rare: '...a hardened guerrilla leader of such long experience, who was famed for his toughness.... The FPL [was] the toughest and most intransigent of the five groups forming the Farabundo Marti Front for National Liberation (FMLN).'[52] If Carpio symbolised the age of 'hard ideologies', his tragedy symbolised and contributed to its end.

What were the prospects of the Salvadoran Revolution? What was at stake and what was irretrievably lost in the intertwined tragedies of Ana Maria and Carpio?

On President Reagan's first inauguration day revolution appeared to be spreading across Central America. The Sandinistas were consolidating their hold over Nicaragua and guerrillas in El Salvador and Guatemala were on the move. America began thinking that Central America could become another Vietnam.[53]

By 1983, the rebels were actually winning the war.[54]

Jorge Castaneda provides the clearest itemisation of the state of the Salvadoran revolutionary movement and its assets and strengths: '[The FMLN] had become the strongest military grouping in the history of the Latin American armed left.'[55] This would remain so throughout the decade. James LeMoyne, the *New York Times* correspondent in Central America from 1984 to 1988, confirmed it: 'The Salvadoran guerrillas are now the best-trained, best-organised and most committed Marxist–Leninist rebel movement ever seen in Latin America.'[56]

The strengths and potentialities of the revolutionary struggle in El Salvador resided in the combination of five factors:

(1) The 'charismatic' nature of the leadership. Carpio was famous in Latin American revolutionary ranks as a labour activist from the working class who had joined the communists in 1948 and risen through the ranks to become the party general secretary. He was a former political prisoner who had undergone torture and the author

of a dissenting yet resolutely militant introduction to a 1969 edition of Che's famous book *Guerrilla Warfare*.

A courtly man, 'Marcial' as his comrades later called him, had spent time in a seminary and according to his friends appeared impelled by a mystical force... The Farabundo Marti Popular Forces of Liberation... [was] an organization with Guevarist and Maoist tendencies that began to prepare for armed guerrilla struggle... His age was advanced for a guerrilla commander.... His political writings generally fall into the 'rigid' Marxist category and reflect a definite Leninist point of view.[57]

Carpio's seniority, experience and sheer prestige had earned him the sobriquet of the 'Ho Chi Minh of Latin America'.

(2) The military strength of the FMLN. Castaneda writes:

In the course of 1980 and through 1982 several thousand, perhaps upward of 10,000 weapons with ammunition were brought into El Salvador. So much arrived that some fighters had two arms each. The first country that donated weapons was Ethiopia... The largest number of weapons came from Vietnam, abandoned by the US in 1975. These were the best guns... Cuba was instrumental in organizing the operation....[58]

In comparison with their precursors, the Salvadorans are in a league of their own, accomplishing what no armed group of the sixties had been capable of[59]

... the most distinctive feature of the FMLN in the firmament of the Latin American armed left: the veritable construction of a lasting, viable, standing army in opposition to a sitting government's constitutional armed forces.[60]

(3) The political and social strength of the revolutionary movement. Castaneda continues:

... during their entire formative years they flaunted their guerrilla vocation, while at the same time developing what many would later qualify as the most important mass movement in Latin America since the Popular Unity in Chile. Day after day throughout the seventies, before elections or after, during strikes or protests over price increases, the Salvadoran extreme left finally put into practice what many Communist parties and Cuban-sponsored groups had recommended but never attained. They were able to combine the armed struggle with the peaceful one, the fight in the country with that in the city, spectacular armed acts with broad based mass action. In a sense, and with the exception of the Sandinistas in Nicaragua, the Salvadoran political-military organizations achieved the highest degree of success in implementing the policy laid out after the defeats of the previous decade; the unity of 'Cubans' and Communists, alliances with other forces, particularly the Church, and a combination of the armed struggle with traditional forms of mobilization.[61]

(4) The contributory role of the Church. El Salvador was 'where the Church and specifically the Jesuits, became most involved with the left and politics in Latin America'.[62]

(5) The social 'accumulation' and human resource profile: 'The FMLN is an impressive organization led by some of the country's most talented people.'[63]

The historic potential of the Salvadoran Revolution as a factor in the struggle between the forces of imperialism and global revolution is attested to by the unprecedented degree of international involvement by anti-systemic states. Hitherto, military assistance from socialist states was limited to other states and to movements against colonialism or apartheid. Almost never (with the exception of Cuba) did a socialist state in the post-Comintern decades grant active material support to a social revolutionary (as distinct from a 'national liberation') movement. That changed with the Second Cold War and the policies of Ronald Reagan. El Salvador was the laboratory of the new internationalism.[64]

But there remained buried political contradictions. The substantive disagreements were over negotiations and a fusion into a single party with the other organisations that were unopposed to negotiations.

In the past few months – and indeed years – a vigorous ideological debate has been going on within the FPL and between the FPL and other guerrilla groups. One of the issues to have aroused most controversy has been whether to negotiate with the Salvadoran government.[65]

Returning from a visit to Vietnam, Ana Maria was in favour, and according to some reports, had won the inner-party battle. Carpio was opposed. 'Marcial distrusted the negotiating posture; his partners favoured it'.[66] '... the position Carpio had presumably espoused: against negotiations, in favour of protracted armed struggle to the death'.[67] 'Marcial ... did indeed oppose a political solution rather than a tactical gesture.'[68]

Castaneda records the fall of the axe and the decapitation of the revolution:

In April of 1983 [erroneously recorded as 1984 on this page (DJ)] the leader of the Fuerzas Populares de Liberacion (FPL), Salvador Cayetano Carpio ('Marcial') was found dead in Managua with bullet hole through his heart or his head (depending on whose version one believes), a suicide note on his desk, and myriad unanswered questions. All of this occurred just days after he had attended the funeral of his deputy, Melida Anaya Montes ('Ana Maria') also found dead in Managua, in her case with eighty-three ice-pick inflicted stab wounds in her body and a bloodied bedroom as the only clues to her murder. The Sandinistas blamed the CIA, then threw a veil of silence on the affair, finally providing a harrowing explanation...[69]

... Rogelio Bazzaglia, one of his faithful co-conspirators, decided to take advantage of Marcial's absence in Libya and assassinate Ana Maria, seeking to make the crime as gruesome as possible so it could then be attributed to either the CIA, another organization of the FMLN, a lover, a maniac, or all four together. Marcial returned from Libya as soon as he was apprised of the situation. When the Sandinistas confronted him with the evidence of his backers' guilt, and of his own at least tacit responsibility, the ageing revolutionary took his own life rather than face the prospect of a trial, prison and disgrace.[70]

According to Sheldon Liss,

It is ironic that this strong critic of unnecessary violence became its victim. In April 1983 his colleagues in the Popular Forces of Liberation blamed him for the execution of his comrade Melida Anaya Montes or Ana Maria. They claimed that his exaggerated sense of self-importance led him to see himself as a revolutionary purist who could not tolerate her increased leadership powers. Once the evidence was laid before him, Cayetano Carpio committed suicide.[71]

This wreaked devastation on the Salvadoran struggle. Carpio was 'El Salvador's oldest and most famous guerrilla leader.'[72] 'Many FPL members, including the nucleus in San Salvador and much of the international network, left the organisation, disgusted...'[73] 'The FPL had the most publicly known leader and was the most powerful of the groups.'[74]

The sheer force and potential of the Salvadoran guerrilla movement is best seen in the fact that in November 1989 it launched the most spectacular offensive seen in Latin America, outside of the victorious Sandinista-led insurrection of 1979. FMLN fighters attacked throughout the country and smashed into San Salvador. US military advisors sheltered in the Sheraton hotel had to be escorted to safety by the guerrillas! Had the FPL not decapitated itself and been debilitated by the ensuing erosion of morale and exodus of cadre, one can easily imagine that victory would have been obtainable a few years earlier – with the regional and global consequences feared by the US. However, by the time the 1989 offensive took place much had changed. The goal was now no longer revolutionary victory but to drive the Salvadoran regime to the negotiating table and to obtain the best possible deal for the FMLN at that table. Something had snapped, died within.

... The FMLN's bitter factionalism, and the consequent ugly political executions robbed the movement of its political legitimacy and hindered its becoming a cohesive force. The Salvadoran rebels long ago lost their moral imperative and were beaten back as much by their own errors as by government repression and US policies.[75]

A HALF-CHANCE IN CHILE[76]

History would provide a postscript – one last chance, or half a chance – in Chile. In the early to mid-1980s the window of revolutionary opportunity half-opened, and then closed, never to reopen.

At the World Conference of Youth and Students in Moscow in the summer of 1985, at the dawn of the Gorbachev period, the mood was still one of militant optimism among the participants from liberation organisations worldwide.[77] There were three main reasons – the Sandinistas were still in power, having won an election the year before; the Manuel Rodriguez Patriotic Front (MRPF) had gone into action, indicating a positive turn on the part of the hitherto cautious yet strong Chilean Communist party; and the downside of the economic transformation initiated by the 'Chicago school' had manifested itself in a major outburst of violent mass protest:

In May 1983 discontent erupted in a surge of popular protest... Since 1982 an urban sabotage campaign by armed revolutionaries has renewed... At the root of Chile's political divisions is the West's second largest Communist party. With support in mines and factories the party historically has opted for an electoral road to power. But in 1980, after the adoption of a new Constitution, the election of Reagan and the Sandinista triumph in Nicaragua, a new, militant party leadership stunned many allies and members by proclaiming that all methods, including violence should be used to overthrow Pinochet. A clandestine affiliate, the Manuel Rodriguez Patriotic Front, began a campaign of urban sabotage... By turning to violence, the party has gained critical new support among the urban poor.

In Chile today despite 11 years of harsh anticommunist policy, the Communist party is far stronger than ever before. And it has drawn on the despair of Chile's shantytowns and their legions of unemployed to embark on an increasingly successful strategy of insurrection – one that almost cost President Augusto Pinochet his life in early September.[78]

In 1985, in an interview granted to the Mexican newspaper *Excelsior*, Fidel Castro analysed the socio-economic situation in the southern cone of Latin America, and in particular in Chile, identifying it as the ripest in the region for violent upheaval: 'Chile may explode with such force that it will cause more damage than has been known anywhere else...'[79]

For three days in mid-1986, Chile was paralysed by a combination of protests and urban guerrilla actions by the MRPF. The quasi-insurrectional moment (July–August) climaxed with the September 1986 attack on Pinochet. Repression followed, its impact enhanced by the lack of unity on the Chilean left.

In the Allende period and in the years following the coup the Chilean left was divided between the Socialist party (of Allende), the Communist party and the MIR. By 1977, however, the rifts showed signs of healing as the Communist party ceased its criticism of the MIR. By the latter part of 1980 the strategic lines had begun to converge, with the Communists shifting to an armed struggle perspective as younger leaders operating underground took over from an older generation in exile. In September 1980 armed sabotage was initiated by Communist and MIR militants, working together. A decade after the military coup, from May to August 1983, there was a flare-up of violent mass struggle in Chile.[80]

Had the militant left solidly united, it could have been well placed to spearhead this upheaval, catapulting it to higher levels. The socialists, Communists and the MIR formed a bloc known as the Popular Democratic Movement, and Communist and 'Miristas' co-operated closely during the MRPF days, but there was no solid MRPF–MIR fusion, which could have become the unitary politico-military vanguard of the urban popular upheaval. Instead the MRPF and the MIR did not go beyond close co-operation. By 1988–89, when the party shifted to a moderate line, the MRPF split into two and the MIR into three groups.

Given the universal revulsion at the Chilean junta and its moral isolation, the social polarisation generated by the Friedmanite monetarist model, the crisis of that model in the 1980s in Chile, the availability of the works of Gramsci and the counsel of Castro, a victorious recovery of the Chilean left was well within the realm of feasibility. Had the vanguard unified and the struggle moved into high gear, the strong historic ties between the Chilean Communist party and the ruling CPSU would have meant that the Soviet Union would have been drawn into supporting it propagandistically and politically:

Chile is a special case where the Kremlin backs the pro-Soviet Chilean Communist Party (PCCh) and other leftists utilizing a combination of armed struggle and peaceful united front tactics to oust the government of Augusto Pinochet. In addition to the pro-Soviet PCCh backing of armed struggle, the PCCh is connected to a violence-oriented splinter group called the Manuel Rodriguez Patriotic Front (FPMR). The FPMR has been engaging in terrorist activities aimed at destabilizing Pinochet's government, while Moscow has been supporting the FPMR with pronounced propaganda support.[81]

Thus, relinquishment of Third World struggles would not have come as readily and as early as it did to Gorbachev. The links between the US and the Chilean junta, taken together with the strategic and economic significance of Chile to the US, would have placed the latter in the position of either having to support a reviled ally or abandon it and incur a loss. The struggle – and the American reaction – would have also strengthened the hand of the relatively more combative elements in the CPSU.

NEGATION BY SUICIDE

By the time the FMLN's November 1989 offensive came, the continuity of the third revolutionary wave had been broken and the historical conjuncture had changed. In the latter half of that year, the Berlin Wall came down and Eastern European socialism dissolved in front of the television cameras. In early 1990, the besieged and bled-out Nicaraguan Revolution would be voted out by the war-weary populace. In 1991, the Soviet Union collapsed. It was over. For socialism the end of History had arrived. Socialism, the negation of capitalism and imperialism, had been negated.[82]

At a time when a US military invasion of Central America seemed imminent under Reagan, the powerful anti-intervention movement in the US coined a slogan that read 'El Salvador is Spanish for Vietnam'. However, El Salvador did not become another Vietnam in the sense that Che intended it, while Vietnam itself had become enmeshed in Kampuchea and lost its lustre as a beacon for revolutionary struggle. If El Salvador did not become Vietnam, Vietnam was no longer 'Vietnam' either.

Commenting on the fall of the Soviet Union, Castro remarked that it was not a case of homicide, but of suicide: 'Socialism did not die from natural causes. It was a suicide.'[83] 'The truth is that they destroyed the socialist bloc with the cooperation of the socialist bloc and the USSR. It was a case of suicide and self-destruction....' [84]

As El Salvador exemplified and personified, the death of socialism involved both homicide and suicide. But given the fact that the homicides, on an individual or a colossal collective scale, took place within the spectrum of anti-systemic forces, the collapse of global socialism as a whole could be said to validate Castro's verdict on the USSR: suicide, not homicide.

The comment on the collapse of Soviet socialism was Castro's second characterisation of the unravelling of a revolutionary experiment as 'suicide', that is, self-inflicted. The first, as we saw, was made about Grenada. The two uses of the term suicide indicate clearly the two types of behaviour that Castro thought self-destructive of revolutions: on the one hand, fratricidal strife, internal bloodletting fuelled by political and ideological fundamentalism – as in Grenada; and on the other, endless compromise and dilution, the lack of political will to fight for the survival of socialism and the continuation in power of the revolution – as in the USSR. Castro strove to avoid both extremes, or as the Marxist lexicon has it, 'deviations'.

Looking back at the Cold War in a CNN/BBC interview (19 March 1998) years after the collapse of the Soviet Union, Castro's main conclusions constitute a distinctive perspective and stance on contemporary history: though Marx, Engels and Lenin did not envisage 'socialism in one country', the Soviet leaders were not wrong in adopting it because they needed a mobilising slogan and task in an international situation that left them no choice; not only was there no Cuban–Soviet master plan, but had there been one, the outcome of the Cold War would have been different; the USSR was neither consulted nor informed of the Cuban internationalist mission in Angola; the only instance of co-ordinated Cuban–Soviet military action was in support of Ethiopia and repelling the Somali invasion; the USSR did not support Cuba's policy towards the revolution in Latin America; that revolution had better prospects than the ones initially faced by Castro and the Cuban Revolution; had the Latin American revolution won, it would have changed the outcome of history not least because of its impact upon the United States, which would have equalled that of the Vietnam War; the Latin American revolution did not succeed largely because of the Sino-Soviet struggle and the competing pulls it exercised on the Latin American communist movement; the USSR collaborated in the demise of socialism in that country; the main factor in the defeat of socialism and the victory of capitalism led by the US in the Cold War was the split between the Communist parties of the USSR and China.[85]

Viewed in retrospect, there were not two contending centres of world socialism/communism, but three: Moscow, Beijing and Havana. Of the three, it is the last that proved most durable, surviving into the twenty-first century.

The corruption within the Catholic Church resulted in radical schisms and bloody violence between the establishment and schismatic sects. To eschew the two extremes, the corruption and hypocrisy of the established hierarchy, and the fanaticism and/or fundamentalism of the rebellious sects: such a standpoint is rare but attainable in the world of ideology and politics: see Marx, Engels, Lenin, Gramsci, Ho Chi Minh, Amilcar Cabral, Samora Machel, Fidel Castro and Che Guevara. In these individuals, political daring and resolute determination were not consumed with fanaticism and fundamentalism. The political thought and philosophy of Fidel Castro warrants scholarly inquiry, because of his political longevity, his role in contemporary history and, most importantly, his avoidance of the disastrous polarisations of many revolutions. Castro has never felt the need, or resisted it if he did, to be cruel and bloodthirsty to survive against tremendous odds. Nor did his lack of dogmatism, his innovativeness, flexibility and even spontaneity, lead to the liquidation of regime and system as they did in the case of Gorbachev. The retention of the *élan vital* did not require the colossally nihilistic experimentation of China's Cultural Revolution. But stability, continuity and rootedness did not result in ideological sclerosis as in Soviet bloc Communism or the relative quiescence and conformism within the capitalist world system, of contemporary China and Vietnam. Castro is the empirical evidence that none of these outcomes were inevitable.

Socialism was only in its historical infancy, so perhaps the internecine strife was but a murderous 'infantile disorder'? Perhaps it was an inevitable function of the economics of scarcity – revolutions having been made in relatively backward societies rather than the economically and culturally advanced Western metropoles? Such historicism and 'sociologism' are as unsatisfactory as 'economism' in understanding the fate of socialism. They do not answer the question of how two revolutions, Cuba and Nicaragua, decades apart and situated in the global South, were able to avoid or resist such temptations. All the factors that bedeviled other revolutionary processes were present here: a revolutionary movement with internal differentiation and unevenness – in the case of the Cuban, the 'sierra' and the 'llano', the guerrillas in the mountains and the urban fighters and support groups; and in the case of the Nicaraguan, three rival tendencies, Marxists, non-Marxists and not-so-Marxists; complex relations between the Communist party, other leftists and the armed revolutionary vanguard; imperialist plots, encirclement and armed counterrevolution. In most other situations, any one of these factors (and certainly a combination of them) degenerated into internecine lethal violence. Yet neither the Cuban nor the Nicaraguan Revolution turned lethally on itself or on its brothers. Neither bore the mark of Cain.

Castro himself is very conscious that the avoidance of violent internal struggle and bloody purges constituted an exception and a historical merit of Cuba's revolution: 'Someone once said that the revolution was like Saturn, who devoured his own children. But this revolution does not devour its own children; we, the men who started this revolution are here.'[86]

Castro was the most consistently exemplary leader of the revolutionary left since Lenin; he was also the one who made the fewest lethal blunders and committed the fewest crimes. He led and won his revolution, which places him in fairly exclusive historico-political company; he built and has sustained a socialist state; he did so in an utterly and unalterably adverse geostrategic and geopolitical setting; he did not isolate himself and Cuba from the rest of the world and instead pursued an actively engaged, high-profile articulate policy of international engagement; no members of the original revolutionary leadership were bloodily purged; no members of rival left-wing organisations and tendencies were executed.

Above all, Castro bridged the gap between the practice and philosophical endorsement of violence (and at the very least, the refusal to renounce it or commend its renunciation as an option), on the one hand, and humanistic and humanitarian ethics, on the other. His main contribution to Marxism, as I shall now begin to demonstrate, has been the stress on moral-ethical factors in militant political praxis.

Part II

History of *Fidelismo* as Ethos

Introduction

Part II of this study attempts to trace Castro's idea of the importance of the moral factor, of moral superiority as an indispensable strategic factor and feature of liberation struggle. It examines the *Fidelista* concept of moral superiority, with its notion of the right and wrong use of violence at its core, and its working out at the various stages of Castro's revolutionary strivings and Cuba's revolutionary struggle.

The voluminous literature of revolutions clearly shows that every revolution considered itself endowed with an intrinsic moral superiority insofar as it represented the oppressed and fought for a better social order. Revolutionary leaders and ideologues believed that they had justice on their side and fought for progress. By definition, therefore, their project was morally superior to that of the enemy. Other moral themes invoked by Castro, such as those of achieving a more egalitarian economic order, and having a citizenry that was more internationalist, self-sacrificial and altruistic than those of capitalism, the very idea of a New Man, are common to all socialist revolutions. In the ensemble of moral claims, the one idea that is unique to Fidel Castro – and unique not merely in relation to other socialist leaders but to political leaders in general – is the claim to have used armed violence in an ethical and moral manner.

The chapters in this part of the study trace this *Fidelista* idea in its articulation and applications. The survey follows the idea from its genesis, through its appearance in the denunciation of the Batista coup, its application in the Moncada assault, and its articulation and utilisation in the legendary defence speech of Castro after his incarceration following the defeat of the Moncada uprising. The chapter tracks the observance of the *Fidelista* ethic under conditions of tremendous pressure, conditions that usually lead to the suspension of humanitarian restraint in warfare, namely guerrilla war (against Batista) notwithstanding the atrocities of the military; the defence of the revolution against sabotage, assassination attempts and an invasion originating from US soil; and the long-term and large-scale involvement by Cuban military forces on the African continent.

The chapters highlight the use of moral, ethical and humanitarian themes, especially pertaining to the use of violence, in Castro's discourse, and observe the interconnections with actual policies and politico-military practice.

3
Evolution of Castro's Ethics of Liberation

This chapter traces the origins and evolution of Castro's ethics of violence, from his adolescence through his days as a student activist to those of leader of an armed rebellion and head of a guerrilla army. Castro's code, comprising his morality and ethic, is framed by a triangle of major compulsions, motivations or ideas: he is willing to die for a just cause; he is willing to kill for a just cause; but he is not willing to kill just anyone for a just cause.

For Castro, the end – of overthrowing oppression and injustice – sometimes, but not always, justifies the means of armed violence, of killing. Violence is a last resort. It should be used only if other possibilities for change have been closed off. Conversely, if other possibilities for change have been closed off, violence is justified and necessary.

That is why I express my conviction – and I think it would be the conviction of any authentic revolutionary – that violence is the last recourse, when there is no other road, when there is no other possibility of change.[1]

This willingness to use violence – to kill – as a last resort, in the struggle against violent oppression and injustice, demarcates Castro from Gandhi. That is his morality. On the other hand, Castro has always affirmed his belief in the existence of the notion of the innocent. He has always refused to use armed violence against them, or to consider everyone who lives under enemy control or is a victim of enemy ideology as an enemy. He has insisted that the death of the enemy or traitor should not be by cruel methods, and refused to countenance torture, mutilation and dismemberment. He has consistently avoided targeting the enemy in conditions that could predictably lead to civilian casualties. He has never considered the families of enemies as targets. He has insisted that the armed enemy should be treated correctly if captured. All these demarcate his ethics from those of liberation movements that practise terrorism.

THE EARLY FIDEL

The guiding ethics of the Cuban Revolution, its specific ethos, is in large measure present in and product of the ideas and consciousness of its leader, Fidel Castro. The raw materials and specific ingredients of the ideology of Fidel, of *Fidelismo*, are discernible in his early years. As in the case of Marx, Engels, Lenin and most Marxist leaders, the evolution of his political consciousness and convictions did not stem from his social origins, but rather from ideas, examples and reasoning, that is, from a mental and emotional process.

I did not acquire it by having poor, proletarian or farm origins – that is through social circumstance. I gained my political consciousness through reasoning, thinking, by developing feelings and deep conviction.[2]

Ideas, ethics, morality and *reason* are key and intertwined themes in Castro's political thought. Material rewards and material punishment, the policy polarities that socialist states tended to swing between, play little role in his ideology:

I think it's a great merit for a person to give their life for a revolutionary idea and to fight, knowing they may die. Even though one knows there's nothing after death, one upholds the idea, the moral value, so firmly that one defends it with everything one has – without expecting reward or punishment.[3]

Political ideas are worthless if they aren't inspired by noble, selfless sentiments. Likewise noble sentiments are worthless if they aren't based on correct, fair ideas.[4]

Honour was an important ingredient of Castro's spirit. 'Even though I wasn't a model student, I felt morally obligated to pass all my exams. For me it was a question of honour.'[5] Castro was clearly impressed, not by the dogmatic methods of religious instruction – which were unsuccessful in his case, and which he rejects as ineffectual – but by the many aspects of the Jesuits' collective character:

Undoubtedly my teachers, my Jesuit teachers, especially the Spanish Jesuits, who inculcated a strong sense of personal dignity – regardless of their political ideas – influenced me. Most Spaniards are endowed with a sense of personal honour, and it's very strong in Jesuits. They valued character, rectitude, honesty, courage and the ability to make sacrifices. ... The Jesuits clearly influenced me with their strict organization, their discipline and their values. They contributed to my development and influenced my sense of justice – which may have been quite rudimentary, but was at least a starting point.[6]

The Bible, especially the Old Testament, left an indelible mark on him. 'Academically ... he showed a keen interest in religious history, particularly battles like that at Jericho, and the heroic accomplishments of Moses, Joshua and Prophet Daniel.'[7] The parallels with his own experiences are discernible between the lines of Castro's retelling:

I think I first learned about war in Biblical history. That is, I became interested in the art of warfare. I was fascinated by it from Joshua's destroying the walls of Jericho to the sound of trumpets, to Samson's Herculean strength, which allowed him to tear a temple down with his bare hands. Those deeds were really fascinating.[8]

Castro dwells upon ethics far more explicitly than anyone in the Marxist tradition. The dismissal of ethics and morality as class-based and therefore to be rejected by Marxists as ruling-class ideology if not self-serving hoaxes, is radically absent in Castro's thinking. The class dimension is clearly present but as a violation by the ruling and exploiting classes, of universal ethics and standards. This conforms to Gramsci's notion of hegemony: the identification of the interests of a class or party with that which is general and broad rather than the narrowly conceived class interest.

Ethical values came from my education, that is from school, from the teachers and, I would say, from my family, from home. I was told very early in life that I should never lie. There were clear ethical values. They weren't Marxist and they did not seem from an ethical philosophy. They were based on a religious ethic. I was taught what was right and wrong, things that should and should not be done. ...

Later on, my experiences in life began to create a feeling of what was wrong, the violation of an ethical standard, and a sense of injustice, abuse or fraud. So, I received not only a set of ethical standards, but also some experience of the violation of ethical standards and what unethical people were like. I began to have an idea of what was fair and unfair. I also began to develop a concept of personal dignity.[9]

What had I brought from that school, what had I brought from my home, what did I take to the university? A profound sense of justice, a certain ethic. That ethic had Christian precepts, which I learned fighting injustice from a very early age, with a sense of equality in my relationships from an early age, and undoubtedly because of a rebellious temperament, however you want to describe it, I reacted; I never resigned myself to abuse and the imposition of things by force.[10]

The picture that emerges, then, is of a rebelliousness but one that was not unrestrained; one that was tempered by a strong notion of ethics; one that not only sprang from but was suffused by a notion of fairness, of right and wrong. 'If you mix ethical values with a spirit of rebellion and rejection of injustice, you begin to appreciate and place a high value on a number of things that other people don't value at all.'[11]

Castro's own political consciousness and his acquisition of it was not at the hands of a mentor, which doubtless assisted him in evolving his own brand of Marxism and avoiding the ideological grip of Soviet Marxism even while embracing a strategic alliance with the USSR. It would have also helped him withstand the collapse of socialism, maintaining his own course.

I think that what I was telling you about faith – the ability to reason, to think, to analyse, meditate and develop feelings – is what makes it possible to acquire revolutionary ideas. In my case there was a special circumstance: nobody taught me political ideas. I did not have the privilege of having a mentor. Most of the people who have played a role in our history had mentors, outstanding teachers or professors. Unfortunately I've had to be my own mentor all my life. ... I've had to continue on my way – a long way – to develop my revolutionary ideas, and they have the immense value of being conclusions reached on my own.[12]

EARLY INTERNATIONALIST SOLIDARITY

Ingredients in the early years of Castro's politics were a strong sense of solidarity with struggles throughout Latin America, a readiness to join (irrespective of political rivalries) expeditions and efforts at armed rebellion against dictatorial usurpations, and the attempt to counter the influence of US dominance in the region.[13]

While he was a rebel, an anti-imperialist, a critic of the character of the prevalent democracy, he was not Communist in the sense of belonging to a Communist party. Following the Comintern line of the Popular Front, the Cuban Communist party had allied with Fulgencio Batista. Fidel does not criticise the Popular Front as an international policy and general line except to say that it was belated in the case of Europe: if the purges in the USSR had been avoided and the Popular Front line adopted earlier, it may have prevented the victory of Nazism. But he criticises the misapplication of that policy by the local CP, to ally with a corrupt dictator like Batista.[14]

This is perhaps the source of Castro's bypassing of the Communist party, though a strategic reason was also present: Cold War propaganda pervaded Cuba, making the designation 'communist' a dangerously unpopular one to the point of being politically fatal. While he avoided affiliation with the Communists, who on Havana University campus were suspicious of this Jesuit-educated son of a large landowner, as a university student Castro was heavily influenced by Marxism, disclosing that he 'gradually built up a complete Marxist-Leninist library of my own' while still at the University of Havana.[15] He describes himself as a socialist student, albeit a utopian one.

The role of a solitary rebel, maintaining his stand in the face of tremendous odds and gravest of physical risks, was assumed early in Castro's political life – and recurs as motif in his defiant stand after the collapse of his ally the Soviet Union and the disappearance of global socialism. While on campus Castro was isolated by the pro-Grau San Martin government forces, and was in danger of physical attack, even elimination. His isolation was compounded by considerable jealousy among student contemporaries. In an almost Gethsemane-like moment, he portrays himself, at the age of 20, as crying in solitude on the beach, and then as taking the existential decision to return, alone – and armed.[16]

This was his first episode of wielding a weapon in a political context, and significantly it is in *self-defence*. Thus the wielding of arms is readily resorted to as *armed resistance* against a threat of lethal violence and against considerable odds. However, this act semi-spontaneously caused others to rally around him, thus giving an illustration of the force of example. More: it was early proof or perhaps the seed of his idea that if one is willing to raise the standard of resistance and rebellion even against seemingly impossible odds, if one is willing to make the ultimate sacrifice, others will come forward to support the cause and the isolation would be broken by solidarity.[17]

The extent of Castro's armed political activism, his ready acceptance of recourse to arms in resistance to and rebellion against acts of injustice backed by lethal coercion, even before the Batista coup, is usually insufficiently appreciated in popular accounts. Already active in support of Puerto Rican independence, when Trujillo seized power in the Dominican Republic Castro joined an expedition to fight there. That it was a foreign country in which he might die posed no obstacle; no domestic political ambition led him to eschew the risk. Despite the fact that the expedition to the Dominican Republic was organised and funded by unsavoury political elements in Cuba belonging to the governing coalition, and despite the presence of his political enemies in the venture, Castro volunteered.

Naturally, seeing that the battle against Trujillo was about to begin and being the President of the Dominican Pro-Democracy committee I did not think twice. I packed my bags, and without saying anything to anyone, went to Cayo Confites to enlist in that expedition. Perhaps the most important factor in all this was that I signed up alongside the vast majority of my enemies. ... The action I took of doing my duty as a student won their respect.[18]

This last characteristic prefigured Castro's active participation in the Non-Aligned Movement, with heterodox ideological and political forces.

Though the expedition was a fiasco and collapsed owing to internal power struggles among the backers, chiefly between the Grau San Martin government and the army, 'I almost started guerrilla warfare in the Dominican Republic; I was already thinking of the possibility of guerrilla warfare in the mountains of Dominican Republic. That was in 1947.' He was only 21 years old.

Castro tried in 1948 to organise a Latin-American students' conference in Colombia, parallel and in opposition to the US-inspired formation of the Organisation of American States (OAS). It was during his dramatic experience in Colombia that two major strands of his thinking, armed rebellion and discriminate use of violence within such rebellion, come together. When he was in Colombia organising the Latin American students' meeting that embraced a number of anti-imperialist themes such as the return of the Panama Canal, the return to Argentina of the Malvinas, and the independence of Puerto Rico, he met the charismatic populist leader of that country's Liberal party, José Elicier Gaitan, who was widely tipped to win the imminent election. A day later, just as Fidel and he were to meet again, Gaitan was assassinated and a spontaneous popular uprising, later known as the *Bogotázo*, erupted. Castro joined the uprising, acquiring a weapon as soon as he could and urging rebellious policemen to take the military offensive against troops loyal to the conservative government. 'I still had my rifle and also a sword, a cutlass. ... I had around nine bullets and my police greatcoat, my militiaman's beret (the cap without the visor) and the sword.'[19]

The CIA's foremost Cuba hand, Brian Latell, emphasises the importance of the Colombian episode in understanding Castro. 'Fidel's participation in the violence was of enduring significance for him and Cuba. The *bogotazo* instilled a number of lessons – strategic, doctrinal, tactical and personal.'[20]

Without much contemplation, Fidel decided to join the rioters, plunging headlong into the mayhem. It was not enough to be just an anonymous body in that roiling mass; he moved quickly up to a position in the vanguard, at the front lines of the rioters where he could more easily assert a leadership role. He had no difficulty arming himself, at first with a tear gas gun and later with a rifle. He remained in the fray for about two days, first in the streets with the mobs, attacking and ransacking government buildings and police stations, and then overnight at a hillside redoubt, firing and being fired upon and for a period of time actually leading a squad of men ready to resist an army assault.[21]

... His... responses to the situation reflect the unique character traits he has exhibited in dangerous and stressful situations ever since. Few other foreigners caught in the maelstrom reacted as he did. Nearly all fled or hid... To have participated in the violence would have been insane by almost anyone's standards, especially for one who had no stake in Colombian politics. Fidel did not give it a second thought. His decision to join the rioters and the subsequent choices he made to stay and fight with them were entirely consistent with his mind set, convictions, personality framework, and proclivity for violence. His response was completely in character.[22]

A second strategic lesson of more enduring significance for Cuba and many other countries was that Fidel's internationalist vision was cemented in Bogotá. Cayo Confites had been a dress rehearsal; Bogotá was the real thing. The commitments he made to fight for another people were fixed with certainty.[23]

While Latell is indeed correct in underscoring the significance and representative nature of Castro's experience in Colombia, he overemphasises one dimension, namely Castro's spontaneous propensity for violent engagement and a frontline role. In truth, several key ideas crystallised out of his Colombian experience. The uprising was ended following an agreement between the Conservatives and the leaders of the Liberal party. However, troops loyal to the Conservatives hounded and eliminated rebellious Liberal loyalists even after the agreement had been announced. To Fidel, this was a betrayal, not least by the Liberal party leadership. Castro also obtained a first-hand experience of a popular uprising, with its parallels in his mind with the French Revolution.

Most pertinently, Castro saw episodes of violence emanating from within the rebellion that ran counter to his concept of violent revolution. While he was surer than ever about the moral rightness of the use of arms and the necessity for offensive tactics that would seize the initiative in a confrontation, for the first time lines began to be drawn in his mind between the correct and the excessive or incorrect use of violence within an emancipatory struggle. The latter included acts of popular revenge on individuals, mob violence and looting. While the impulse was partly against anarchy and in favour of greater organisation in an insurrection, there was an important moral dimension:

I saw people breaking shop windows and other things. This began to worry me, because I already had some very clear, very precise ideas about what should and shouldn't happen in a revolution. I began to see expressions of anarchy here on 7th Avenue... around midnight or 1:00 in the morning an incident occurred that I still remember. The Liberals found a certain policeman and tied and beat him on the floor where I was. I was disgusted. They called him a *godo* [Conservative Party supporter]... They insulted him and beat him several times. I didn't like that.[24]

In his retrospective view of Colombia, Castro reveals his self-concept and the importance of the ethical dimension in his ideological makeup:

Why did I stay, knowing it was suicidal and that they were making military mistakes? Because I had a sense of honour, idealism, a moral principle. That night the tanks kept going by and an attack was expected every half hour. I knew that if an attack came, everybody there was going to die because it was a real mousetrap. And even though I disagreed completely with what they were doing from a military point view, I stayed. I was going to die there anonymously, but I stayed. I'm proud of that; I acted in accord with my moral principles, with dignity and honour, with discipline and ... selflessness.[25]

Already this sense of honour ruled out certain uses of violence:

... *The greatest influence* those events had on me was in Cuba's revolutionary strategy, the idea of educating the people during our struggle so there wouldn't be any anarchy or looting when the revolution triumphed, *and the people would not take revenge.*[26]

THE RESPONSE TO BATISTA'S COUP

Fidel Castro had imparted training, including weapons training, to over a thousand activists, clandestinely using space at the University of Havana. His response to the Batista coup contained many of the elements of his thinking: rebelliousness, Jose Marti's nationalist resistance, armed revolt, mass appeal and mobilisation, the issue of legitimacy and the moral-ethical dimension. The last two aspects are evidenced in the manifesto that he clandestinely drafted and distributed, attacking the coup:

We have suffered misrule for many years awaiting the constitutional opportunity to exorcise the evil. And now you, Batista, you who fled for four years and then played useless politics for another three, appear with your perturbing and poisonous remedy, tearing the constitution into pieces when there are only two months to go before arriving at our goal by adequate means.[27]

Whatever Prio did in three years you have been doing for eleven years. Your coup is thus unjustifiable. It is not based on any serious moral reason or on a social or political doctrine of any kind. Reason is found only in force, and justification in lies. Your majority is in the army but not in the people. Your votes are in rifles never in will. With all that, you can win a military takeover but never clean elections. Your assault on government lacks principles that give legitimacy. ... Laugh if you will, but principles are, in the long run, more powerful than cannons. The people develop and are nourished on principles. For principles they die...[28]

Fidel filed a petition in the courts arguing that Batista should be sentenced to a hundred years for his coup, and the ringing conclusion of that petition provides a glimpse of his world outlook and motivations:

I do not commit any offence in stating these things with the greatest respect and sincerity; not to say so is bad, to resign oneself to a reality that is tragic, absurd, without logic, without values, without sense, without glory and honour, without justice.[29]

This must be taken together with his indictment of the conduct of the Orthodoxo party hierarchy in respect of the Batista coup, an indictment that indicates those values and mores that he reviles:

From above the tumult of cowards, the mediocre, and the poor of spirit, it is necessary to pass a brief but courageous and constructive judgement... Whoever believes that up to now everything has been done well, that we have nothing to reproach ourselves for, is a man who demands little from his conscience.[30]

The moral factor enters Castro's condemnation of 'politics as usual' and his celebration, by contrast, of the revolutionary alternative. The latter is placed higher on a scale of values and the differentiation could be described as existential:

... The moment is revolutionary and not political. Politics is the consecration of the opportunism of those who have the means and the resources. The Revolution opens the way to true merit, to those who have sincere courage and ideals, to those who risk their lives and take a battle standard in their hands.[31]

Fidel Castro always strove to maintain a moral asymmetry between himself and his foes. The concluding sentence of the short speech he made to the rebels who were about to attack the Moncada barracks under his leadership (remarks that Haydee Santamaria refers to in her reminiscences) is utterly telling and is indicative of Castro's criteria for the use of lethal violence: 'Those who are determined should go forward. The watchword is not to kill except as the last resort.'[32]

MILITARY DEFEAT INTO MORAL VICTORY

The assault on the Moncada army barracks – the country's second largest – which Castro hoped would raise the standard of a more general rebellion, ended in failure. In a dialectical move, he was able to avoid the military defeat from becoming a political defeat – and was subsequently able to transmute it into a political victory – by transferring the battle to the moral arena. He reversed the political consequences of a military defeat by winning a moral victory, which in turn enabled him to win the battle for public opinion.

Those who had met in combat confronted one another once again. Once again, with the cause of justice on our side, we would wage the terrible battle of truth against infamy! Surely the regime was not prepared for the moral catastrophe in store for it![33]

Fidel Castro's 1953 speech before his judges ('History Will Absolve Me'), conducted in the prison infirmary, is replete with references to the moral-ethical dimension. He makes a moral indictment of the regime, posits a moral superiority on the part of his fighters and cause, and perhaps most significantly, makes explicit reference to morality in armed combat, contrasting the behaviour of his fighters with that of the Batista forces and going on to make a general statement of principles about ethical and humane behaviour in warfare.[34]

The moral asymmetry of the *Fidelista* revolutionaries and the Batista regime is striking. The extreme brutality of the Batista forces is amply documented. In the aftermath of the defeat of the Moncada uprising,

61 captured militants were tortured, mutilated with their genitals and other body parts ripped out, and murdered.[35] These included Abel Santamaria, Castro's deputy, whose eye was plucked out and shown to his sister Haydee, also a captured revolutionary militant. Secret photographs of the corpses were published in the respected magazine *Bohemia*, generating a wave of revulsion at the repression. During the civil war the government forces engaged in what one independent writer calls 'State terror and corruption, bestial torture and murder of political opponents as well as non-participants ...'[36]

Castro's self-image is clearly that of a moral man:

This was an incredible situation, honourable judges: Here was a regime literally afraid to bring an accused man to court; a regime of blood and terror that shrank in fear of the moral conviction of a defenceless man – unarmed, slandered, and isolated.[37]

... I want to clear the field for an assault against all the endless lies and deceits, the hypocrisy, conventionalism, and moral cowardice that have set the stage for the crude comedy which since March 10 – and even before then – has been called justice in Cuba.[38]

Castro spends a large portion of the speech contrasting the conduct of his revolutionary combatants with details of torture and execution of prisoners, and killings of uninvolved civilians by the Batista forces, then goes on to mention a handful of honourable exceptions.

Everyone had instructions, first of all to be humane in the struggle. Never was a group of armed men more generous to the adversary. From the beginning we took numerous prisoners – nearly twenty – and here was one moment when three of our men – Ramiro Valdes, Jose Suarez, and Jesus Montane – managed to enter the barracks and hold nearly fifty soldiers prisoners for a short time. Those soldiers testified before the court, and without exception they all acknowledged that we treated them with absolute respect, that we didn't subject them to one scoffing remark. In line with this, I want to give my heartfelt thanks to the prosecutor for one thing in the trial of my comrades: when he made his report he was fair enough to acknowledge as an incontrovertible fact that we maintained a high spirit of chivalry throughout the struggle.[39]

The moral dimension of his speech resides not only in the explicit references to morality but in the argument of the right to overthrow a regime that had seized power in violation of the constitution, and in Castro's indictment of a social system that heaps injustice and misery upon the mass of its citizenry – an indictment of what we might term *structural or systemic immorality*.

Society is moved to compassion when it hears of the kidnapping or murder of one child, but it is criminally indifferent to the mass murder of so many thousands of children who die every year from lack of facilities, agonizing with pain… and when the head of the family works only four months a year, with what can he purchase clothing and medicine for his children? They will grow up with rickets with not a single good tooth in their mouths by the time they are thirty; they will have heard ten million speeches and will finally die of misery and deception.[40]

Castro implicitly sets out a code of conduct in revolutionary warfare, indeed warfare in general:

Let me mention two important facts that facilitate an objective judgement of our attitude. First: we could have taken over the ranking officers in their homes. This possibility was rejected for the very humane reason that we wished to avoid scenes of tragedy and struggle in the presence of their families.[41]

… Neither a real soldier nor a true man can degrade his code of honour with lies and crime.

In wartime armies that murder prisoners have always earned the contempt and abomination of the entire world. Such cowardice has no justification, even in a case where national territory is invaded by foreign troops. In the words of a South American liberator: 'not even the strictest military obedience may turn a soldier's sword into that of an executioner'. The honourable soldier does not kill the helpless prisoner after the fight, but rather, respects him. He does not finish off a wounded man, but rather, helps him. He stands in the way of crime and, if he cannot prevent it he acts as that Spanish captain who, upon hearing the shots of the firing squad that murdered Cuban students, indignantly broke his sword in two and refused to continue serving in that army.

The soldiers who murdered their prisoners were not worthy of the soldiers who died… when Cuba is freed, we should respect, shelter, and aid the wives and children of those courageous soldiers who perished fighting against us.[42]

Here, when he speaks of the decisions and choices including those of location of operations made by his rebel force, it is apparent that Castro's code is imbued with a spirit of chivalric honour.

PRISON: COMBINING REASON WITH MORALITY

The combination of honour with rationality is a feature of Castro's ethics. Take the case of his prison letters, reproduced in Mario Mencia's *The Fertile Prison*. He emphasises the moral factor motivating his understanding of his enemy, himself, the nature of the national crisis, the struggle and tasks that engage him, and the many challenging strategic and tactical decisions he is called upon to make. Crucially the self-image built up in these writings is of a man in whom 'calm cold reason' and 'strong moral feelings' are combined:

There is a law of inertia in the moral as well as the physical world, and both worlds also have their laws of gravitation; a thousand forces tend to slow you down, and sometimes you have to combat them with every ounce of psychic and spiritual energy... the physical must submit to the moral, the innate rebel ever at war with calm, cold reason, which in turn is based on strong moral feelings.[43]

The comparative silence of society concerning Batista's depredations was seen by Castro not only in political or social terms but also in moral ones.[44]

Rejecting a conditional amnesty (the condition being the renunciation of anti-regime activism), Castro wrote on 19 March 1955 a statement that was published in *Bohemia* on 27 March:

There is not the slightest doubt that after nearly two years in prison, solitary confinement etc, I would be prepared to go through another similar period – and as many more as may be necessary – rather than give the slightest ground to those who would undermine our moral stature... I write this from an upright conscience...[45]

...What moral right do men who have spent three years publicly stating that they made their coup d'etat to bring peace to the republic have for saying that...? Those officials in the comfortable, well paid posts they would like to keep forever, have the gall to use such terms to men a thousand times more honourable than they, who are kept behind bars....[46] We will not give up one iota of our honour in return for our freedom.[47]

In 1954, writing from prison to Melba Hernandez and Haydee Santamaria on 18 June, Castro returns to the issue of moral asymmetry as a criteria for deciding on who should assume power after the overthrow of Batista and rules out on that basis a return of the oligarchy, the old elite. He speaks in terms of what may be called a moral mandate, which has been forfeited by the old ruling class but has been won by the young revolutionaries:

...return to power of men who were morally and historically finished and who were fully responsible for the country's plight. Remember always that our prospects for victory are based on the certainty that the people will back the efforts of men with integrity, who will from the start formulate their revolutionary laws. Men who have deceived and betrayed the people cannot hope for such backing... we have had to fight alone before, during and after the events of the 26th. Now we represent a lofty and unblemished ideal, and we have the right be the vanguard of the future. We shouldn't sell our souls for a mess of pottage.[48]

In September 1956, Fidel signed the Mexico Pact with the Revolutionary Directorate headed by Jose Antonio Echeveria, the manifesto of which committed the July 26 Movement and the directorate jointly to the armed overthrow of Batista, a cause for which they sought broad unity of 'all the revolutionary, moral and civic forces of the country, the students, the workers, the youth organizations, and all worthy people of Cuba, to assist them in this struggle'.[49]

In his defence speech after the abortive attack on the Moncada garrison, Castro retraced the military and organisational errors and misfortunes that led to the failure of the attack. One of these was that a large group of the attackers, travelling in a convoy of vehicles, simply lost their way and did not participate in the assault. A key participant, Haydee Santamaria, reconstructed the Moncada experience decades later to a Havana University student audience in 1967, disclosing that some members of the group of rebels had refused to participate upon hearing of the plan, because they thought it suicidal. Castro gave them permission to leave the base camp, a farm in the Siboney area in Santiago de Cuba, on the proviso that they were the last to leave the premises after all the others had proceeded for the planned attack. However, Haydee is virtually certain that this group of reluctant ones left earlier than they had been told to, and their vehicle turned off in the direction of Havana, unintentionally misleading the group of volunteers who were proceeding to the Moncada in another column of vehicles. Seeing the first vehicle turn, the column of rebels did so too and lost their way in an endless detour. They were arrested, tortured, some murdered and others imprisoned after the Moncada attack. Later, says Haydee, when Castro knew of this, he did not denounce the ones who declined to participate and turned around, despite the fatal damage their action had caused. Haydee uses the recollection to make a point about Castro's quite distinctive ethics and morality in the matter of armed struggle:

Those ten... but I cannot say how many there were. It was not brought out into the open, because Fidel, with his tremendous understanding, did not wish to hold them up to public scorn. Names were not mentioned much; the action had not been forced on anyone. For even in that crisis Fidel had the same sensibility and human fibre that never left him, even in the face of the most crucial decisions.

One of the things he said then [in his speech before the Moncada attack] was 'Don't shoot for pleasure; don't kill for pleasure'. And the quality that led him to say 'don't kill, don't shoot', also kept him from pressing men who were not ready to fight. He refused to brand them as traitors, considering only that they were not, at that time, ready to go along with the plan.[50]

Castro had spent his time in prison conducting political education for fellow prisoners and, by means of smuggled communications, strengthening the underground movement. He had refused any offers of release that were conditional upon changed political behaviour on his part, and accepted only an unconditional amnesty.

POST-PRISON STANCE

Castro left jail a tempered and resolute revolutionary, utterly unrepentant – which is why his first act upon release is so striking. Castro's conduct upon his release from prison was illustrative of his values and notions of revolutionary behaviour.

At the prison gate, surrounded by friends, relatives and reporters, he embraced the chief of the prison guard Lieutenant Perez Diaz, and told reporters, 'This is a spontaneous and sincere gesture without histrionics, because this officer is a gentleman in the full sense of the word'. It was a gesture similar to the tribute he had paid to Lieutenant Sarria and Captain Tamayo in 'History will absolve me'.[51]

An article written after his release indicates his resolution to keep his mind free of bitter vengefulness despite two years in prison, including four months in solitary confinement:

... We said of the prison that although we were mistreated without end, we were leaving it without prejudice in the mind or poison in the soul – which could becloud our thoughts on the path to follow – and that the people of Cuba could always expect a calm and dignified attitude worthy of the circumstances from us. Those who spoke in that manner remained in the national territory with honour and a clean conscience, as can only be done by those who know how not to fear, have no blemish on their souls and know how to fulfil their duty simply and naturally. While I was still in prison some spoke about amnesty with conditions. We rejected them energetically even if it meant indefinite imprisonment. When the amnesty was finally decreed without conditions, our statements had no hatred, baseness or vengeance. If we reply to humiliation with dignity, to a decent act we reply with decency.[52]

In another article, polemical in nature, in the same period, Castro engages in another collective self-description, couched in explicitly moral terms: 'It does not matter that our hands are without weapons. Today we are the moral columns of the fatherland, and as columns we shall collapse rather than fall individually.'[53]

Later Castro lists the values and attributes he regards as central to armed revolutionary movements: 'Stubborn fools are those who believe that a revolutionary movement can be measured by the millions available to it and not by reason, idealism, determination and the honour of its fighters!'[54]

Writing in *Bohemia* magazine in 1955, Castro quotes the words of the prosecutor at his trial, with regard to the Moncada rebels' conduct during their attack:

... On the part of the revolutionaries, it is not difficult to say that they acted with honesty. They were sincere, courageous and patriotic in their confessions. They also behaved with generosity and honour. One example is right here in the Palace of Justice where they respected the lives of a group of armed forces members whom they could have killed...[55]

The acknowledgement by the prosecution, that is, the enemy, of the comportment of insurrectionists and their humanitarian conduct in the heat of armed insurrection is both a historical rarity and proof of Castro's achievement of moral-ethical hegemony even in military defeat.

CASTRO AS MILITARY LEADER

Fidel Castro's views on the correct and incorrect use of violence are of major significance precisely because he was, by any international standard, a successful practitioner of war on a large scale and a politico-military leader of great courage and skill. Castro was at home in warfare. Though he had no military training, he was familiar with firearms, having been a hunter while an adolescent. He protected himself from deadly gangs on campus by carrying a weapon. He joined armed expeditions to overthrow dictators, and when one such was called off, he jumped ship and swam ashore, submachine gun around his neck. When stranded in Colombia he participated in the uprising following the assassination of Eliecer Gaitan, and his first instinct was to find a firearm.

Inspired by the Cuban heroes Cespedes, Maceo and Marti, he saw little point in any form of resistance against manifestly oppressive systems, other than armed rebellion and warfare. He called for an organised armed revolution, rejecting as both unviable and undesirable other options because they would not lead to a total transformation.

While in the Sierra, Fidel's *nom de guerre* was Alexander, and later in life, in his middle years, he would name his sons with variants: Alex, Alexei etc. Sir Leycester Coltman, a long-serving British ambassador to Cuba, says that Alexander the Great exercised a compelling hold on Castro's imagination. Like Stalin, Trotsky, Mao and Giap, Castro had no formal military training. In 1958, as rebel leader fighting in the mountains, he beat back the all-out offensive by Batista's army, an army that was one of the largest and best armed (with American planes and using napalm bombs) in Latin America.

With him as commander-in chief, the post-revolutionary Cuban armed forces proved to be one of the finest fighting forces in the world, evoking favourable comparison with the Israeli Defence Forces:

With the exception of Israel, no other small country has tallied as many stunning battlefield victories as Cuba has. Not even the Israeli military has ever exhibited the long-range force projection capabilities that Cuba's did in the 1970s, when tens of thousands of troops were dispatched first to Angola and later to Ethiopia, both many thousands of miles from Cuban shores. It was Fidel, to be sure, who was the grand strategist of those interventions and who astutely calculated the geopolitical benefits and risks.[56]

The very fact of his military successes, in Cuba and overseas, proves that the selective, discriminate use of violence in the differing contexts of guerrilla and counter-guerrilla war, and large-unit mobile-conventional warfare, does not detract from military efficacy, and indeed may enhance it.

Brian Latell places Castro's skills as commander-in-chief in perspective:

There is no disputing that throughout his career he has acted courageously, beginning at Cayo Confites and Bogotá. He is not known to have flinched or lost his nerve in any of the innumerable crises he has experienced. He was sharp and in command during the Bay of Pigs, moving Cuban forces around the island like chess pieces. He made all the strategic decisions during Cuba's military interventions overseas. And he seems to have been no less capable as he aged Into his sixties and seventies. In the summer of 1994, for example, during the worst anti-regime rioting that has ever occurred in Cuba, he went to the scene at Havana's seaside Malecon Boulevard in an effort to calm the protestors and personally direct the security response.[57]

Castro's military skill, achievement, physical courage and Hemingwayesque 'grace under pressure' – attested to here by a hostile source – combines with humanitarian conduct to form a specific code of conduct, ethic and way of being.

REVOLUTIONARY WAR AND TERRORISM

Castro's military vocation, and the intertwining of moral and martial impulses in the man's thinking, were exemplified in the revolutionary war he waged against Batista. In a document published in the magazine *Bohemia* in 1955, while Castro had not yet been amnestied, he clarified the reasons that made war politically and morally inevitable and necessary, thus meeting the criteria of a 'just war', although, as argued earlier, there is no evidence that his argument derived from, rested upon or was a conscious application of just war theory.

We are not professional troublemakers nor are we blind proponents of violence. We would not resort to violence if the better homeland that we yearn for could be achieved with the weapons of reason and intelligence. ... No people would follow a group of adventurers who sought to plunge the country into civil strife unless injustice held sway, unless there were no peaceful legal means provided to all the citizens in the civic battle of ideas. We agree with Marti that 'he who starts a war that can be avoided is a criminal as is he who fails to start a war that is inevitable'.[58]

When, after his release, Castro broke in March 1956 from the leadership of the Orthodox party, he reiterated his convictions on the use of violence and the justification for armed rebellion:

It is not our fault if the country has been led into an abyss from which it can be saved only by revolution. We do not love force. Because we hate force we are not willing to be governed through force. We do not love violence. Because we hate violence we are not willing to continue to put up with violence, the violence that has been used against the nation for the past four years.[59]

Castro's discriminating, critical view of the way in which violence was to be used even against an oppressive government, already evidenced in his reactions in Colombia, once again makes an appearance in response to events in Cuba in 1955. Castro had just been released from Batista's prison as a result of a massive publicity campaign and the dictator's own need for legitimacy. He had few illusions that anything had changed, that a genuine liberalisation had taken place. It is at this time that a rash of bombings takes place in Havana. In his first news conference given upon his release Castro condemns these acts. His condemnation stems partly from a suspicion that these were acts of *agents provocateurs*, partly from a classically Leninist rejection of individual terrorism (Lenin denounced the Narodniks and SRs). However, there is an unmistakeable moral revulsion in Castro's denunciation, a moral judgement that would surface throughout his political life and manifest itself in his response to the 9/11 attacks on his great foe the USA more than half a century later:

...Terrorist acts, because they are inhuman, antirevolutionary and indirectly beneficial to the government... No one with any sense can think that setting off a bomb in any old doorway can cause the fall of a government.[60]

The second occasion was in June 1955. A Batista opponent, Jorge Agostini, was murdered upon return from exile, and Castro had openly accused the government of responsibility. When bombings followed the assassination he wrote an article entitled 'Against Crime and Terror', which contained an unambiguous denunciation:

The greatest service that can be performed for a dictatorship that stresses order is to use the barbaric and inhumane method of dynamite, because the oppressors are then given the justification for terrorism... I am so convinced of the immense harm that they are doing to the struggle against the dictatorship, that I would not hesitate to publicly denounce the bunch of savages who render such a valuable service to Batista while pretending to be revolutionaries.[61]

Revolutions are based on morals. A movement that has to rob banks or accept money from thieves cannot be considered revolutionary.[62]

If a revolution robs a bank to get funds, the enemy will call us gangsters. If the Revolution accepts aid from embezzlers who have plundered the Republic, the Revolution will be betraying its principles. If the revolution solicits aid from vested interests, it will be compromised before it attains power... Any form of collection by means of coercion or violence is entirely alien to our methods.[63]

A serious competitor to Castro's guerrilla project arose from among militant university students, calling itself the Revolutionary Directorate (DR). Its strategy was that of assassination and urban terrorism, redolent of the Russian Narodniks and their successors the Socialist Revolutionaries, referred to in Part 1 above. Castro's response by-passed the three options that are most widely practised in such contexts: he avoided a coercive or imitative competition, or endorsement of such tactics:

Apart from personal rivalry, there were some policy differences between Echeverria and Castro. Echeverria favoured assassination as a prime weapon in the struggle against Batista. Castro was more cautious. Without ruling out assassination in exceptional circumstances, he argued that assassination usually meant replacing one individual with another who would follow the same line, while the perpetrators forfeited public sympathy. In planning the attack on Moncada, he had considered seizing the high-ranking officers in their homes but had rejected this option. 'We wished to avoid scenes of tragedy and fighting in the presence of their families'.[64]

Castro made a public criticism of the DR's tactics. His criticism of the killing of a top Batista police officer illustrated his notion of targeting and based itself on the fact that the man was not a notorious torturer.

A few weeks after Castro's meeting with Echeverria, their differences over assassination became public. The DR shot dead the new SIM chief, Colonel Antonio Blanco Rico, when he was leaving a nightclub. In the aftermath numerous people were killed, including ten men who had sought asylum in the Haitian embassy. The Colonel was a questionable target, being a reforming officer who since his appointment had tried to put an end to the practice of torture by SIM interrogators. Castro publicly condemned his killing. 'Such acts must not be indiscriminate…from a political and revolutionary standpoint, his assassination was not justified. Blanco Rico was not a Fascist executioner.'[65]

Castro's critique of assassinations went further, and even encompassed a DR attempt on the life of Batista.

In March 1957, the DR launched an attack on the presidential palace, and came close to achieving their objective. If Batista had not by chance taken a concealed lift from his office to his private third floor apartment just before the attack he would probably have been killed. Thirty-five DR militants were killed at the palace before the police regained control. Echeverria himself, after trying to make a broadcast from a radio station, which had also been occupied by DR militants, was killed by the police in the streets afterwards. Fidel Castro once again publicly dissociated himself from the attempted assassination. It was 'a useless spilling of blood. The life of the dictator does not matter.... I am against terrorism. I condemn these procedures. Nothing is solved by them.'[66]

As we shall see in Chapter 7 below, Fidel Castro's condemnation of terrorism remained consistent throughout his political life.

CASTRO'S CONCEPT OF CONDUCT IN WAR

Let us examine how Castro carefully delimits and explains the underlying logic of the use of violence by his military forces.

Does it seem illogical in the midst of the war to free enemy prisoners? This depends on the war itself and the concept one has of war. In war one must have a policy for the enemy just as one must have a policy for the civilian population. War is not merely a matter of rifles, bullets, cannons, and planes. Perhaps that belief has been one of the causes of the failure of the tyranny's forces.... Since we landed in the Granma, we have adopted an unchanging policy toward the enemy. That policy has been fulfilled rigorously, indeed as probably very few times in history. From the first battle that of La Plata on January 17, 1957, to the last battle in Las Mercedes during the first days of August there were over six hundred members of the armed forces in our hands in this front of the Sierra Maestra alone. *With the legitimate pride of those who have known how to follow an ethical norm, we can say that without one exception the fighters of the rebel army have honoured their law with the prisoners. Never did a prisoner forfeit his life, and never was a wounded man left unattended. But we can say more: Never was a prisoner beaten. And further: Never was a prisoner insulted or offended. All officers who were our prisoners can verify that no one was submitted to interrogation due to our respect of their condition as men and soldiers. The victories achieved by our troops without murdering, torturing, and even without interrogating the enemy demonstrate that abuse to human dignity can never be justified.* [Italics in original]

This attitude, maintained during twenty months of struggle, with over one hundred encounters and battles, speaks itself for the conduct of the Rebel Army. Today in the midst of human passions, it does not have as much value as it will when the history of the Revolution is written. To have followed that policy now when we are strong is not as meritorious as when we were a handful of men persecuted like beasts in the rugged mountains. It was then, during the days of the battles of La Plata and El Uvero, that to have respected the lives of prisoners had profound moral significance.[67]

While waging a full-scale guerrilla war for the seizure of power (and not merely armed propaganda actions, such as the ANC's military wing Umkhonto We Sizwe would undertake), Castro's forces were humane in their treatment of prisoners – only spies and torturers were executed.

Castro and his comrades showed no mercy however, towards farmers who acted as spies for the Batista regime. In one case, which served as a warning to others, they were able to prove that a scout of theirs, Eutimio Guerra, had accepted 10,000 dollars from the army to lead the guerrillas into a deadly ambush and kill Castro with his own hands. Castro sentenced him to death.[68]

That sentence was carried out by Che Guevara.

In 1958, after a revolt by reformist naval officers, B-26 planes bombed the city of Cienfuegos and regime troops re-entering it shot 33 officers and tortured captives. By contrast, after the strategically important victory at El Uvero, the advancing Rebel Army

… executed one notorious overseer who had murdered landless peasants and rebel sympathisers; and they distributed captured livestock to the campesinos, thereby ensuring their own supplies. Batista's army by contrast, spread only fear and terror among the rural masses, wreaked only murder and destruction as they combed the land for insurgents.[69]

During Batista's big push in 1958 against Castro's forces in the Sierra, the government's aircraft used napalm bombs.

In his categorical rejection of the Miami Pact signed by several moderate anti-Batista parties, Castro lists four reasons why the July 26 Movement is entitled to the leading role in recomposing the armed forces following a victory. The first reason is its military strength and prowess, 'with over 20 victories over the enemy'. The second of the listed reasons is moral, and relates to restraint in the use of violence. It reads:

Because our fighters have shown a chivalrous spirit free from any hate of the military, invariably respecting the life of the prisoners, healing their wounds, never torturing an adversary even when knowing that he is in the possession of valuable information. They have maintained this conduct in war with unprecedented equanimity.[70]

Enrique Meneses, a Spanish journalist who spent months with Castro and his guerrillas in the Sierra Maestra mountains as early as 1957, wrote a long report for *Paris Match*, and later a book that was hostile to Castro's subsequent radicalisation, provides in the book an eyewitness account of the treatment of prisoners in the guerrilla camp:

The first time I went down to Havana to send a story I took with me letters from the prisoners to their families. In many of them Celia Sanchez had enclosed a hundred-peso note. The prisoners suffered no ill treatment, and when some of them wanted to fight for Castro he turned them down, not only because he hadn't got the arms to equip them but also because he didn't think they should fight against their former comrades. The news these prisoners sent to their relations made a magnificent advertisement for Fidel Castro and his cause.[71]

As referred to in the Introduction to the present study, Michael Walzer excerpts from the *US Marine Corps Gazette*, an eyewitness report by a well-known journalist of Raul Castro's handling of prisoners, in a classic application of Fidel's policy:

That same evening, I watched the surrender of hundreds of Batistianos from a small-town garrison. They were gathered within a hollow square of rebel Tommy-gunners and harangued by Raul Castro: 'We hope that you will stay with us and fight against the master who so ill-used you. If you decide to refuse this invitation – and I am not going to repeat it – you will be delivered to the custody of the Cuban Red Cross tomorrow. Once you are under Batista's orders again, we hope that you will not take arms against us. But if you do, remember this: We took you this time. We can take you again. And when we do, we will not frighten or torture or kill you... If you are captured a second time or even a third... we will again return you exactly as we are doing now.'[72]

While he categorically rejected a military coup, in the victorious closing stages of the civil war Fidel Castro had a number of exchanges of letters with officers of the armed forces. Though the letter-writing may be said to be tactical, the contents of the letters and their tone significantly illuminate Castro's well-defined code of conduct within revolutionary war, and warfare in general:

Dear Friend,

It was difficult to imagine that you and I, seeing each other at the University, would someday be fighting each other, in spite of the fact that perhaps we do not harbour different feelings with respect to the fatherland, which I am sure you venerate as much as I do.

Many times have I remembered that group of young soldiers that attracted my attention and awakened my sympathies because of their great desire for culture and their efforts to continue their studies. I knew how to appreciate it when in my mind the things that are occurring now are far away.

I did not have then, as I do not have today – in spite of the sad circumstances which have placed the armed forces beside the most nefarious politics in our history – any hatred of the military. I have judged with harsh words the behaviour of many in general and the army in particular, but never have my hands or those of any of my companeros been tarnished with the blood or degraded by the mistreatment of an imprisoned soldier. In one of our battles at Uvero, there were thirty-five prisoners; none was mistreated, and today all of them are free and in service. However, on that same occasion, one of our wounded men was left with the military doctor due to his critical state, but once cured he was not freed as an elemental gesture of reciprocity towards those who had freed thirty-five adversaries. That companero, invalid as the result of the wound inflicted, is today in the Isle of Pines....

What a surprise to know that you are around here! And even though the circumstances are difficult, I am happy even to know about one of you, and I write you these lines without thinking of them, without telling you or asking you anything, only to salute you and wish you, very sincerely, good luck. Your friend, Fidel Castro.[73]

Unique in irregular warfare at the time, and rare even in current times, was the handing over of wounded prisoners to the International and Cuban Red Cross. This indicated the humanitarian norms and guidelines to which Castro, Che and others adhered even in the heat of war. The definitive statement of Castro's concept of war and on the code of conduct in warfare, buttressed by a report of his fighters' behaviour, is contained in 'Report on the Offensive: Part 2'. He is acutely aware of the distinctiveness of the conduct of his army, its long-range historical significance and its moral worth. He is also conscious of the intersection of moral and strategic value of a humanitarian policy. Finally, Castro understands that a humanitarian policy in war is a necessary insurance against brutalisation of the future society, one that arises from the civil war. In that he is radically different from those who eschew violence and advocate a non-violent strategy in order to avoid such social distortions. Castro's philosophy of rebellion, unlike that of others, particularly other Marxists, does not ignore the issue of the effect of violence on future society. His solution is neither adherence to pacifism nor blindness to the consequences of violence, but rather a code that guides the practice of violence, serving almost as a Hippocratic Oath:

... To kill makes no one stronger. Killing has made them weak; not to have killed has made us strong. Why do we not murder prisoners? (1) Only cowards and henchmen murder the enemy once he has surrendered. (2) The rebel army cannot use the same tactics as the tyranny we fight. (3) ...What would be convenient for the dictatorship is not for us to cure wounded soldiers and respect the lives of the prisoners, but rather to murder them all without exception so that each member of the armed forces could then see the need to struggle to the very last drop of blood. (4) If in any war cruelty is stupid, in no war is it more so than in a civil war, where those who fight one another will have to live together someday and the executioners will meet the sons, wives and mothers of their victims. (5) Before the shameless and depressing examples given by the dictator's murderers and torturers, we must place the example that our fighters have given before the coming generations as an edifying achievement. (6) Right now we must sow the seed of fraternity, which must rule the future fatherland that we are forging for all and for the good of all. If those who fight honestly know how to respect the life of an enemy who surrenders, tomorrow in peace no one can feel he has the right to practice revenge and political crime....[74]

In a humanitarian practice that was probably without precedent in an unconventional war or a war waged by unconventional forces, and in an example that has hardly been followed in other parts of the world either by guerrillas or governments from Lebanon to Sri Lanka, Castro released enemy prisoners into the care of the International Committee of the Red Cross, and did so unconditionally, and without an exchange of prisoners, that is, without reciprocity.[75]

When victory was in sight, and doubtless deriving from his experience in Colombia, the Castro forces actively discouraged popular revenge. Already in November with victory in sight Castro had told the Cuban people:

No one must take revenge on anyone. Those who have committed inhuman acts against the people will be detained and imprisoned and later tried by revolutionary courts. In the decisive moments which are approaching, the people must give the highest proof of civic sense, patriotism, and a sense of order so that later no dishonourable accusation can be made against our revolution which, because it is the highest goal of the Cuban nation and the most extraordinary proof of the people's desire for peace and of their dignity, must suffer no blemish.[76]

THE ABSENCE OF INTERNECINE VIOLENCE

Castro's doctrine of violence also included a doctrine of non-violence. Armed violence was not only to be deployed in a selective and ethical manner; it was to be limited to certain *types* of conflict. Violence was not to be applied to other types of contradictions and conflicts.

Castro deployed armed violence against the enemy, but not against competitors and rivals – and he did not confuse the latter with the former. This is all the more striking given that he was convinced of the moral superiority of his project, and was determined that his revolutionaries should lead Cuban leadership and that his vision for Cuba should prevail. His political will was utterly resolute, and yet that quality did not translate itself, as it did in all other revolutions starting with the French Revolution of 1789, into a practice of violence against all rival tendencies and competing projects of governance. In Castro, resolute will did not lapse into fanaticism or fundamentalism.

Julia Sweig lays bare the complexity and competitiveness of the political milieu in which Fidel Castro strove to make his revolution.[77] Despite the high level of competition among anti-Batista forces, some of whom would agree to participate in elections held by the regime, and others who would resort to terrorist and adventurist armed tactics, both groups thereby jeopardising the cause in his eyes, Castro was firmly against the use of armed violence to resolve political or ideological disputes within the oppositional space: 'We are against violent methods aimed at persons from any opposition organization that disagrees with us. We are also radically opposed to terrorism and personal assault. We do not practice tyrannicide.'[78] Castro's attitude in practice towards other revolutionary organisations is manifest years later in the letter he sent a group of guerrillas, independent of the July 26 Movement, fighting in Las Villas. The letter is one of cordiality, advice and offers of concrete support, including directions as to how to seek a tie-up with Castro's force in case of need.[79]

What makes this even more striking is that, as Sweig notes, the contradictions and tensions that existed in the run-up to the overthrow of Batista, echoed throughout the years in power. Yet, despite the historicity of these contradictions – and here the contrast with the Russian Revolution in power is noteworthy – Castro never succumbed to the temptation to kill as a means of resolving the contradictions.

The different approaches to ousting Batista were represented by, among others, the various factions and offshoots of the Ortodoxo and Autentico parties, the radical, armed opposition, and armed insurgents fighting for tactical and strategic superiority in the drive not only to unseat the dictator but also to rid Cuba of corruption and longstanding politiqueria or dirty politics... A number of the subsequent political conflicts in the 1960s, particularly between what came to be the three primary revolutionary forces, Castro's 26th of July Movement, the DRE and the Communist Party, known as the Popular Socialist party (PSP), had their roots in the conflict within and among those three groups during the anti-Batista insurgency.[80]

John Dorschner and Roberto Fabricio track the event of the final weeks of the Cuban Revolution, providing fascinating testimony about the fierce political competition that was under way to prevent a Castro victory.[81] Elements within the armed forces, a variety of civilian politicians, rival armed rebel organisations and finally the United States engaged in feverish initiatives and manoeuvres to grab power, heading Castro off and forcing him to compromise. The account also shows that Castro had spotted the moves and even anticipated them, and was determined that his Rebel Army and what they represented would not be thwarted of total victory. Thus his was not a moderate, pluralist, power-sharing paradigm. He was determined and resolute in his counter-moves. His determination makes all the more remarkable his non-recourse to lethal violence against rival political forces even at this decisive eleventh hour, though he was ready to continue the war unabated to forestall or resist a military coup, a civilian–military restoration of the old establishment, or US military intervention.

When in the immediate aftermath of the revolutionary victory, the DR felt marginalised, their contribution unrecognised (to their mind) and excluded from the victory parade, they seized a large quantity of weapons and stored them on the Havana University premises. The situation was potentially similar to the conflict that exploded between the Bolsheviks and the SRs, or Khomeini and the radical Fedayeen. Yet Castro resolved it by peaceful means, bringing to bear the weight of public opinion, which he had roused in a speech.

Then without naming the DR, Castro started to whip up the crowd against them. He said some people had seized weapons from a military base, which was under the command of the Rebel Army. The weapons should be returned to the barracks where they belonged. Why had these weapons been taken? Against whom were they to be used? The crowd shouted their indignation. Once again Fidel's magic worked. The pressure of public opinion, strengthened by a demonstration of mothers' calling for the handing in of weapons, enabled Castro to bring the DR to heel without resorting to overt force.[82]

Two great revolutions of differing social character, the French and Russian, were characterised by lethal violence between competing tendencies, as was the Chinese revolution at a subsequent stage (the

Cultural Revolution). The Spanish Civil War of the 1930s, in which the elected Republican government strove unsuccessfully to protect itself from the onslaught by Franco's Fascists who were supported by Hitler, was marked on the Republican side by debilitating strife between the 'pro' and 'anti' Soviet/Stalin formations of the left. There are a few allegations that Ho Chi Minh's Communists deployed violence against the Vietnamese Trotskyists or directed the attentions of the French colonial authorities towards them. Tito's Yugoslavia bloodily eliminated pro-Stalin/Cominform elements, while other post-war Eastern European regimes eliminated pro-Tito elements during the same periods the late 1940s.[83] As Chapter 2 above underscored, the devastating effect of internecine violence in the ranks of victorious or strongly ongoing revolutionary struggles in the 1970s and 1980s contributed significantly to the defeat of socialism in the Cold War. In contrast to this pattern of brutal and ruthless violence against political competitors, Castro's practice of making an appeal over the heads of his armed radical competition to the general public, occupying the moral high ground, and outmanoeuvring and neutralising his rivals without recourse to violence, is unique in the history of revolutions. Had Castro's practice been the norm, might not the history of these revolutionary projects been different?

4
Defending the Revolutionary Regime

The preceding chapters in this part of the study have dealt with the enunciation and practice of Castro's ethic of correct and incorrect use of armed violence in the context of the armed revolutionary struggle. To what extent, and how, has this ethic been sustained after his accession to state power? The task of this chapter is to investigate the elaboration in policy and practice, of Castro's idea of moral superiority and the ethical use of violence, with particular reference to the defence of the revolutionary state against armed invasion and domestic counterrevolution; the transition to socialism, issues of foreign policy and the projection overseas of Cuba's power. It deals not with Castro's wielding of power in general but in relation to the specific idea or doctrine of his that is under study.

THE USE OF VIOLENCE IN VICTORY

According to the testimony of British journalist Edwin Tetlow, Castro's was 'one of the best behaved armies you could imagine... To a man they behaved impeccably'.[1]

In the weeks and months after the victory of the revolution the people expected one thing above all else a settling of accounts with Batista's paid torturers and murderers.[2]

'Paredon! Paredon! Paredon!' – Up against a wall – shouted several hundred thousand voices at a mass rally in Havana on Jan 22 1959.[3]

In the wake of the revolutionary victory, acts of violent anarchy persisted only until the rebel forces arrived in the area. The post-revolutionary punitive actions, including executions, were based on files that the fleeing Batista left behind, with copious information. These executions followed a legal process of a trial.

Also left behind were mountains of documents that testified to the corruption and crimes of the Batista regime, so that the *barbudos* would have an easy job demonstrating the necessity and legitimacy of their revolution, as well as proving the guilt of thieves and murderers from the old regime, who were apprehended and brought before a revolutionary court. The documents also revealed the extent of the co-operation between the United States government and Batista's criminal regime.[4]

How did the Castro regime handle the situation? There were no lynchings. There was a solitary incident, according to the new US ambassador, Philip Bonsal, for which Raul Castro was solely allegedly responsible, in which 70 ex-Batista prisoners were summarily executed. However, even the US ambassador admits that Castro intervened and 'the Castro procedure of setting up special tribunals to try the cases of people who on the basis of Nuremburg principles were accused of serious crimes, could have been an improvement over the earlier method'.[5] Meanwhile, 'Soldiers and officers who had a clean record were integrated into the new Fuerzas Armadas Revolucionarias (FAR).'[6]

Most striking and conclusive is the comment made by Tad Szulc:

Cuban revolutionary trials… bore no resemblance to the real bloodbaths that followed the Mexican, Russian and Chinese social revolutions in the twentieth century… By the same token the Cuban revolution refrained from institution-alised mass killings such as those perpetrated against hundreds of thousands of Chinese in Indonesia in the aftermath of the 1965 army anti-Communist coup, or those attributable to Chilean military authorities when they overthrew the Marxist president, Salvador Allende Gossens, in 1973… It is quite remarkable that violence-prone Cubans remained so un-violent.[7]

Samuel Farber makes the points that the executions prevented informal lynchings, were overwhelmingly approved of by a majority of Cubans 'of almost all political inclinations', and, most relevant to the present study, 'torturers and assassins were properly identified, and no innocent bystanders fell prey to the revolutionary settling of accounts'.[8]

This imperative to spare the innocent entailed special sensitivity to the treatment of children. In a speech to schoolchildren Castro explained that:

They can go to our schools even if their fathers committed crimes and even if their fathers killed somebody. Those children are not to blame for that. You know yourselves that the children themselves are innocent. At school even though some child may be the son of one of the soldiers from before, he should be treated as a brother. Any child who is so unfortunate as to have had a father who committed crimes is not to blame for that. The child is a victim himself.

At school you must not have bitter feelings towards any of your classmates, because all children are innocent.[9]

In the aftermath of the French, Russian and Chinese Revolutions, class origin was regarded as a stigma passed down through the generations, and the sins of the parents were visited on the children. In the case of the Cuban Revolution, Castro opposed any notion of shared or transmitted guilt and collective punishment.

USE OF VIOLENCE BY THE REVOLUTIONARY STATE

On 10 March 1959, only two months after he had entered Havana, five days after Castro had met the new US ambassador, and much before any expropriation of US property business interests in Cuba, the US National Security Council had 'already reviewed modalities for "bringing another government to power in Cuba." The record of this review exists in the classified NSC archives...'[10]

As we have noted, since the bloody suppression of the first experiment in the revolutionary rule of the working masses, the Paris Commune of 1871, Marxists were determined that a victorious revolution would be defended against all comers and at any cost. In the collective consciousness of rebels everywhere was a historical memory as it were, of what a victorious counter-offensive by former rulers would entail – the crucifixion for mile upon mile of Spartacus and his rebels being a notorious early example.

Castro's commitment to the defence of the revolution was absolute, but he remained uniquely restrained in his methods. He combined resoluteness with restraint, in a synthesis of political will and humanitarian norms. This synthesis, so evident during his armed uprising and guerrilla war, remained throughout the Cuban Revolution's transformation into a state. Castro did not relax his norms of humanitarian conduct when the revolution had emerged and consolidated itself as a state; not even when that state faced a serious armed challenge, an invasion, which threatened its very existence, and everything that the rebels had fought and sacrificed for. That synthesis of political determination, military prowess and morality gave him a significant strategic advantage, countering disadvantages of a more tangible military and economic sort.

The propensity of Castro to make for the moral high ground can be seen in the immediate aftermath of the Bay of Pigs invasion, an attack that had used napalm bombs. A total of 1,189 attackers surrendered and were imprisoned. They included a number of wanted killers from the Batista days. Fourteen were tried for their activity under Batista, a mere five were executed, and nine sentenced to 30 years' imprisonment. In an unprecedented event, Castro personally discussed and debated the invasion and the Cuban Revolution with the prisoners, in the full glare of TV cameras. Twenty months after the invasion they were released in exchange for US$ 53 million worth of medical supplies.[11]

Castro's treatment of prisoners came into the full view of the world after the Bay of Pigs invasion. Castro had played a major role in repelling the invaders, speaking to a young pilot and motivating him to bomb the crucial troop and supply ships, driving down to the forward command post and basing himself there during the fighting. Castro's forces had lost over two hundred dead in repelling the invasion.

More than any other Castro knew the consequences of victory for the invaders: certain death for him and his followers, and a bloodily vengeful reversal of his revolutionary reforms. Most other leaderships in this situation, having beaten the invaders, would have inflicted an exemplarily harsh punishment – as commended by Machiavelli – in order to deter anyone signing up for future incursions. Castro chose to make an example, but of a different sort.

… Over the following four days the interrogation of prisoners was shown live on television, with a panel of journalists putting the questions…. Some prisoners remained defiant, criticising Castro for failing to hold elections. But this at least indicated that they had not been ill treated or intimidated. … On April 25 Castro himself took over the questioning, walking among the prisoners with a microphone like a talk show host. 'Be honest' he said to one prisoner, 'Surely you recognise that you are the first prisoners in history who are allowed to argue with the head of the government you came to overthrow, in front of the whole country and of the whole world!'[12]

Tad Szulc, author and Latin America specialist of the *New York Times*, documents Fidel's swift occupation of the moral high ground at this historic crucial moment:

Castro spent Thursday the nineteenth on the breach in Giron satisfying his curiosity by inspecting enemy positions and talking to the prisoners. There were so many prisoners that quite a few still had their weapons with them as they surrounded Fidel to answer his questions. Fernandez, who knew most of the Brigade officers personally from the old days, says that the prisoners first feared immediate execution by their captors, then 'were surprised that they were treated with total correctness... human dignity was scrupulously observed.'

... Castro had decided while the battle was still progressing that the prisoners would not be harmed, and he did not wish to damage the image of revolutionary purity and generosity with brutality, summary executions, or a mass trial....

... Fidel came up with another sensation in his drama by allowing ten of the men to fly to the United States on May 20 to support his demands. The prisoners were personally told by Castro that ten of them, chosen by the whole group, could go to Miami and Washington for seventy-two hours, or longer if required for the negotiations, on their word of honour as officers and gentlemen that they would return to Cuba. He stunned them with this offer when he visited the captives just after being awarded the Lenin Peace Prize... The other touch was that they travelled in their Brigade camouflage battle uniforms, clean and shaved, a gesture of military honour Castro always applied to his foes in war. They brought mail for the families of those left behind when they flew back to Havana a week later, and they were allowed to carry 660 pounds of gifts for their fellow prisoners.[13]

Castro later said: 'Our Marxist-Leninist party was really born at Giron.'[14] If so, as its father, he made certain that its birth was attended by a gift of moral capital.[15]

THE QUALITIES OF THE *FIDELISTA* FIGHTER

Combat, warfare, requires hatred of the enemy. All military training seeks to inculcate such hatred in the psyche of the soldier. However, such hatred itself often results in excess, in atrocities, because hatred involves the dehumanising to some degree of the enemy. If the enemy has to be destroyed, then any and all means of doing so seem valid, indeed called for. In a guerrilla or counter-guerrilla war, the temptation to excess is greater than in most other forms of struggle. Insofar as the regime tends to resort to torture and to target civilians suspected of being sympathetic to the cause of the rebels, the rebel forces too tend to seek revenge by visiting torture on the enemy in captivity and targeting civilians working for the enemy. A revolutionary regime waging war against counterrevolutionary insurgents not only has the problem of identification that bedevils any regime, but is motivated to root out the resistance with a view to defending the fledgling revolution.

Revolutions (and significant progressive experiments) are replete with examples of insufficient decisiveness and resoluteness in their defence, and therefore of failure (for example, the Paris Commune, Spain, Guatemala, Chile). Similarly, revolutions also provide examples of unrestrained force resulting in the undermining of the moral standing and support base of the revolution, also leading to collapse (Greece's civil war, 1947). Castro strove for a 'golden mean'. Brian Latell identifies one aspect of Castro's vision of the model revolutionary:

... He has always expected other revolutionaries to emulate his behaviour. Zealotry in the pursuit of his revolutionary causes would be the fundamental requirement. He believes true revolutionaries must plunge willingly, heroically into action without getting bogged down in needless contemplation or theorizing. He came to expect fanaticism from those charged with defending the revolution at home and in pursuing revolutionary internationalist causes abroad. In Fidel's mind, at least, the decision to stay and fight on Bogotá's Monserrate Mountain provided the model for all future revolutionary internationalists.[16]

Fidel Castro and Che Guevara sought to create the kind of fighter who would be motivated by hatred towards the enemy but would not yield to the temptation to torture enemy captives or target civilians. In his Message to the Tricontinental, Che referred to the need for 'hatred' and the transformation of the guerrilla into a 'cold, selective killing machine'. The adjective 'selective' marks such a fighter out from those who use terrorism in support of the cause of liberation. Given the scale and scope of the operation of the Cuban armed forces, the achievement of Fidel in inculcating this doctrine of 'hatred plus humanism', of creating a fighter who was a zealot, even a fanatic with a difference – one who would not shed the blood of the innocent or torture captives – is a remarkable one, especially when seen against the backdrop of the atrocities committed by US forces in Abu Ghraib and Guantanamo.

Colonel Victor Dreke, who served as Che Guevara's deputy in the Congo and later headed the Cuban military mission in Guinea Bissau,[17] provides testimony of the ethic of the *Fidelista* combatant. Speaking of the fight against US-supported counterrevolutionary guerrilla bands in the Escambray Mountains, he says:

There's something about the anti-bandit struggle that I think is important for everyone to understand: Our troops never abused a single prisoner. We never mistreated a single one, even though these prisoners had committed a great many murders and we hated them. ...They were assassins and criminals. We never mistreated anyone; the captured bandits were never beaten or abused. But they were taken to serve their sentence, according to what each had done.[18]

A rare glimpse into the formation of the *Fidelista* fighter is provided by Ulises Estrada, who fought alongside Che Guevara in the Congo, in his account of the training as underground militant of Tamara Bunke alias Tania, who died as a guerrilla fighter in Che's campaign in Bolivia. Estrada talks about instructions given in the use of explosives:

We emphasised that in the Cuban situation the use of explosives as weapons of war – though never for terrorist attacks – had been important in confronting the enemy's troops and repressive forces... According to Pascual, in their first conversation he explained to Tania the innumerable risks involved in handling explosives and the importance of adhering to strict security measures. Going by his own experience in the Cuban insurrectionary struggle, he also emphasised that these deadly weapons should be only used in direct attacks against the repressive forces of the enemy and should never cause injury to innocent people or civilians.[19]

There is a telling contrast between the use of explosives in the *Fidelista* practice and concept of liberation war, and those of al Qaeda, Hamas, Hezbollah and the Tamil Tigers, who either wittingly target civilians or have no compunction about the use of explosives amidst civilians. The Cuban doctrine is not limited to insurgency. Though the Cuban air force was extensively used in the Angola campaign, there was never even an allegation of an air-strike that targeted or caused non-combatant civilian casualties.

The *Fidelista* notion of morality included truthfulness in propaganda. Not even to boost the morale of the fighters and supportive populace was exaggeration permitted. As Dreke says:

And unfortunately in many liberation movements – not just in the Congo but in other places too – the companeros have a habit of exaggerating. If they capture a rifle they say they captured ten rifles. If they kill a soldier they say it was twenty soldiers. This wasn't true of the Cuban Revolution. In reporting on events we never claimed a single extra bullet, a single extra enemy killed, a single extra prisoner.[20]

Another source of moral superiority of the Cuban Revolution was the frontline role and presence of the leaders; an indication of courage and responsibility. Dreke puts it thus:

One thing that shocked us was that the main leaders of the Congo liberation movement were not there on the front lines. But when you look more deeply at the liberation struggles in Africa, you see that the same thing was happening all over. All the African liberation movements were based in the neighbouring countries. We didn't understand this. We were young people accustomed to Fidel being with us day and night, side by side, or Almeida, who was in charge of operations in the Escambray. The companeros were right there on the front lines of battle.[21]

However, Castro's notion of morality did not involve denying any human worth to the enemy, thereby demonising him.

At the high point prior to the victory at Playa Giron, Castro pointed out the counterrevolution had 1,000 armed men in the Escambray who were experts in evading our forces. I won't call them cowards. There can be people who are mistaken and even very mistaken who are personally brave but not personally moral.[22]

He was ready to acknowledge qualities such as courage, but did not view courage alone as conferring morality. Morality required the service of a cause that was moral, but it also meant conduct in a manner that was moral in the service of that cause.

The use of violence by the Cuban armed forces, in a combination of prowess and the avoidance of atrocities, is most striking in Africa. Cuba's role in Africa, and especially Angola, is comparable to that of the US military in Vietnam.[23] In that comparison the Cubans come off infinitely better, both in terms of military achievement as well as observance of humanitarian norms, or at least the absence of atrocities and massacres.[24] The fact that the Cuban army, unlike the American, was a 'socialist' army is of no decisive importance, as the performance and conduct of the Soviet Red Army in Afghanistan demonstrates. If socialist ideology, as distinct from capitalist or imperialist, was a factor, then it is the specific type of socialist ideology inculcated by Fidel Castro (and his brother Raul, the Defence Minister), with its strong ethical-moral component, that seems to be pertinent. Nor can the factor of military training alone, explain it. The post-Vietnam US army, as deployed in Iraq, is an all-volunteer professional force, unlike the draftees of Vietnam. Few military formations have as rigorous a professional training as the US Marine Corps. However, the Haditha massacre in Iraq, in which 23 unarmed civilians including six children were massacred, was perpetrated – according to footage by a Marine cameraman – by a unit of the US Marines, a unit headed by a lieutenant-colonel that had a reputation for serious human rights abuses.[25]

As the evidence in this part of the study shows, the *inculcation* of the ideology of armed struggle in the Rebel Army by Fidel Castro includes the *inoculation* against the use of violence against certain categories and in certain circumstances. Fidel Castro was the founder and commander of the Revolutionary Armed Forces, or FAR, known at the time as the Rebel Army. He has remained the commander-in-chief throughout. He 'led personally' the victorious fight-back against the invaders at the Bay of Pigs,[26] and as the data in this part of the study shows, strategically (and sometimes tactically) commanded the Angolan operation, particularly in its decisive stages, such as the battle of Cuito Cuanavale in 1988. As Nobel prize-winning author Gabriel Garcia Marquez writes in his essay on the Angolan expedition, 'Operation Carlota' (named symbolically after a black woman slave fighter for Cuban independence and initially transported on a Cuban ship named 'Vietnam Heroico'), Castro gave a pep talk to and personally saw off every contingent of the Cuban fighters who went off to Angola.[27]

While Fidel Castro was the founder and commander-in-chief of FAR, its chief organiser and the Minister of Defence has been his brother Raul Castro, while Ernesto Che Guevara was an illustrious *commandante*, theorist on strategy,[28] frequent writer for the army journal *Verde Olivio*,[29] and heroic role model. Both these personalities, Raul Castro and Che Guevara, shared Fidel Castro's ethic of violence, and as such, the composite influence of the trio Fidel, Raul and Che, shaped the ethos of the Cuban military. Of the three it is Fidel who demonstrates the earliest, most consistent and frequent insistence on the right and wrong use of violence – and therefore should be taken as the pre-eminent influence in this regard.

One of the ideologues of Cuba's armed forces and role model after his death was Che Guevara. His ethics of violence, indistinguishable from that of Fidel, is summarised by his son Camilo Guevara in the introduction to a new edition of the *Bolivian Diary*:

Che never ceased believing that revolutionaries, even if they are being massacred sadistically, should invoke the use of force only when absolutely necessary, and even then, should never accompany it with cruelty. This idea is directly proportional to the condition of being a revolutionary.[30]

On the face of this evidence, it is difficult to attribute – as a principal factor – the Cuban armed forces' discriminating, surgical use of violence to anything other than the ideology of Fidel Castro and the elaboration of that ideology into an ethic and collective practice.

MORALITY AND FOREIGN POLICY

Cuba's achievement on the world stage was unique. H. Michael Erisman opines that 'Never before, at least not in the twentieth century, had such a small country exerted such influence on the international balance of power. Never before had a Latin American nation left such deep marks in world politics.'[31] Erisman builds on the judgement of scholars such as Jorge Dominguez and others to rank Cuba as unique among the actors to emerge on the international scene in the latter half of the twentieth century.[32]

The Cuban revolution had burst on the world from a small Caribbean island, gradually becoming one of the central issues in international affairs.... Its leaders commanded world attention; its policies had to be monitored by statesmen everywhere; its people could be found throughout the globe. The stage of the Cuban revolution had become universal as its concerns and policies impinged on millions of its friends and foes in many countries.[33]

How does the moral factor figure in that foreign policy achievement, especially in the context of the Cold War and complex crises? Having examined several significant and contentious episodes in Cuba's external affairs, this portion of the chapter argues that realism did not drive out ideals and ethics, and that a hallmark of *Fidelismo* is precisely the combination of realism and idealism, even in that domain in which realism is said to be the overwhelmingly dominant consideration in decision-making, namely that of state behaviour in the international system or foreign policy.

THE MISSILE CRISIS

It is now amply documented that the decision to station Soviet missiles in Cuba was against the backdrop of a US plan for the invasion of the island, and that the decision to station the missiles was entirely a Soviet one, which Castro agreed to with some misgivings. Both the misgivings and the acceptance contained a moral dimension, a factor that is hardly present in any Leninist analysis of the 'conjuncture' (the contradictions and balance of forces in a concrete situation) and decision-making:

We did not like the missiles. If it were a matter of our defence alone, we would not have accepted the missiles here. But do not think it was because of the dangers that would come from having the missiles here, but rather because of the way in which this could damage the image of the revolution in Latin America.... I thought: if we expected the Soviets to fight for our cause, to take risks for us, and if they were even prepared to go to war for our sake, it would have been immoral and cowardly not to allow the presence of the missiles here.[34]

... But when I walked away from that table I was already convinced that morality left us no other alternative but to accept the presence of the missiles here. I immediately convened a meeting with all the comrades and explained the content of the conversation and the Soviet proposal. I also explained my point of view and the analysis I had made of the moral and ethical content of the situation. Every comrade without exception agreed: comrade Osvaldo Dorticos who was then the president of the country, Raul, Che and a number of other leading cadres of the revolution. That same day, I met again with the Soviet envoys. My answer was: 'If this is to strengthen the socialist bloc, and, in addition, defend the Cuban revolution, we are prepared to accept all the missiles that need to be established here'.[35]

The desire never to cede the moral high ground, combined with an astute understanding of the link between the moral factor and strategic advantage, made Castro oppose Khrushchev's decision to dissemble, to lie to the Americans about the stationing of missiles:

If our conduct is legal, if it is moral, if it is correct, why should we do something that may give rise to a scandal? Why should it seem that we are doing something secretly, covertly, as if we were doing something wrong...? We're giving *imperialism* the initiative; we're giving the *enemy* the initiative.[36]

The Russians had assured the USA that only defensive weapons would be employed in Cuba.

It did us a lot of harm. Kennedy trusted in what he was told... so in the eyes of world public opinion, Kennedy gained moral force... What other advantage did it give him? That when the missile sites were finally discovered on 14 October, the United States had an enormous advantage... the initiative in the military realm was put in [their] hands. They ... could afford to choose one option or another, a political option, quarantine, or a surprise air attack on those installations.[37]

Theodore Sorenson confirms Castro's fine-grained understanding of the nexus between the moral and the strategic, saying that a publicly admitted stationing of Soviet missiles in Cuba in response to the stationing of US Jupiter missiles in Turkey aimed at the USSR would have made it 'much more difficult [for President Kennedy] to have mobilized world opinion on his side'.[38]

In his 1998 interview in the CNN/BBC series on the Cold War, Castro returns to this issue and makes a general point on politics and morality quite contrary to that of Machiavelli's advice to a new prince in a new principality:

Actually the Soviet leader resorted to deception and, in any political dispute or any dispute for that matter, deception is negative and fruitless. It demoralizes the one who lies, the one who deceives. Worst of all Kennedy had believed word for word what Khrushchev had told him and he was reacting to all the pressure in his country on the basis of the assurances he had received from the Soviet government.[39]

The moral factor re-emerges in the most intense moments of the missile crisis, and in a complex manner. Castro sent a message to Nikita Khrushchev on 26 October 1962, which he refers to in his 1998 CNN/BBC interview as 'the most passionate letter in history',[40] arguing that in case of an all-out US invasion of Cuba, the USSR should not wait for a US first strike on it but should seize the initiative. The Soviet leader understood this to mean that Castro was urging him to launch a nuclear first strike on the USA, to which Castro replies on 31 October:

I may have tried to say too much in too few lines. We were aware that in the event of a thermonuclear war we would be wiped out... I did not mean to suggest, Comrade Khrushchev, that the USSR should have been the aggressor, because that would have been more than wrong, it would in my view have been immoral and disgraceful; ... I meant to say that after imperialism had attacked Cuba, the USSR should act without hesitation and never commit the mistake of giving the enemy the opportunity to carry out a nuclear strike against it.[41]

What is most noteworthy is that this is not a public speech or interview of Fidel Castro's. It is a top-secret communication between two Communist leaders and at a moment of high-intensity crisis, of survival or obliteration for Cuba and certainly for the revolution and its leadership – perhaps never meant for publication. In this context, the stress on the moral-ethical aspect ('That would have been more than wrong... It would have been immoral and disgraceful'), a rarity in exchanges between two leaders in such a context of severe danger, assumes great significance and is evidence of its centrality to Castro's thinking and world outlook.

Castro's final judgement on the missile crisis is instructive:

It was Khrushchev's fault that the crisis developed as it did. If he had the common sense to do as we suggested and operate publicly, then the position of the Soviet Union before international opinion would have been very strong.[42]

It clearly confirms the premium Castro places on the occupation of the moral high ground in any confrontation with the enemy.

CZECHOSLOVAKIA 1968

How then is Castro's support for the Soviet intervention in Czechoslovakia in 1968 to be understood? Was it a blatant contradiction of his striving to occupy the moral high ground? Castro's moral-ethical criteria operated within a larger ethic of fighting against oppression and injustice, a prime embodiment of which was 'US imperialism'. Not only was it encircling and attempting to destroy the Cuban Revolution, it was raining destruction on the people of Vietnam. Taken together with its history of intervention in Latin America on behalf of the privileged and iniquitous systems, it was in Castro's eyes an immoral empire and a mirror image of how Reagan would see the USSR: an evil empire.

While Cuban society under Castro in the 1960s was hardly the grey-on-grey of Eastern Europe, and as such he would not have any objection to a more attractive model of socialism in the Soviet bloc, Castro had two problems with the Czech reforms. Firstly, the reformists were 'soft-liners', conciliators in foreign policy. Khrushchev's and Brezhnev's 'peaceful coexistence' was bad enough, having done considerable damage to the peoples of the Third World by giving the US a blank cheque, but the Czech reformers were even more conciliatory towards the US and the West than the Soviets. Russian action was therefore a flicker of resoluteness and confrontation on their part, which should be encouraged. Secondly, the Czech reforms were headed in a wrong direction, towards more marketisation and material incentives.

Castro's stand in August 1968 was similar to that of Mao Ze Dong in relation to Hungary in 1956. Mao's emerging differences with Khrushchev after his secret ('de-Stalinisation') speech to the 20th Congress of the CPSU didn't stand in the way of his applause for Russian resoluteness in relation to the West. Furthermore, though Mao had criticised Stalin just that year for the 'incorrect handling of contradictions among the people', that is, for the excess use of violence in domestic disputes, and while he had authored a policy of the Ten Great Relationships, arguing for a less centralised economy, he still felt that the Hungarian reforms were too far, too fast and in the wrong direction. Thus Mao both urged and endorsed Soviet action. Castro did not urge Soviet action in Prague, but came round to supporting it as a rebuff to the US and possibly a wake-up call to the Soviets themselves for the incorrect policies of market liberalisation that the Czechs had taken a step further.

Far from negating the importance of the moral-ethical factor in Castro, this stand in 1968 only underscores its importance because it is a reminder that the moral-ethical criteria and delimitations were part of the ideology of a man who was resolutely and tough-mindedly committed to the anti-imperialist struggle and the confrontation between capitalism and socialism on a global scale.

It was painful to have to use military force but necessary and right to do so when socialism was under threat…. He was privately gratified to see that the Soviet Union still had the nerve to take decisive and controversial action to uphold the strength and unity of the Socialist camp…. Like Margaret Thatcher, Castro always viewed a particular event in the context of the wider conflict between ideologies. Whom would it benefit? The western camp or the Socialist camp? Us or them? … Justice was not a question of legal technicalities, but of moral conviction.[43]

Fidelismo was no pure romantic idealism, but a complex combination of idealism and realism, virtue and power.

ANGOLA AND APARTHEID

From the earliest days of the emergence of Revolutionary Cuba, military assistance was rendered throughout the Third World to liberation movements and states deemed progressive. This ranged from support to the Algerian FLN, through Guevara's missions to the Congo and Bolivia, to Castro's admission of weapons induction into the Cuban embassy in Santiago so as to assist Salvador Allende if he chose to arm detachments of loyal workers (which he did not).

The best known of Cuba's external military involvement is of course Angola. In none of these cases did the host movement or state pay Cuba; the Cuban government paid its own soldiers. In none was there any allegation, even by the US, of atrocities committed by Cuban soldiers, almost 300,000 of whom served over the years in Angola alone, out of a larger total who served outside Cuba's shores.

Cuba's Angolan mission was neither at the behest of nor with the foreknowledge of the USSR. What is more pertinent is that Cuba's relations with the US had shown signs of distinct improvement prior to the Angola mission. The Cuban involvement there, independent of the USSR and damaging to an embryonic and much-desired relaxation of tensions with the USA, doubtless had as a causative factor a need to enhance Cuban influence and prestige by means of power projection, but it also contained an aspect that can only be described as moral-ethical. This was the reversal of Cuba's history in which black slaves were brought to work in plantations. It was a historical restitution: a blow against white racism and for black emancipation.

Sir Leycester Coltman sketches the background and summarises the results of Cuba's involvement:

Angola was a far away country about which the Cubans knew little. But ... how could he reject an appeal from a fellow revolutionary threatened by both the United States and the apartheid regime of South Africa? He did not hesitate for long... He gave a pep talk to every departing contingent, urging them not to fail in their historic mission. About half the soldiers were black, and especially sensitive to the message that Cuba's duty was to save a black south African country from the claws of the South African racists and American white supremacists... he devoted almost all his time and energy to the Angolan expedition, poring over maps in his office and personally ordering every deployment and every action... The Cuban expeditionary force saved the MPLA from destruction... The rapid advance northwards of the South African forces was halted, destroying the myth of South African invincibility.[44]

The salience of the factor of black fighters defeating hitherto undefeated white supremacist troops is confirmed by Swiss sociologist Jean Ziegler:

In November 1975, Cuban regiments, three fourths of which were made up of black troops, disembarked at the port of Luanda and pushed the invaders back... Black Cubans had blocked the way of white South African tanks and paratroopers.[45]

Thus, the practice of internationalism, which in Castro's version contained a pronounced moral imperative, took precedence over improved relations with the USA despite the potential economic benefits of such improvement. It also took precedence over the wishes and interests of his Soviet patron and ally, whose détente relationship with the USA – bringing recognition of coequal partnership and the possibility of global condominium – was jeopardised by Castro's Angolan intervention.

Perhaps Angola provided the most dramatic example of the extent of Castro's achievement. In the most detailed study of Cuba in Africa,[46] Piero Gleijeses writes that while all the Cuban soldiers in Angola were volunteers, there was a ban on members of the Central Committee volunteering because there was such a rush to do so. Instead the leadership made the decision. The seniormost party official in Angola, Jorge Risquet, had official complaints made against him by his colleagues because he turned up for a meeting with a photograph of himself with African liberation leaders taken in 1965 when he was liaising between Havana, Africa and Che Guevara's mission in the Zaire/Congo. Risquet brought the photograph as evidence of his familiarity with Africa's liberation movements, but his comrades protested that he was lobbying. He got the job.

Gleijeses notes that Cuban officers and troops were paid only their regular salary, and that by the Cuban government, not the Angolan. He quotes an official South African army history to the effect that the Cubans 'fought cheerfully until death', and documents in painstaking detail the military defeat of the powerful South Africans at the hands of the Cuban volunteers. This exemplifies the Thermopylae mentality of the Cuban Revolution, for both Fidel Castro and Defence Minister Raul Castro have made repeated reference to the example of the Spartan resistance against Xerxes' massive force, immortalised in Herodotus' *Histories*. But scholars and journalists also report that Cuba's various revolutionary anniversaries, including its national day, are celebrated by huge open air all-night parties hosted by Fidel and the leadership, with bands on every street corner.

Castro's consistent attempt at counterattacking by establishing a moral superiority over his foes and subjecting them to withering fire from a moral high ground is illustrated in one of his replies to US criticisms of his interventions in Africa:

What moral basis can the United States have to speak about Cuban troops in Africa? What moral basis can a country have whose troops are on every continent… when their own troops are stationed right here on our own national territory, at the Guantanamo naval base? It would be ridiculous of us to tell the United States government that, in order for relations between Cuba and the United States to be resumed or improved, it would have to withdraw its troops from the Philippines, or Turkey, or Greece, or Okinawa or South Korea.[47]

As noted, Cuba could have benefited materially had it not sent its fighters to resist apartheid South Africa's forces when they invaded Angola in 1976. Cuba could have had the pressure ease up on her if she did not fight against the South African invaders once again in 1988 in the battle of Cuito Cuanavale on the Namibian border – a battle that was won, expediting negotiation for Namibian independence and Nelson Mandela's release from prison, because, as Mandela said, it was the news that the invincible South African army had been militarily beaten back by Cuban forces that shattered the morale of the white supremacist regime of Pretoria. Conventional wisdom attributes the liquefaction of the apartheid system to the collapse of the USSR, the end of the Cold War and the resultant end of South Africa's threat perception. However, the ANC was unbanned and Mandela released in 1990, before the USSR collapsed in winter 1991.

Arguably the most moral political leader of our time, Nelson Mandela is perhaps the most reliable and credible source with regard to the moral capital accumulated by the Cuban Revolution:

Your consistent commitment to the systematic eradication of racism is unparalleled. ...

We come here with great humility. We come here with great emotion. We come here with a sense of a great debt owed to the people of Cuba. What other country can point to a record of greater selflessness than Cuba has displayed in its relations with Africa? How many of the countries of the world benefit from Cuban health workers or educationists? Where is the country that has sought Cuban help and had it refused? How many countries under threat from imperialism or struggling for national liberation have been able to count on Cuban support?

It was in prison when I first heard of the massive assistance that the Cuban internationalist forces provided to the people of Angola, on such scale that one hesitated to believe, when the Angolans came under combined attack of South Africans, CIA financed FNLA, mercenary, UNITA and Zairian troops in 1975.

We in Africa are used to being victims of countries wanting to carve up our territory or subvert our sovereignty. It is unparalleled in African history to have another people rise in defence of one of us.

We also know this was a popular action in Cuba. We are aware that those who fought and died in Angola were only a small proportion of those who volunteered. For the Cuban people internationalism is not merely a word...

The crushing defeat of the racist army at Cuito Cuanavale was a victory for the whole of Africa! The defeat of the apartheid army was an inspiration to the struggling people inside South Africa! Without the defeat of Cuito Cuanavale our organizations would not have been un-banned! The defeat of the racist army at Cuito Cuanavale has made it possible for me to be here today! Cuito Cuanavale has been a turning point in the struggle to free the continent and our country from the scourge of apartheid!

The decisive defeat of Cuito Cuanavale altered the balance of forces within the region and substantially reduced the capacity of the Pretoria regime to destabilize its neighbours. This in combination with our people's struggles within the country was crucial in bringing Pretoria to realize that it would have to talk.[48]

Mandela's testimonial to the moral worth of Cuba's action contrasts with the moral fragility of Cuba's Western critics on the twentieth century's defining issues of apartheid and racism.

THE OCHOA EPISODE

Heroic as the Angola experience was, a shadow crossed its aftermath. Arnaldo Ochoa was the commander of Cuban forces in Angola, a decorated veteran of the Cuban armed forces and popular among the soldiery. Against the backdrop of US allegations of drug running by or via Cuba, and Castro's own vehement denunciation of the charge, the Cubans conducted an investigation as a result of which Ochoa and several other officers were arrested and charged. Following a televised trial (according to some, televised only in parts), and a confession by Ochoa, who however claimed that these actions were not for personal aggrandisement but for the upkeep of the Angola expedition, Ochoa and his confederates were executed by firing squad.

It is possible that Cuba embarked upon this drastic course of action to pre-empt an American action on drug smuggling charges. However, Cuba has shown no signs even during the 1962 Missile Crisis, of panic, of being militarily intimidated by the United States, and certainly not to the extent of sacrificing its own military commanders. In his long interview with Tomas Borge, Castro criticises Stalin for his purges of the party and the Red Army in the 1930s, which, he noted, weakened the army, party and state in the face of the Nazi enemy. It is highly unlikely that Castro would have risked such a weakening, when only 90 miles from the US, and a US that was governed at the time by a Republican administration.

Some commentators speculate – albeit with no evidence whatsoever – that the Castro brothers wanted to head off a threat from within the armed forces. Another version is that a pro-Soviet faction in the armed forces was being promoted by Moscow to undertake a coup and initiate *perestroika* and *glasnost* in Cuba. Both versions are hardly tenable.

No historic founder-leader of a revolutionary state has been deposed in his lifetime. No revolution has witnessed a serious bid for power by a contender from a successor generation, outside the historic leadership core of that revolution. It is difficult to believe that Ochoa, who was popular within the armed forces but certainly nowhere near as popular as Castro, the founder of those armed forces, and hardly a household name among the Cuban people, let alone the world outside, would put himself forward as an alternative.[49]

Even if this were the case, that would have been a far stronger charge, of mounting or planning a straightforward coup – so characteristic of Latin America and so reviled among Marxists – rather than one of drug smuggling. It is also unlikely that if there were indeed disaffection in the army Castro would have stoked it by arresting a popular officer.

As for the notion of a pro-Soviet coup, that does not fit the known facts. Mikhail Gorbachev's relations with Cuba were known to be good. The elements in the USSR who would have had the most contact with the Cuban armed forces were those in the Soviet defence establishment, and these were precisely the elements known to be most supportive of the special relationship with Cuba, Fidel and Raul Castro. Those in the USSR and the CPSU who were opposed to the equation with Cuba were the Yeltsinites, who had no links with the Cuban army. If indeed the Ochoa group had planned a pro-*perestroika* coup, there is no reason to think that Castro would not have crushed it decisively and denounced it as such – just as he did the power bid by the general secretary of the pro-Moscow Cuban Communist party, Anibal Escalante, in the 1960s.

Before the revolution, the Cuban coast was used for smuggling contraband, including alcohol. With the exponential growth of the drug trade, Cuba could either have participated in it clandestinely or looked the other way as the cartels used the coast for smuggling. This would have not only brought in much-needed foreign currency for hard cash-strapped Cuba but could conceivably have eased the attacks against it launched by anti-Castro exiles in Florida, given the nexus between these elements, the Mafia and the CIA.

The entire venture could have been justified as revolutionary expediency and any damage to the main drug-consuming country, the USA, could have been regarded as an undermining of capitalist society. Arguments of these sorts are the staple of guerrilla movements that do countenance or are in alliance with the drug trade, the most notable being the FARC of Colombia. However, Castro's Cuba firmly rejected these options. The Ochoa trial itself shows the repeated invocation by Fidel and Raul of the ethical virtue of the Cuban Revolution.

HUMANITARIAN INTERNATIONALISM

In the first years of Revolutionary Cuba, especially on his visit to the USA, Castro defined his revolution as 'humanism'. Whatever propagandistic utility he derived from that definition, his socialism was marked by a humanistic streak. For Castro, internationalism was to be understood in ethical and moral terms, and his use of 'conscience' was unique in the Marxist tradition:

There have been times when we had to build a road in another country when we were in need of roads in ours, or we built an airport when we ourselves were short of airports. ... First of all internationalism is also a matter of conscience, and it implies doing without many things in order to help others who are more in need than us.... Help others even if nobody helps us. It's simply a moral duty, a revolutionary duty, a matter of principle, of conscience, even an ideological duty. To contribute to humanity even if humanity has done nothing for us.[50]

Castro practised what he preached, despite the sharp differences with the USSR by that time, and the costs to Cuba of Soviet retrenchment from its commitments both strategic and economic:

When the Chernobyl nuclear disaster struck the Soviet Union, Castro offered to look after any children affected by the radiation. In quixotic fashion, he was ready to take any number of children, for any length of time, and to give them the best available medical treatment and nursing care, at no cost. More than 13,000 children came to Cuba, some staying many years. In the tropical sun and with the loving care of Cuban nurses, the condition of many children improved dramatically. Children who arrived looking thin, haggard and miserable, returned to the Ukraine looking healthy and fit.[51]

Despite the strong animosity between the George W. Bush administration and Cuba, especially in relation to the President's brother Jeb's long-standing relations with the most violently anti-Castro Cuban émigré organisations, Castro's immediate reaction to 9/11 was an example of both his ethico-moral humanism and his occupation of the moral high ground as a strategic factor in confrontation with his enemy.

When Castro received news of the terrorist attacks on the United States on 11 September 2001, he was not for a moment tempted to take satisfaction from the misfortune of his old adversary. Indeed he realised at once that the destruction of the Twin Towers would be counter-productive in terms of the war against 'imperialism'.... His immediate reaction, conveyed through Foreign Minister Roque, was to condemn and reject the attacks, to express sympathy and solidarity to the American people, and sincere condolences to the victims. He offered the use of Cuban airports for the diversion of aircraft in American airspace. Cuba also offered to give blood plasma and other humanitarian assistance for the victims of the attacks. Later, in a more measured statement, Castro said Cuba would never allow its territory to be used for terrorist attacks against the United States. Cuba was the country that had suffered most from terrorism. Cuba was against terrorism; but it was also against war... On 6 October 2001 Castro held a ceremony to mark the 25th anniversary of the destruction of a Cuban airliner near Barbados, with the death of 73 people. The two Venezuelans who planted the bomb were almost certainly agents of the CIA. The ceremony was Castro's way of reminding the world that Cuba had indeed been a victim of terrorism.[52]

Castro's response was utterly consistent with his stance of occupying the moral high ground, and bore considerable similarity to his reaction to the assassination of President John F. Kennedy, an adversary. He condemned the act, sent condolences to the victims and offered assistance, while reminding the US (and the world) that it, rather than Revolutionary Cuba, had engaged in or encouraged the kind of terrorism that it now was the victim of, in the company of Cuba. The denunciation of terrorism and its human cost was also a denunciation of US imperialism, but solidarity with the victims demonstrated that a common humanity had, for Castro, a higher value than ideological and political enmity. Because it was not mere propaganda but was backed up by a concrete offer of help, placing the onus of acceptance or refusal on Washington was also an oblique critique of the US government.

Part III

Analysis

Introduction

Fidel Castro's doctrine of violence figures in this study in several ways and is utilised for several purposes. The doctrine illustrates the illegitimate and legitimate use of violence. I think it has to be placed at the centre of any contemporary argument concerning the possibility of the ethical use of violence. Castro's doctrine, I want to argue, delineates a contemporary theory of 'just war' for both anti-state organisations and states. It is also been used as illustration of the strategic utility of morality and ethics in politico-military practice. On the basis of this 'working model' of a leftist political ethos, I want to suggest that a fusion of realism, romanticism and ethics in progressive political thought generally is both desirable and possible.

'The revolution's capital is its moral supremacy', observed Isaac Deutscher.[1] It will be discerned that within world socialism the Cuban example proved qualitatively stronger, because it was a cleaner, more humane beacon, combining an age-old moral force, reaching back to the Prophets of the Old Testament, with the most exciting experiments of modernity. History may also judge that the greatest leader of humanity's socialist experiment, after Lenin, was Fidel Castro, who handled with far greater wisdom and far less discredit the problems of post-revolutionary society than did all others. Castro's revolution gave the lie to the thesis of the inevitability of a period of terror.

Castro independently put into practice one of Gramsci's most important innovative contributions to political thought. It is Gramsci who argued that the proletariat, or any rising class for that matter, had to think in terms of hegemony, of authentic leadership and 'direction' rather than simple domination, and that hegemony had to be achieved in intellectual and moral-ethical realms.[2] That is what Castro did as a young rebel after the Moncada defeat. It is what he has done throughout his revolutionary life. It is the essential secret of the success of the Cuban Revolution in the face of impossible odds. As argued in Chapter 2, the inability to maintain intellectual and moral-ethical hegemony is also the quintessential secret of the collapse of socialism throughout the world, and the failure of socialism's experiments in the twentieth century. Castro and the Cuban Revolution have always striven to occupy the moral-ethical high ground in relation to their foes, capitalism and US imperialism.

5
The Moral High Ground

'There is a morality of politics – a difficult subject and never clearly treated', says Jean-Paul Sartre,[1] while his one-time friend, contemporary and critic Raymond Aron points to the difficulty of preventing an 'ethics–politics of rebellion from sliding into the fascist cult of violence'.[2] This part of the study suggests that Fidel Castro provided precisely an 'ethics–politics of rebellion' (in fact, of violent rebellion) as well as rulership that did not degenerate into 'a cult of violence', and in so doing, provided the outlines of a viable 'morality of politics'.

In this chapter, the contention is that Castro demonstrates it is possible to be an effective contender for and wielder of state power, and yet be restrained and discriminate in the use of violence. Indeed, his moral and ethical dimension vitally inheres in his capacity to achieve and maintain state power, and to survive in the face of unprecedentedly overwhelming odds.

The chapter situates Castro's contribution to Marxism. It notes his novel introduction of the moral factor in Cuba's transition to socialism. It discusses Castro's stress on moral hegemony within his wielding of power. It examines Castro's distinctive code of honour, and his framing of Che Guevara's contribution in quintessentially moral terms. It evaluates Castro's revaluation of historical figures in the communist tradition as exemplifying his unique synthesis of the realist and moral-ethical perspectives.

The chapter then goes on to identify the sources of accumulation of moral capital by Castro and examines its role in his success in sustaining socialism. It appraises the interplay of nationalism and internationalism in his thought and practice, and suggests that his ethics of revolution marks the Cuban from all other revolutions, making it the 'exceptional revolution'.

FIDEL'S MARXISM

This study accepts Donald E. Rice's definition of *Fidelismo* as 'Fidel's particular construction of Marxism', and a 'global perspective'.[3] In my view, much of the confusion about Castro's communism and his commentary on it – what did Fidel Castro know about communism and when did he know it? – stemmed from the fact that here was a Marxism that did not issue from Moscow or Beijing; it didn't emanate from a Communist party of Comintern provenance. Nor, however, did it belong to the known strands of dissident revolutionary doctrine such as Anarchism, Trotskyism or Titoism. It was the beginning of a New Left, a new communism or socialism, independently evolved by the independently evolving Fidel Castro, Che Guevara and Raul Castro. It outstripped Titoism as a model of independent socialism despite Yugoslavia's founding role in the Non-Aligned Movement because its revolutionary role was far less muted than Tito's (given the latter's functional relationship with the USA and the West).

The debate on Castro's Marxism embraces two positions. There are those who argue that he was certainly, up until the revolution, a radical democrat, populist or nationalist, but not a convinced Marxist. This school of thought subdivides into those who consider Castro to have betrayed his original democratic programme, and those others who feel that he was needlessly pushed towards Marxism by the United States. The contending school of thought holds that Castro was, even before the revolution, a communist, or communist agent, by which is meant a member or agent of the pro-Soviet Communist party and by extension, Soviet Russia.

The truth seems to lie in between. Castro was not anti-communist, but he was never a member of the party, unlike his brother Raul perhaps, nor was his politics even remotely a part of a Communist party or Soviet conspiracy. He was however undergoing a process of radicalisation, which brought him in touch with Marxism at university, turned him into a socialist, and by the time he left the university, had made him a Marxist-Leninist.

His was an independent Marxism-Leninism, not that of the Communist party. The moderation of the programme that he presented in his famous trial speech 'History Will Absolve Me' and after, during the civil war, is overblown. It contained many radical elements that ran counter to the economic interest of the elite and the United States, and aspects of a transition to a further stage. These programmes can be understood as corresponding to the democratic or first stage of the revolution as conceived of in Marxist and particularly Leninist theory. It corresponded to the state of popular consciousness in Cuba at the time, but was part of a process that in

Castro's thinking would culminate in the setting up of a new type of state and society.

Lionel Martin, ABC and CBS correspondent who covered Castro for sixteen years, painstakingly assembles the evidence, which gives great credence to Castro's own repeated contention that by the time of the Moncada uprising of 1953, and indeed before he had left the university, he was not merely acquainted with Marxism-Leninism, but was also a conscious Marxist-Leninist.[4] Castro says himself that when he left the university in 1950 he was already a convinced Marxist.[5] Martin concurs, but dates 1951–52 as the period when Castro's Marxist socialism had unmistakeably crystallised. Batista seized power in 1952, and Castro immediately made preparations for a mass movement and an armed response to the coup, a response that would culminate in an armed uprising. In 1985 Castro asserted that he had been a Marxist even then: 'We were Marxist-Leninists since before March 10, when Batista's coup d'etat took place – I want you to know that, I've said it before, we were Marxist-Leninists before.'[6] In his most recent statement, in what is most likely to be viewed as his last years, Castro clarifies the matter conclusively:

In the university, where I arrived simply with a rebel spirit and some elementary ideas of justice, I became a Marxist-Leninist and acquired the sentiments that over the years I have had the privilege never to have felt the slightest temptation to abandon.[7]

Brian Latell confirms this claim, going against the received wisdom that Raul's Marxism antedated Fidel's, and that Raul and Che prodded Fidel towards Marxism. His reconstruction from intelligence sources as well as the testimony of Fidel's sister Juanita is that Raul's conversion to Marxism, which came in 1951, was initiated by Fidel.[8]

Raul's personal and ideological transformation began in 1951. It was then, under Fidel's prodding that he undertook a precocious conversion to Marxism-Leninism. … Raul later confirmed much of his sister's account of the timing of his ideological conversion and of Fidel's motivating role in it. In an interview with the Mexico City newspaper *El Dia*, he stated: 'I first came into contact with Marxism around 1951'. He said that until then he had been anti-communist like most Cubans – though not Fidel – at that early, tendentious stage of the Cold War. It was Fidel, he says, who gave him a copy of one of Engels's treatises on Marxism and encouraged him to read it and appreciate it. He recalled that it was *The Origins of the Family, Private Property and the State*. 'I read it twice. It was not a difficult book to understand,' and referring to Fidel, he added, 'He explained some questions to me.'

In the *El Sol de Mexico* interview in 1991, Raul confirmed his earlier account. He said: 'It was Fidel who influenced me into becoming a communist... [H]e explained communism to me and gave me books.'[9] Latell concludes: '... more recently I have come to believe that Fidel's ... own Marxist and Leninist convictions were solid by the early or mid-1950s'.[10]

Still more striking is the testimony of Ulises Estrada who spent considerable time with Che Guevara in a safe house in Prague, on the way back from the failed enterprise in the Congo. 'Che considered Fidel to be the person who had converted him into a true communist.'[11]

Thus, while conventional wisdom long held that Che and Raul were committed Marxists well before Fidel and converted the latter to their doctrine, new scholarship tends to undermine and even reverse that conception.

Though it may be supposed that Fidel's Marxism, or his assertion of such early conversion, were either a concession to the *Zeitgeist*, or an attempt to secure the backing of the powerful socialist bloc, such reasoning is contradicted by his clear reassertion of his Marxist convictions after the fall of the USSR. Following the fall of the Berlin Wall in 1989, through to the party congress in 1991, the year of the collapse of the USSR, he not only reasserted his Marxism but changed and further radicalised his decades-old slogan of 'Patria O Muerte' (Fatherland or Death!), to 'Socialismo O Muerte' (Socialism or Death!)[12]

In the Master Lecture delivered at the University of Venezuela, Caracas in February 1999, Castro took pains to reiterate the periodisation of his conversion to Marxism and Leninism, reiterating a quintessential ideological continuity from the Moncada attack and even earlier, as he graduated from university:

... We had already read almost a whole library of the works of Marx, Engels, Lenin and other theoreticians. We were convinced Marxists and socialists. With that fever and that blind passion that characterises young people, and sometimes old people too, I assumed that basic principles that I learned from those books and they helped me understand the society where I lived. Until then it was for me an intricate entanglement for which I could not find any convincing explanation... I was discreet, but not as much as I should have been because I would explain Marx's ideas and the class society to everyone I met... Towards the end of my university studies, I was no longer a utopian communist but rather an atypical communist who was acting freely.[13]

What is relevant about the periodisation of Castro's ideological evolution is that from just before the Moncada attack or at least from the Moncada attack onwards, to this day, his political thought must be reckoned within the Marxist-Leninist ideological universe. Therefore his explicit emphasis on moral-ethical factors does not take place essentially prior to a conversion to Marxism-Leninism. Nor could he have found it within the existing Marxist-Leninist frame of reference, since the ethical and moral dimension in the form of a sense of right and wrong, and specifically of the right and wrong use of violence, hardly existed within the Marxist-Leninist canon. Thus it can be understood as Fidel Castro's specific contribution to Marxism-Leninism; a specific feature of his Marxist revolutionary thought; and hallmark of his Marxism.

THEORY OF TRANSITION: THE MORAL FACTOR

It would be tempting to dismiss the references to morality and ethical criteria as belonging to the ideals held by the youthful Fidel Castro, which he betrayed, abandoned or outgrew with his conversion to Marxism-Leninism. Not only is that interpretation belied by the counter-argument of Castro's own statement that he was already a socialist, operating with a Marxist-Leninist framework at that time, but also by the persistence of these criteria throughout his political life. Particularly telling is the interweaving in Castro's perception of a moral dimension with an issue that is squarely within the realms of strategy, ideology and Marxist theory; namely, that of the transition from a democratic or nationalist phase/stage to the socialist phase/stage of the revolutionary process. In Lenin, for instance, the transition from the February Revolution to October, from the democratic to the socialist, is analysed in terms of the balance of class forces and the concrete situation, including the factors of popular consciousness, preparedness of the vanguard party (and according to Zizek, the need to stay ahead of popular consciousness, give it a push and take the existential risk of a leap). Lenin's essays of 1917 illustrate this.[14]

The historical-social transition was signalled by Castro's speech in April 1961 when, marshalling the Cuban people to resist the Bay of Pigs invasion, he publicly proclaimed, for the first time, the socialist character of the Cuban transformation. Speaking on 26 July 1973 on the twentieth anniversary of the Moncada uprising, Castro refers to April 1961, framing it in moral terms:

Thus on April 16, 1961, our working class, marching to bury their dead on the eve of the invasion, with their rifles held high, proclaimed the socialist character of our revolution, and in its name they fought and shed their blood. An entire people were ready to die. A decisive leap in political consciousness had come about since July 26, 1953. No moral victory could be compared to that one in the glorious history of our revolution, because no people in the Americas had been subjected by imperialism to such an intense process of reactionary indoctrination of destruction of a nationality and its historic values. No people had been so deformed over half century, and here was that people standing up like a moral giant before historic oppressors to sweep away in a few years that ideological burden ...[15]

Fidel Castro is the only one among leading Marxist political figures who sees an explicitly *moral* dimension in the transition from the democratic to the socialist stage (or phase) of the revolution.

HEGEMONY, RULERSHIP AND REPRESSION

Antonio Gramsci makes a famous distinction between the societies of Eastern Europe, where the state is everything and civil society is nothing, and those of the West, in which civil society is broad and thick, complex and weighty. Pre-Revolutionary Cuba was not Tsarist Russia.[16] As noted earlier in this study,[17] in Batista's time there were many Cuban political parties, personalities and factions in kaleidoscopic convergences and divergences. Castro had to face a number of competitors within the militant opposition to Batista, and many more in the moderate opposition. He also had to handle the divergences between the urban and rural/mountain guerrilla wings of his own movement: the 'sierra'/'llano' distinction made famous by Guevara.

Gramsci recommended a move by which hegemony would accrue to the revolutionary forces within civil society through the accretion of consent gained by leadership in political, intellectual, cultural and moral-ethical realms. This was meant to be a prolonged prelude and preparation for a subsequent shift to a strategy of frontal assault against the state. Interpreters of Gramsci have turned the two sequential yet interlinked phases/stages into two opposing models:

one of the protracted achievement of hegemony, essentially peaceful, and the other of insurrection.[18]

Fidel Castro combined the two, restoring some of Gramsci's scheme, but telescoping the first movement radically. He conducted an insurrectionary frontal assault on the state, shifted to guerrilla warfare, while manoeuvring in the civil and political spheres, gaining consent and building consensus, cumulatively yet rapidly achieving hegemony. Most importantly, he did so, indeed understood that he could only do so, by non-military, peaceful political means, without recourse to lethal violence against his rivals and competitors.

But how does Castro square his moral-ethical emphasis with his system of rule?

While the behaviour of oligarchic dictators (such as Batista and Chile's Pinochet) outraged Castro's sense of fair play, he viewed the democracy that existed in Cuba and Latin America with a sharply critical eye. Castro's aversion to competitive multiparty electoral democracy dates back to his youth, and is rooted in his own experience of the kind of corrupt democracy practised in Cuba. The sources of disillusionment were several. Castro saw how elections were organised through ward-heelers and orchestrated by the army in the rural areas. His father influenced the votes of his employees in favour of a rich friend, who was a candidate, by dispensing large sums of money. Castro himself helped in the campaign of one of his half brothers, which gave him a close-up view of electoral politics. Young Cubans were aware of the powerful behind-the-scenes role played by Fulgencio Batista in controlling successive Cuban administrations. The outwardly reformist government of Grau San Martin was also pervasively corrupt as evidenced in its practices at the University of Havana.[19]

Even so scathingly a critical account of Fidel Castro and Revolutionary Cuba as that of Ben Corbett concludes with a strikingly affirmative assessment of Castro's contribution when seen in relation to the Cuba that he inherited:

Before Castro, people were slaughtered indiscriminately. Political assassinations occurred daily in the power vacuum. Life was cheap. Peasants were abused. Soldiers shot and killed humans as if they were rodents. ... The violence before Castro indicates there was a desperate need for Cuba to free itself from its neo-colonial chains. ... One leader was needed in Cuba, and Castro became that leader. And when he came he said 'Stop! Let's see what we have here. Let's find the best part of the Cuban character and let it shine. Let us focus our pride.'

Because of this belief, human life is now very precious to all Cubans. Over the past four decades, the island has enjoyed enough peace and stability that the culture has been able to focus on slowly defining itself. The price of freedom is sacrifice.[20]

Thus Castro's critical indictment of that system and society that preceded him and his insistence that illiberal revolutionary rule is ethically superior to parliamentary democratic, in reality capitalistic rule, cannot be dismissed as merely opportunistic or as 'false consciousness'.

Castro considers his system of rule as morally superior in at least three respects. In the first place he is possessed of a sense of a mandate from the masses, based upon genuine and enduring popularity and the dynamic of interaction between himself and the Cuban people. He sees, in the second place, a social and moral contrast between pre- and post-Revolutionary Cuba. In the third place, he draws a contrast between the social gains of the Cuban Revolution and the privations and inequities he sees in capitalist societies.

When he offered to resign [in 1970 after the failure of the target of 10 million zafras of sugar] why did so many people shout for him to stay? Why did they not just keep quiet? Part of the answer lay in the 'Achievements of the Revolution', the new schools, new roads, new hospitals. But more important was Castro's own personality. He seldom stopped talking, teaching, arguing, discussing. His 'direct democracy' might look like crude manipulation in the eyes of foreign observers, but it undoubtedly made millions of Cubans feel involved and consulted in a way that had never happened under previous governments, even those which had been elected in relatively free elections.... Castro's road to socialism was proving steep and stony, but most Cubans still preferred to stick to it. Only a minority, constantly reduced by emigration, were sufficiently disillusioned to want to bury the revolutionary project.[21]

Commingled with the moral justification is the tough-minded determination that the revolution will remain in power, that the revolutionary state will not be undermined, that Revolutionary Cuba's security will not be jeopardised in the face of ceaseless attempts at counterrevolution by the neighbouring superpower.

In his lifetime Castro has experienced the success of US-backed attempts, mainly violent, to unseat left-leaning and/or nationalistic governments in Latin America and throughout the Third World, from Arbenz through Lumumba to Allende. His own revolution has been a target of invasion and terrorism. He has warned against (from the 1960s) and then observed the peaceful undermining and unravelling of socialism in the USSR. He is determined that none of those outcomes would prevail in Cuba, which means that none of the methods used, nor any combination, would be permitted.

Nor can we afford to make idealistic mistakes in the present situation, which contains bigger threats, greater risks and worse difficulties than ever. We aren't going to play around with our country's independence and security or with the Revolution, pretending that circumstances are ideal and dreaming up idealised forms of leadership and political organisation that can't be applied in the present circumstances... We won't help reactionary, counterrevolutionary, imperialist views to spread among our people, because we aren't going to help imperialism or create conditions that are propitious for imperialism's acts of aggression. Let the economic blockade against our country, the United States's threats and attacks, the campaigns against Cuba and the war against Cuba end, and then in those different conditions, we might even seek different political formulas for our country. But we can't do this in the midst of a decisive battle, a battle of life or death... Not only the existence of the Revolution but also that of the Cuban nation has been at stake. We aren't going to be so stupid as to give means of expression to those who want to destroy the Revolution and our country.[22]

Castro attempts to maintain the moral high ground even on the issue of democracy, human rights, governance and political freedoms by focusing on the average quantum of violence in everyday life and governance in electoral democracies, and by drawing attention to the restrictions on security grounds in those democracies, making the point that Cuba is under even greater security threat. He makes this point not just while preaching to the converted in Cuba, but to Western audiences. To give just one example, he did so in a hostile interview by Maria Shriver of the NBC, with the otherwise argumentative interviewer having no rejoinder.

In Cuba the police, the forces of law and order, have never broken up a demonstration. Every day you see that in the United States, in England, in Spain, in France, in Italy, in West Germany, they are repressing workers on strike, pacifists, and demonstrators. Not once in 30 years has tear gas been used against the people; not once in 30 years has a single shot been fired against the people; there has never been a single blow, a single rubber bullet, a single dog. And we see that every day in Spain, in France, in Italy, in England, in West Germany, in the United States.

When you do away with tear gas, beatings, and dogs; when you do away with water jets, when you do away with repression, then you can speak about human rights. None of that has ever happened in Cuba, not even once. I believe there is greater respect here for human rights than in the so-called democratic societies.[23]

While Castro's handling of dissent has been coercive, what is notably absent is the use of lethal violence.[24] His treatment of individual dissenters has been harsher than that in any First World democracy, but less so than in most Third World societies, both undemocratic and democratic, some of which are allies of the United States. While poets have served jail sentences in Cuba there have been no equivalents of Ken Saro Wiwa of Nigeria, who was murdered by the military authorities. Castro's treatment of collective protest has, however, been far more lenient than almost any country including the USA and other First World democracies. There has been nothing like the scenes outside the Democratic convention in Chicago '68, or firebombing of the MOVE headquarters in Philadelphia where incendiaries were dropped by police helicopter on a building housing members of a black cult, including women and children. Nor have scenes such as those in Seattle 1998 been witnessed in Cuba.

Castro's handling of the Bay of Pigs prisoners was all of a piece with his response to demonstrations. Decades later, when faced with rioters who wanted to migrate to the USA, Castro didn't resort to the East German option of enclosure and lethal action. He did the opposite – the Mariel boatlift[25] being the best known but not the only example (a smaller version took place under President Clinton). Thus Castro re-took the moral high ground: he was not preventing people from leaving; on the contrary, the USA was refusing to grant visas to legal migrants, but encouraging illegal immigration by admitting anyone who came clandestinely from Cuba, and now he, Castro was opening the doors and the US was refusing to take the departing Cubans in.

An obvious counter-argument to Fidel's criticism of violent crackdowns on public protests in the West would be that in Cuba people do not have the freedom to demonstrate while in the Western democracies they do. But Castro's contention soon passed the test. His NBC interview was given to Maria Shriver in February 1988, before the fall of socialism, and in 1994, after its fall, when Cuba was isolated and struggling for survival, a major riot broke out in the capital city. Yet Castro's doctrine of zero or minimum force was observed scrupulously.

An account by Alma Guillermoprieto, based also on accounts by reliable Mexican journalists, sheds light on what John Kane calls 'moral capital' accumulated over the years by Castro, and his adroit reinvestment of that capital for even greater gain, because moral capital, like capital in general, brings in considerable returns not when it languishes but is put to productive use.

In August of 1994, when the Habanazo – or first full-fledged riot against the regime broke out on the streets of downtown Havana, he stopped the rock throwers in their tracks by appearing, on foot, in the very thick of the fray. As the observant and thoughtful correspondents of the Mexican weekly Proceso noted at the time, the protesters' tune changed the moment Fidel appeared on the scene. 'This is over, El Caballo [The Horse, a favourite name for Fidel] has arrived' someone said, and another man was heard to murmur, 'He really has balls, coming here.' Yet another: 'The Old Man doesn't change. There's no overthrowing him'. The ability to inspire feelings of intimacy and awe in equal measure is what has kept Fidel Castro in power even through the years of awful hardship that followed the collapse of the Soviet Union...[26]

There were no shootings, skull-cracking, CS gas and police dogs set on crowds, unlike in almost any other country. Instead, in what seems a unique gesture, Castro led an enormous counter-demonstration and, in a dramatic encounter, debated the issues with the riotous youth.

And sure enough, in the middle of the crowd was the unmistakable figure of Fidel Castro... He had performed a remarkable piece of political theatre, turning the country's first anti-Castro demonstration into a much bigger pro-Castro demonstration. The riots fizzled out slowly.... The uniformed police played a minor role and were very restrained trying to talk the rioters into desisting. At one point a police van stopped near a group of stone-throwers; the police jumped out and managed to seize one of the rioters. As they walked him to the van, he asked if he could take his bicycle, since if it were left in the street it might be stolen. Two policemen duly accompanied him to pick up the bicycle and helped him to load it in the back of the van, before the van drove off. Some of Castro's supporters complained that the police had been ineffectual. They suggested that if the police had appeared more quickly and acted more vigorously, the riot would have ended much sooner. Castro defended the police strongly.[27]

Castro's statement on this occasion is the most succinct summation of his conscious intertwining of the moral-ethical and the power ('realist') dimensions, of his acute awareness and conscious use of moral capital:

The officers behaved very well. They did not use violence. They were cool, calm and persuasive. Our enemies want to provoke violence and make us lose our head. I am proud of the way our people behaved.... We have to exercise great self-control. In that sort of situation it is better than our own side should be the ones suffering casualties. We cannot abuse our power when we are fighting unarmed individuals. I am convinced of this political principle. I realise that some people are more radical and want what they call an iron fist. If we let ourselves be carried away, we are giving the enemy a tool to use against us, to try to isolate us in front of world opinion by presenting us as repressive murderers and all that... Can you imagine how advantageous it would have been for them if a police battalion had dispersed the riots by firing a few shots and killing ten or twelve people? When it is the people themselves who respond, that is different. I have always believed in the importance of letting the masses deal with such challenges. Weapons should be reserved for invaders or mercenaries.[28]

While it takes place in 1994, Castro's response is not a born-again conversion to non-violence, and as we have seen, in complete consonance with his earliest political thinking. But its context is of great relevance. This was three years after the fall of the USSR. Castro was initially in sympathy with Gorbachev's desire to reform and breathe new life into socialism, and even after the fall refused to denounce Gorbachev himself as a conscious counterrevolutionary in terms of intention. He had nonetheless warned by 1986 and 1987 that the Soviet Union was headed towards doom, and when the collapse took place, Castro had already (in 1987) restored Guevara's vision of the new Socialist Man as inoculation against the bacillus of Soviet-type *glasnost* and *perestroika*. He had reaffirmed and sharpened Cuba's commitment to the socialist, Marxist-Leninist, communist option, unconsciously returning perhaps to his Jesuit roots and attempting an ideological counter-reformation.

However, Castro's response to the riot also showed that he had rejected the Chinese option of forestalling Soviet-style liquidation: the Tien An Men solution. He did not think that the way to forestall socialism's fall was more repression, and did not believe that the Eastern European and Soviet outcomes could have been averted had those ruling elites resorted to greater levels of violence and coercion.

The bloody crushing of the civic protest in Tien An Men Square impacted upon the societies of Eastern Europe and the USSR, swinging them away from any version of socialism and towards dramatic regime change. One cannot help but speculate as to the impact on the peoples and thus the events of Eastern Europe and the USSR, had the Chinese Communist leadership handled the demonstrations with the sensibility of Fidel Castro. Zhao Zhiyang, the Chinese Prime Minister, who attempted dialogue with the protesting students, neither had the moral authority to convince the students nor the political authority to convince his colleagues of the need for dialogue. They sent in the tanks to crush the student demonstrators while he himself was incarcerated and died years later, while still under house arrest.

Moreover, Castro engaged in a risky opening up of the regime to the airing of contrary perspectives, by permitting the Papal visit of 1998, and also by dint of his regime's increased promotion of youth culture: more discos, open air rock concerts and a statue of John Lennon in a park in Havana. (This was unveiled by Castro himself, to the strains of 'Imagine'.)

Castro thus seems to have adopted the combination of 'consensus and coercion', deriving from Machiavelli's Centaur and commended by Gramsci to the Modern Prince, the Communist party, as a prerequisite for 'hegemony'. While Machiavelli's Centaur is a supreme symbol of Realism, this is but one strand in the ideological fusion that is Castroism.

CODE OF HONOUR

Fidel Castro brings in categories, such as 'fair' and 'honourable', rejected by Realism as 'romantic' and condemned by Marxism as 'idealistic', into his most serious and intimate political reflections. In his conversations with fellow senior revolutionary Tomas Borge, Fidel Castro looks back at his famous speech 'History Will Absolve Me', delivered at his trial after the Moncada attack, and explains his choices as well as his understanding of the historical process in heterodox terms, quite foreign to 'the materialist conception of history':

... When I said 'History will absolve me'... that was an expression of confidence in the ideas I was defending as the fairest ones, and of the cause I was defending as the most honourable one. I meant that the future would recognise this because, in the future, those ideas would be made realities; in the future, people would know everything about what happened: what we did and what our adversaries did, what goals we sought and what goals our adversaries sought, and who was right – we or the judges who were trying us, who had acted dishonestly in discharging a public trust who had abandoned their oath of loyalty to the

Constitution and were serving a tyrannical regime. I was challenging them, absolutely convinced that the ideas we were defending would triumph in our homeland someday – a conviction I still have, that humanity's legitimate causes will always advance and triumph eventually.[29]

Revolution is a zero-sum game and a radical overturning of values, and yet, that most consummate revolutionary, Fidel Castro displays values of honour and chivalry, which are not only unheard of in Marxism, especially Marxism-Leninism, but are rare in warfare and almost unknown in modern political discourse whatever its ideological orientation.

The Marxism of Marx and Engels, particularly the latter, did display traces of courtly values, but Marx's explicit critique and rejection of Don Quixote as archetype indicated a tough-minded scientific outlook that made no place for romanticism. For his part Lenin was – as Gramsci defined him – the Machiavelli who came after Marx. Mao Ze Dong and Ho Chi Minh celebrated valour and had a clear code of conduct in warfare, but that code was manifestly functional and strategic, and did not form part of, still less stem from, a personal ethos of honour.

For Castro, valour is not enough. 'Honour' and 'gentlemanliness' are important even in the midst of struggle, and even towards the enemy. Who could doubt the USA's posture of deadly enmity towards the Castro regime? The Frank Church Committee is among the many sources to document the attempts by the US to assassinate Fidel Castro during the Kennedy administration. Apart from a great many plans for invasion, a number of actions of terrorism with considerable cost of life were perpetrated against Cuba during that period. However, in a fascinating ambiguity, Kennedy and Castro occasionally had communication through back channels. While this is not unprecedented, what is most striking is the testimony of one of these intermediaries, *L'Express* journalist Jean Daniel, about the spontaneous reaction of Castro to the news of the assassination of Kennedy, a man who presided over an administration that tried to murder him.

'What? Assassination?' Daniel heard his host ask, visibly disconcerted. Everyone gathered around the radio, and shortly afterwards it was reported that Kennedy was dead. When the American national anthem was then broadcast, Castro and his guests stood up and silently remembered the Cubans' archenemy.[30]

It is significant that the following remarks come not from a Castro interview with a Western journalist whom he is trying to charm or win over, but in conversation with Tomas Borge, the Sandinista leader, an old revolutionary and guerrilla commander who had close military dealings with Castro; in other words, a fellow Marxist, revolutionary and guerrilla:

We were very upset by his death. Kennedy was our adversary, and we were adversaries of Kennedy. If you're any kind of gentleman, you're sorry if your adversary has been assassinated, and you've lost him – you miss him. The way they killed him hurt... Kennedy was our adversary but we had to acknowledge that he was an intelligent man, with good qualities. The news of Kennedy's death made me bitter – not at all pleased, even though he had taken harsh measures against Cuba, had wronged us and attacked us.[31]

Castro's notion of honour and honourable conduct in warfare led him to the kind of value judgements that are quite original for a modern political leader and certainly for a Marxist-Leninist, a stubborn communist. Though the voluminous military writings of Engels do contain references to the valour of fighters belonging even to the side that Marx and he adjudges reactionary, and there is a strong indictment of the brutality of British colonialism, while acknowledging its progressive historical functions, the criticism is not explicitly couched in terms of honour. Honour is neither yardstick nor category.

From Lenin onwards, even these nuances disappear and war is judged just or unjust on the basis of the character of those forces at play, with any indictment of conduct being solely of the reactionary force. There is no paradox, such as is present in Castro's judgement.

Castro repeatedly locates himself extending the long tradition of Cuban wars of independence against Spanish colonialism. He criticises the United States for intervening in the terminal stages of the independence wars, to seize for itself (in the form of the Guantanamo Bay base) the fruits of victory and impose a neo-colonial settlement on Cuba. But he finds occasion to indict the US and speak with sympathy of the Spanish colonialists, on quite different grounds: that of conduct in war. He speaks of a naval combat during the concluding stages, when Spanish ships, under the command of a valiant officer but following erroneous orders from Spain, gave up a defensible position and sailed singly and suicidally out of the Santiago de Cuba harbour, straight into the mouths of the cannon of the American fleet. He indicts the US for the virtual massacre that ensued, displaying the values that he cherishes even in the middle of bitter combat:

The North Americans should be ashamed to boast of such victory. That kind of victory brings no glory, because it was obtained in very uneven conditions, under absolute superiority and engaging each Spanish vessel separately. The Spanish fleet was in no condition to win this battle. Even if it had fully deployed it would have been hopelessly sunken. Only in this case, it was sunken boat after boat, one by one and all against one. I believe that this was a moral victory for those Spanish sailors, a heroic deed honoured by a people like ours, who cherish heroism.

... We even paid tribute to the US sailors killed in the 'Maine' in the 100th anniversary of its explosion in Havana harbour.[32]

Unsympathetic US commentators, especially official ones, tend to decry Castro's speeches as merely rabble-rousing, but it is hardly the case that those addresses are used to whip up pure hatred. Castro attempts to educate his public (including on the most emotive occasions and while invoking the most militant and martial spirit) in his notions of honour in war. For example, on 3 October 1965, in his solemn televised ceremony to present the members of the Central Committee of the newly formed Communist party, and explain the absence of Che Guevara, an address made in the presence of Guevara's family and famous for its disclosure of Che Guevara's farewell letter to him, Castro stresses that

... there is no better tactic, no better strategy than to fight with clean hands, to fight with the truth. Because these are the only weapons that inspire confidence, that inspire faith, that inspire security, dignity, and morale. And these are the weapons we revolutionaries have been using to defeat and crush our enemies.

... Who has ever heard of a lie from the lips of a revolutionary? Lies are weapons that help no revolutionary, and no serious revolutionary ever needs to resort to a lie. Their weapon is reason, morality, and truth, the ability to defend an idea, a proposal, and a position.[33]

The theme is recurrent and echoes through the decades. In a speech on 16 April 1996 commemorating the Bay of Pigs victory, in which he invokes the spirit of resistance so as to strengthen Cuban resolve five years after the USSR's fall and in face of the blockade tightened by the Helms–Burton and Torricelli amendments, Castro significantly says: 'moreover, one has always to be gentlemanly, even when one fights against wretched people....' He refers to the Cuban revolutionaries as having been turned by history into 'solitary soldiers of humanity's most just cause, clean soldiers, pure soldiers'[34]...who may 'fall, but we'll never falter! We will fall, but we'll never take one single step backwards! We will fall, but we will fall with our banners and our ideas held high!'[35] It is a poignant description revelatory of both self-image and the role Castro strives to inculcate in the Cuban people.

FIDEL AND CHE

Che Guevara, renowned for his acerbic frankness and lack of lush sentimentalism or adulation, provides the best testimony of the unique contribution of Fidel Castro. In his famous farewell letter Che refers variously to 'the way of thinking and of seeing and of appraising dangers and principles' and 'the teaching and example' of Fidel:

... Reviewing my past life, I believe I have worked with sufficient integrity and dedication to consolidate the revolutionary triumph. My only serious failing was not having had more confidence in you from the first moments in the Sierra Maestra, and not having understood quickly enough your qualities as a leader and a revolutionary.

I have lived magnificent days, and at your side I felt the pride of belonging to our people in the brilliant yet sad days of the Caribbean [Missile] crisis. Seldom has a statesman been more brilliant as you were in those days. I am also proud of having followed you without hesitation, of having identified with your way of thinking and of seeing and appraising dangers and principles.

I state once more that I free Cuba from all responsibility, except that which stems from its example. If my final hour finds me under other skies, my last thought will be of this people and especially of you. I am grateful for your teaching and your example, to which I shall try to be faithful up to the final consequences of my acts...[36]

This is re-echoed even more poignantly in the penultimate passage of Che's legendary 'Message to the Tricontinental', better known by its main slogan 'Create Two, Three, Many Vietnams!'

... if some day we have to breathe our last breath on any land, already ours, sprinkled with our blood let it be known that ... we are proud of having learned from the Cuban Revolution, and from its maximum leader, the great lesson emanating from his attitude in this part of the world: 'What do the dangers or the sacrifices of a man or of a nation matter, when the destiny of humanity is at stake.'[37]

It is natural that some of Castro's key ideas and attitudes emerge in his remarks on Che Guevara. Some of these themes emerge in the immediate aftermath of his death and are revealed in Castro's treatment of it, while others are discernible in later years when Fidel reminisces about Che. In the exceedingly emotion-laden and politically difficult, complex moment of acknowledging Guevara's death before the Cuban people in a televised address on 15 October 1967, Castro says that he opted for full disclosure irrespective of any benefits that could have arisen by permitting doubts to linger about the veracity of the reports, and goes on to make a general point about his art of revolutionary governance and the factor of moral standing.[38] Almost two decades later Castro was to say to the Brazilian priest Frei Betto that 'in short, I'd say that if Che had been a Catholic, if Che had belonged to the Church, he would probably have been made a saint, for he had all the virtues'.[39]

It is clear in retrospect that the Jesuit-trained Fidel Castro consciously canonised Che Guevara, but what is far more crucial is his unorthodox identification of the moral factor as the most crucial determinant in the revolutionary and communist project. This posture is apparent in his understanding of Che's most enduring value as a moral figure:

As a revolutionary, as a communist revolutionary, a true communist, he had a boundless faith in moral values. He had a boundless faith in the consciousness of human beings. And we should say he saw, with absolute clarity, the moral impulse as the fundamental lever in the construction of communism in human society...[40]

This cruelly prolonged Che's agony until a sergeant, also drunk, killed him with a pistol shot to the left side. Such a procedure contrasts brutally with the respect shown by Che, without a single exception, towards the lives of the many officers and soldiers of the Bolivian army he took prisoner.[41]

He was a person of absolute moral integrity, of unshakeably firm principles, a complete revolutionary who looked toward the future, toward the humanity of the future, and who above all stressed human values, humanity's moral values.[42]

In his response to the blow and the strong emotions that Che's death would have aroused in him, Fidel Castro not only demonstrates his notion of the power of example, he displays a reading of the importance of moral and ethical example, rare in communist political discourse, alien to the orthodox reading of dialectical and historical materialism and approximated only by Gramsci's Marxism:

The imperialists too know the power, the tremendous power, of example. They know that while a person can be physically eliminated, an example such as Che's can never be eliminated by anything or anyone!

Newspapers of all tendencies and currents have universally recognised Che's virtues. Only in an exceptional case; among hundreds of viewpoints expressed does the vulgar opinion of some scoundrel crop up. For Che's life had the virtue of impressing even his worst ideological enemies, causing them to admire him. It is an almost unique example of how a person can gain the recognition and respect of their enemies; of the very enemies they have faced, arms in hand; of their ideological enemies, who have in turn been almost unanimous in expressing feelings of admiration and respect for Che.

... Isn't it precisely revolutionaries who preach the value of moral principles, the value of example? Aren't revolutionaries the first ones to acknowledge how ephemeral is humanity's physical existence and how long lasting and durable are humanity's ideas, conduct and example – since example is what has inspired and guided the peoples throughout history?[43]

That this idea was neither limited to the emotions of the moment nor an opportunistic move but was a consistent and central feature in Castro's political thought is evidenced almost thirty years later, when Che's remains, dramatically excavated by a team of Cuban forensic scientists and archaeologists, were brought back to Cuba and solemnly enshrined. 'I also see Che as a moral giant', said Castro in a speech marking this occasion, 'who is growing every day, whose image, whose force, whose influence has multiplied throughout the earth. How could he fit under a headstone? How could he fit into this plaza? How could he fit solely into our beloved but small island?'[44] It was also evidenced by Castro's quite extraordinary definition – or redefinition – of socialism, one quite distinct from Marxist-Leninist 'scientific socialism', at a time of terminal crisis for Soviet socialism: 'Socialism is the science of example.'[45]

CASTRO ON STALIN, GORBACHEV

Fidel Castro's quite distinctive synthesis of ethics and realism is evidenced not only in his own deeds and accompanying discourse, but in his evaluation of historical figures, figures belonging to the tradition within which he has placed himself, of communist or socialist leaders. His remarks on the contrasting figures of Stalin and Gorbachev cannot be accommodated within the usual categories.[46]

The evaluation of Joseph Stalin on the left is generally either one of outright condemnation – as the betrayer of Lenin and the fount of socialism's crisis – or one that holds his role in history to have been basically positive. Castro's assessment belongs, on balance and barely, to the latter category, but it is quite distinctive in its reasoning and mix of approbation and blame, blending as it does the ethical with the realistic. Ethical and moral evaluations of Stalin are uniformly condemnatory, while realistic evaluations tend to be justificatory. However, Castro's contains ethical criticisms that are linked to ones that deploy realist criteria. His evaluation, contained most extensively in his long interview given to Sandinista leader Tomas Borge, is unique also because it contains some criticisms made by Trotsky and other dissidents, while twinning them with the kind of defence of Stalin made by Mao, and adding many new critical observations entirely without precedent.

In his 1998 CNN/BBC retrospective on the Cold War, Castro makes a Realist defence of Stalin's 'socialism in one country':

They expected the revolution in Germany and other developed capitalist countries. Socialism in one country, the Soviet Union, emerged because they had no other choice, and as revolutionaries they could not give up. Based on Marx's ideas they tried to build socialism in a country that was industrially very backward, something not contemplated in Marx's conceptions. Their theoretical contributions, however, cannot be overlooked.[47]

This is a position consistently held by Castro, as is seen in his remarks two decades before, to Cuban residents in Moscow in a speech at Lomonosov University:

But, when the first socialist revolution took place in this country and the revolutionary movement was crushed in other parts of Europe, the general circumstances were difficult and the Bolsheviks were faced with one alternative. What was it? The alternative of surrendering or that of building socialism even under very difficult conditions. This historical challenge, this enormous task, was imposed on them. They didn't surrender; they didn't consider themselves defeated by the fact that the revolution had been defeated elsewhere; and, considering the natural resources and the size of the country they opted to build socialism.[48]

The latter quote dating from 1977 cannot be taken as a salute to prevailing orthodoxy in the Soviet camp, because Castro reiterates this interpretation before a Western TV audience in 1998, considerably after the fall of the USSR. It also reveals that Castro in no way attributed the collapse of socialism to the 'original sin' of Stalin's 'socialism in one country', and is likely to have derived inspiration from it when Cuba was left isolated after the fall of the socialist bloc.

It is also Castro who holds that 'revolutionary internationalism is one of the laws of our struggle. We cannot triumph in isolation. Large scale assistance or the simplest support of popular rebellions strengthens us all, since they are the expressions of a new humanity...'[49] He is thus able to hold together two apparently contradictory ideas: that of internationalism as 'the most beautiful essence of Marxism-Leninism', and the concrete historical necessity for socialism in one country, thereby striving for a synthesis of internationalism and patriotism, romanticism and realism. 'It is realists who make the best revolutions, the best and most profound revolutions.'[50]

In the interview given to Tomas Borge, Castro refuses to blame the crisis of socialism on Stalin, and holds that he strengthened the Soviet state that he inherited. He also decries as unfair the attribution of all Soviet successes to Stalin, just as it would be unfair to deny him any credit for those successes and lay all blame for failure solely at his doorstep. In terms of domestic policy Castro believes Stalin erred in permitting and encouraging the distribution of land among the peasantry (though he does say that this policy may have been inevitable owing to the prevalent circumstances) and then, when the consequent and entirely predictable crisis arose, swing to the opposite extreme and engaging in a crash and coercive collectivisation. This criticism is hardly original and was made by Trotsky and the left opposition. What is new, however, is that the policy that Castro commends as one that Stalin should have followed – that of a gradual collectivisation – does not belong to this tradition and is identified with the opposite school of thought, that of Nikolai Bukharin and the right opposition.

Castro's most damning criticism of Stalin in domestic policy was his decapitation of the Red Army's officer corps in a paranoid purge. This, says Castro, severely debilitated the Soviet Union's capacity to resist and roll back the Nazi war machine.

Castro's critique of Stalin's diplomatic and strategic policy is clear but not unique. What is unique is the military conclusion he draws. He is full of praise of Stalin's support to the Spanish Republic and maintains a conspicuous silence, well within a Realist approach, about his role in suppressing the Anarchists and Trotskyists (detailed by George Orwell). However, he is severely critical of the Nazi–Soviet Pact and the invasion and annexation of Poland and Finland by the Red Army. Castro is not only harshly critical of the damage done to the morale and standing of communists the world over, he suggests that in the case of Poland, the USSR should have opened a part of its own territory and permitted its co-ethnics to cross over, rather than invade and occupy that country at the time that it had been subject to Nazi aggression.

Castro's rejection of the Nazi–Soviet Pact is not only – as is usually the case – on moral grounds, but on military strategic ones. He argues that while it was fully understandable that the USSR did not want to fall victim to the West's strategy of pitting Nazism against the Russian revolutionary state, the time bought by Stalin worked far more favourably for Hitler. Had Stalin not decimated the Soviet officer corps, it would have been better for the USSR to have faced Hitler before the Nazi–Soviet Pact had enabled the latter to occupy many countries, including France, and thereby vastly strengthen its military capacities.

Castro is also critical of Stalin's initial behaviour when the Nazi armies were massing and the war broke out. He argues that there should have been a general mobilisation, the shifting of airplanes to the rear, and the mobilisation of the reserves so as to protect the rear while the main army defended the front resolutely. He rejects the notion that such mobilisation would have given Hitler a pretext to commit aggression, and underscores the fact that despite so vast and manifest a mobilisation by them, the Nazis were still able to achieve surprise. He is critical of Stalin's refusal to believe that Hitler had indeed invaded. All these mistakes, he says, resulted in the destruction of the Soviet air force, the capture of huge numbers of Soviet soldiers and the siege of major Soviet cities.

Having made this criticism, which is not original, Castro then blends it with a very positive assessment of Stalin as a wartime military leader, resulting in an evaluatory mix that is quite distinctive in its balance.

Two final observations by Castro are quite noteworthy and revelatory of his distinctive outlook. Had Stalin not made these mistakes in the realm of the moral-ethical and psycho-political (the Nazi–Soviet Pact) as well as the military strategic, the Red Army could have defeated Nazism without or before the Second Front was opened and the US armies arrived in Europe. The war would have ended with the Red Army having reached Portugal, he asserts quite emphatically.

Castro rejects, however, in his long interview given to Gianni Mina, the interpretation common to Trotskyists and radical leftist historians such as Fernando Claudin[51] that Stalin prevented the European Communist parties, notably the Italian and the Spanish, from taking power in the aftermath of World War II. He concludes, very much in the realist tradition, that while such a possibility did perhaps exist after World War I, the balance of forces, especially the powerful military presence of the US in Europe after World War II, was too great to permit such an outcome.[52]

It is clear that Castro considers the combination of ethical, political and military errors to have had consequences that deleteriously affected the course of world history and the world-historic contestation between capitalism and socialism. By implication and extension, the correct combination of political, strategic and ethical policies, a policy that is alert, resolute and yet does not violate ethical norms, would have profoundly positive consequences precisely in terms of the balance of power. This is a highly distinctive perspective, which once again transcends the idealist/realist divide in political thought. Castro makes this explicit by claiming that the Cuban Revolution never made the kind of unprincipled compromise that Stalin did, especially in the realm of international policy.

In his attitude to Mikhail Gorbachev too, Fidel Castro eschews the prevailing polarisation. He neither regards Gorbachev as hero or villain, as liberator of the Soviet people by the dismantling of socialism, nor the conspiratorial counterrevolutionary who single-handedly destroyed the Socialist USSR. Despite the colossal damage done to Cuba by the collapse of socialism in Eastern Europe and the USSR, Castro regards Gorbachev as a well-intentioned reformer who started out on the path of a necessary renovation of socialism.

He does not indict Gorbachev's book *Perestroika* as full of ideological heresy and iniquity but identifies as its crucial error the notion that all reforms had to be simultaneous rather than graduated and sequential. Though well intentioned, the process that Gorbachev unleashed got out of hand. Castro is especially critical of a phenomenon in the realm of ideas and ideology that was not pioneered by Gorbachev but set in as the process departed from its stated goal of a reformed socialism: an attitude of nihilism towards Soviet history, the weakening of the party and 'the authority of the state'. Castro's conclusion is that while

Gorbachev was no villain, he cannot be exonerated of responsibility for what happened. But he views unnamed others as being more directly and wittingly responsible for the destruction of the USSR with its consequences for the global balance.

So far, this chapter treated with themes of power and morality, tracing its working through Castro's ideas and practice of rulership, as well as his judgements about historical figures and global events. Our account now turns from tracing Fidel's ideas and practice, to analysing them in the light of the main concern, that of the moral and ethical dimension, with an ethics of violence at its centre.

THE SOURCES OF MORAL CAPITAL

The record majorities in recent years in the UN General Assembly, against the US embargo on Cuba, represent Fidel Castro's and the Cuban Revolution's accumulation of 'moral capital' on a world scale. Correspondingly, in the domestic sphere, the economic hardships endured by the Cuban people do not seem to have had the effect of eroding the popularity of either Castro or the revolution. As Robert M. Levine, director of Latin American Studies at the University of Miami, writes: 'For their part many Miami Cubans expected their long-suffering relatives to curse Castro in private, but in many cases the Cubans pronounced their fervent support of the revolution, regardless of the hardships caused by Cuba's economic distress.'[53] Thus, tangible, material hardship is counterbalanced by intangible moral strengths.

If the United States, especially with Republicans in the White House, has not been more directly, militarily, aggressive towards Cuba after the fall of the Soviet Union, it stems from two factors. The first has been the knowledge that, unlike Saddam Hussein, the Cuban leadership will not fold, and that the Cuban armed forces and armed civilians will inflict a heavy cost on the US forces who at some point will have to put their boots on the ground. The second factor has been an awareness that the scale of damage the US would have to inflict on Cuba would not only augment the regard with which Cuba is held in Latin America and in the wider (mainly 'Third') world – but also and concomitantly the antipathy or disaffection that exists towards the USA.

A colossally favourable military balance can sometimes be a political liability. Israel's great success from 1948 to 1973 was that it was able to combine a qualitative military superiority with a moral superiority that issued from being weaker in terms of population, size and some quantitative military indicators, thereby projecting itself as David versus Goliath. While the Lebanon invasion of 1982 eroded that moral advantage, its bloody suppression of the first and second Intifadas and the indiscriminate bombing of Lebanon in the 2006 war have led to the steady depletion by Israel of that precious moral capital it had accrued through the horrors of Nazism.

The United States could hardly rely on such asymmetry as a source of moral capital, except at its founding moment, the War of Independence against the British Empire. America's moral assets have been that war of independence, the absence of a bloody aftermath, the enlightened political order it put in place after the revolution, the Civil War and the abolition of slavery, the embodiment of individual freedom and liberties, and the role it played against fascism in World War II.

By definition, every one of the United States' military targets in the post-war age has been far smaller and weaker. In Vietnam this led to a David vs Goliath factor, permitting the Vietnamese to accumulate considerable international sympathy and moral capital. In its post-Vietnam interventions the US has been able to avoid that, by picking on smaller but perceptibly villainous entities of little moral standing (or else those the US has been able to credibly depict as morally reprehensible). It has been able to do this in universal terms, thus neutralising the negative factor of a huge asymmetry in military strength.

However, this strategy cannot apply in the case of Cuba because it has been neutralised by Fidel Castro in a moral-ethical pre-emptive strike. None of the United States' targets so far, from Noriega through Milosevic to Saddam Hussein, hosted former US presidents and allowed them to address the 'captive' nation on national TV uncensored, had a special relationship with the Pope, and successively secured record majorities in the most representative international body, the UN General Assembly. After Ho Chi Minh's Vietnam, Cuba alone – and that because of the personalities of Fidel Castro and Che Guevara – has some echo within, some reach into US society and culture.

Fidel Castro has constructed three lines of defence for his revolution: military experience, proven prowess and mobilisation; a broad social support base; and a visible accumulation of moral capital. These factors are interlinked and feed into one another. Gramsci said that the state is 'hegemony armoured by coercion'. Castro has successfully combined the realist principle of a military defence that can inflict unacceptable casualties on an invader, with the idealist principle of moral standing. From Noriega to Saddam, the US could depict their targets credibly as bad guys, villains, but in the case of Castro it cannot do so credibly to the international community. The disagreement between the US and the rest of the international community over Iraq concerned strategy, tactics and timing, but the disagreement over Cuba would be a much wider gulf: the US would be resorting to action that far surpasses its existing policy, which itself has been resoundingly rejected by the international community, including America's allies.

Moral capital therefore has functioned as a tangible, material, defensive shield or added a layer of protective coating to a military and social defensive capability. The combination of the military, the social and the moral constitutes a capability that serves to maintain Cuba's sovereignty and independence, while ensuring the continuity of its revolutionary identity.

An important source of the moral strength and prestige of Castro is that he, unlike most communist and many democratic leaders, never took his cue from anyone or any power centre. Many societies swing from dependence to isolationism and back. Castro never confused independence with isolationism. He was neither isolationist nor dependent on anyone for his political and strategic decision-making. While not being isolationist, indeed while being very active internationally, he has also been the most independent of leaders, even while economically reliant on the USSR. Even so unsympathetic an observer as Brian Latell acknowledges this fact:

... Fidel never spent a day in his life working for someone or taking orders. He has never subordinated himself to the will of another person. He has never said 'yes sir' not even to his father or the Soviet leaders when, at different times in his life, they were paying the bills... Fidel always managed to keep his distance and maintain considerable independence even while in the bear's hug.[54]

There was a brief and welcome thaw in relations between Cuba and its Northern neighbour during the Clinton administration. As the Elian Gonzales case dragged on, until its resolution in 2000, public opinion polls showed that a majority of Americans supported the return of the boy to his father in Cuba, and the US Justice Department under Attorney General Janet Reno went head-to-head with the right-wing Cuban mobs in Miami. But the thaw was short-lived. Despite opinion polls that show that a majority of US citizens and US corporations support the lifting of sanctions, the Bush administration has ratcheted up the rhetoric and the pressure against the Cuban Revolution and its leadership.

Why does the administration of a country so rich, powerful and successful, perhaps unprecedentedly so, as the United States, at the apogee of that success, hate and loathe little Cuba? Could it be due to the war on terrorism? Castro unequivocally denounced the 9/11 outrage, al Qaeda and terrorism, and offered Cuba's help. Moreover, there has never been a single act of terrorism in the United States sponsored by Cuba, though a great many terrorist actions against Cuba have originated on the soil of its gargantuan neighbour. Could it then be because Cuba has a despotic rule? Why, then, no pressure on Saudi Arabia to democratise? Is it because Cuba has a one-party system, and that party, unlike in the case of Saudi Arabia, is a Communist party? What, then, of the ties, including excellent economic ones, between the US and Communist party-ruled, nuclear-armed China, which has Most Favoured Nation (MFN) status?

A partial explanation is provided by the influence, especially within the Republican Party in Florida and therefore within the Bush administration, of the wealthy anti-Castro Cubans, a group that has sponsored as many acts of bloody carnage (blowing up airplanes, killing athletes etc.) and drug trafficking as has any terrorist outfit anywhere in the world. However, this does not explain the bipartisan character of the tightening of the economic blockade.

Another explanation is that Cuba, an island 90 miles from Florida, sets a bad example by refusing to accept US hegemony, and maintains complete sovereignty and independence. Is it that Cuba gives offence by refusing to subordinate everything to the marketplace and the motivation of private profit? Is Cuba's abiding sin that of protecting a system that has given it far better social indicators than countries that have adopted policies urged by the World Bank and International Monetary Fund – and in some cases such as public health, better social indicators than the US itself?

Is it that Cuba commits an unpardonable crime by speaking out in culturally non-specific, universal terms, in the language of 'critical reason', against injustice, aggression and terrorism from all quarters, and against double standards? Is it that Cuba is an affront because it does not maintain a truculent silence, like North Korea, but speaks out challengingly while lacking any tangible quantitative strength such as the economic and nuclear might wielded by China – and thereby questions the whole worldview of capitalism, which is predicated on material success and power? Is the affront precisely because Castro's challenge is moral and ethical, and has regional and some global resonance? Is it that Cuba cannot be tolerated because Cuba is 'the sling of David' – as Jose Marti, the nineteenth-century 'apostle of Cuban independence', described his own efforts – and Castro's words are argumentative and analytical stones that hurt the rulers of the world?

Selected countries can be arm-twisted into sponsoring resolutions against Cuba at the human rights sessions in Geneva, countries that have incomparably worse records (Mexico, for example, slaughtered hundreds of demonstrating students on the eve of the 1968 Olympics), and can be bought, bribed or threatened. Yet in the far more representative and democratic UN General Assembly, the blockade against Cuba has been voted against by record majorities (in 2004 by 179 to 4), in consecutive years including in 2001 when in the wake of 9/11 the world was fully supportive of the USA.

In voting against the embargo, most countries are registering a protest against the coercive tactics of the USA and asserting the principles of independence and sovereignty. But many are also attempting to repay a collective debt to Cuba. Cuba has never charged for its volunteers, be they doctors, soldiers or teachers – or for its blood shed on foreign soil in support of the liberation struggles and independence of other peoples and nations. While the countries of the global South owe the First World many millions of dollars, which they repay at great cost, they owe Cuba a debt in moral terms, a debt that is greater because of its non-monetary character, its non-quantifiability – the debt one owes a tribune and a champion, a gladiator for the Third World in the global arena.

Cuba's internationalism is acknowledged even by hostile analysts belonging to the CIA.

Once in power, with the capability to assist peoples whom he considered oppressed or exploited, he would never waver in performing internationalist duties. Internationalism would remain his and Cuba's sacred obligation as he provided clandestine and propaganda support, and on some momentous occasions massive military backing, for guerrillas and revolutionaries in about two dozen countries on three continents.[55]

Learning the hard way, I subsequently came to realize that Fidel's abiding commitment to revolutionary causes, dating back to Cayo Confites and the *bogotazo*, was a much higher priority for him than improving relations with the United States.[56]

While it may mean a jeopardising of individual or narrow national interests, the solidarity with Cuba is very much in the tradition of and follows the example set by the Cuban Revolution and its leader, since the socialist state of Cuba has many times sacrificed its own interests, has sacrificed the material rewards and opportunities it may have enjoyed, because of its internationalist principles and practice, its solidarity with causes and the struggles of other peoples.

SUSTAINING SOCIALISM

Following the collapse of global socialism and the triumph of capitalism as a system, Castro conducted a moral offensive against the capitalist option. His offensive proceeded along three axial routes, one of which was widely noted by commentators and scholars: an invocation of Che Guevara, the saint and martyr of the Cuban Revolution and socialism, re-emphasising Che's moral values, his prophetic prognostications of the fate of socialism if it proceeded along the path of market reforms, and his concept of a New Man motivated by moral principles rather than private profit. Less noticed were two important ideological and psychological manoeuvres on the part of Castro: the identification of capitalism with racism and apartheid, and with colonialism and imperialism, two phenomena with which Cuba had bitter memories, and were among the worst outgrowths of capitalism.

For if we are to speak of the most just of causes, it is the cause they [Mandela and the ANC] have represented. If there is anything odious and repugnant in this world, where there are so many odious and repugnant things, it is apartheid. Who invented it? Communists, socialists, socialism? [Shouts of 'No!'] No! ... In what way is apartheid different from the practice in effect for centuries of dragging tens of millions of Africans from their land and bringing them to this hemisphere to enslave them, to exploit them to the last drop of their sweat and blood?

... But the fact is that apartheid was created by the West, by the capitalist and imperialist West. The real truth is that the West supported apartheid; they supplied it with technology, countless billions in investments, and vast quantities of arms; and they gave it political support. No, imperialism did not break ties with apartheid, it did not blockade apartheid... It was Cuba that had to be blockaded, Cuba where the vestiges – that is racial discrimination – disappeared a long time ago. Cuba had to be blockaded as punishment for its social justice – but never apartheid. They took some half-hearted economic measures against apartheid...

Where did colonialism come from if not from capitalism? Where did neo-colonialism and imperialism come from if not from capitalism?[57]

If Stalin's Russia, notwithstanding the horrors of the Moscow trials and the labour camps, accrued significant moral capital in the battle of Stalingrad against the Nazi invaders, Cuba, with far less on its revolutionary conscience, did much the same with the battle of Cuito Cuanavale, and in a sense even more so because it was not defending its soil, its homeland.

Cuito Cuanavale was almost 15,000 kilometres away from Cuba, across a vast ocean and on another continent; the battle compounded the military asymmetry of a Third World country against the industrial might of South Africa, and fighting on the very doorstep of the apartheid regime. Cuba's supply line was nightmarishly extended, while South Africa's was short. Cuba left itself vulnerable to a humiliating defeat in the Angola theatre, while reducing its defences at home, 90 miles from the USA and at a time that the USSR had made clear that the defence of Cuba could not be guaranteed by it. From any conventional Realist point of view the odds were staggering. It is difficult to think of a feat of arms quite so onerous, but Fidel Castro accepted the challenge, and won.

As Mandela was telling you, in this action the revolution put everything at stake, it put its own existence at stake, it risked a huge battle against one of the strongest powers located in the arena of the Third World, against one of the richest powers, with significant industrial and technological development, armed to the teeth, at such great distance from our small country and with our own resources, our own arms. We even ran the risk of weakening our own defences and we did so. We used our ships and ours alone, and we used our equipment to change the relationship of forces, which made success possible in that battle. I'm not aware of any other time when a war broke out at such a distance between so small a country and such great power as that possessed by the South African racists....

...When this new balance of forces developed (and by then we had assembled forces that were invincible and unstoppable), the conditions for negotiations were created, in which we participated for months.

We could have waged big battles there, but given the new situation it was better to resolve the problem of Angola's integrity and Namibia's independence at the negotiating table. We knew – how could we not know! – that those events would have a profound effect on the life of South Africa itself, and this was one of the great incentives that pushed us on.[58]

Once again, former CIA operative Brian Latell recognises both Fidel's extraordinary military achievement as well as the prestige it garnered him internationally:

But in most of the Third World, in Africa, Latin America and the Middle East, his dependence on Moscow no longer mattered much. He was one of them. He was an original, audacious revolutionary hero unlike anyone else on the world stage. The Cuban troops in Angola had secured the revolutionary Marxist regime and then, late in 1975, at the end of a long, dangerously stretched supply line, they had met the racist South African army on dusty battlefields and triumphed. It was the South African dictatorship's Bay of Pigs. The Cubans fought with incredible ferocity, true to their commander-in-chief's uncompromising demands. They 'rarely surrendered and, quite simply, fought cheerfully until death' according to South Africa's leading historian of the conflict.[59]

Castro uses the feat of arms at Cuito Cuanavale to enhance the standing of the regime in the eyes of the Cuban people by giving them a tremendous sense of pride:

And if we fought fourteen thousand kilometres away – however far it was – if we got into the trap at Cuito Cuanavale that the enemies had created and that turned into a trap for them, then here, on our coasts, in our countryside, in our mountains, in our cities, in our cane fields, in our rice fields, in our swamps, we will fight as we fought at Cuito Cuanavale, and we will resist for more years than we resisted in Angola, until victory.[60]

Thus Cuito Cuanavale is also reinvested in a strategic dimension, to deter the US from aggression by influencing the calculus of its military, as well as by stimulating the fighting spirit, confidence and morale of the Cuban armed forces and populace.

CRITERIA OF MORAL SUPERIORITY

Political leadership almost always depicts itself or its cause of the moment as morally superior but does not set up criteria to judge that moral claim. The claim is therefore self-referential and tautological: the leadership or course of action is moral because the enemy is evil and the purpose or cause is just. The justification for Hiroshima and Nagasaki are the classic cases in point. The cause is just because it aims at the defeat of the evil enemy and the setting up of an order that is better or emanates from a system that is more democratic, freer, independent, equitable, etc.

Religious leadership preaches correct conduct. However, religious leadership that is also political, such as the Papacy of old or that of Islamic states, makes the claim of moral superiority on the basis that its religion is intrinsically superior to any other. Such politico-religious leadership limits the criteria of right conduct to the personal realm, away from state policy.

The challenge is to make the claim of moral superiority in a manner that holds itself up to standards and embeds criteria for verification. Such standards would judge conduct and impose limits on conduct – and are usually eschewed by political leaderships (of states as well as liberation movements) because they consider these as fetters that weaken their efforts to prosecute a cause thought to be desirable because it is just or necessary. Moral means are thus seen as a fetter, not an aid, to the achievement of moral ends, and as debilitating to the exercise of political and military force in defence of the state or a cause. Is it possible to conceive of a state or political leadership or doctrine that is strong and effective and yet conducts itself in a moral manner; a political leadership that imposes upon itself, subjects itself to a test of ethical means in pursuit of ethical ends, and is also successful in the exercise of power?

Castro's claim of moral superiority issues from two main sources, intertwined, but with one as decisive in the final analysis. One of the two sources is systemic, and as such is not original, except in that the statistical indictments and claims have been backed up by international organisations such as the World Health Organisation. Cuba's socialist system is superior in its social achievements; capitalism, imperialism and the neo-liberal world order are morally inferior because of increasing and avoidable poverty and inequity, especially – but not only – in the global South.[61] This has been the claim of socialists, Marxists and communists the world over, and they have thought that the case for moral superiority needed no further buttressing by correct action and behaviour. The systemic argument is the stock in trade of political leaders and ideologues of all persuasions: the combination of free market economy and liberal democracy is morally superior as a system, because it ensures individual freedom of choice; the system of Islamic law, Sharia, is superior because it does not allow a sexually permissive society.

Fidel Castro goes beyond the argument of systemic or structural superiority, and adds another dimension, that of conduct, of actual practice. The point is deepened by making it a criterion of moral superiority, and finally, in a bold and unique move, making it the main source and criterion of moral superiority. Within practice, the central issue to Castro is the correct and incorrect use of violence. As is made explicit in his speech to a US audience, at New York's Riverside church on 8 September 2000, that is the very cornerstone of the foundation of his claim to moral superiority – and in this he is unique among modern political leaders and ideologues.

> .... I would have absolutely no moral right to be speaking here now if a single Cuban had been murdered by the Revolution at some point throughout these 40-plus years, if there were a single death squad in Cuba, if a single person in Cuba had been vanished. And I will go even further: if a single person in our country had been tortured – mark my words – if a single person had been tortured in our country. ... You can ask South Africans who were prisoners of our troops if anyone beat them, if a single one of them was executed, because we taught and passed on our war policy to those with whom we collaborated. ... Neither in our war nor on our internationalist missions was any prisoner ever beaten or executed. There are living witnesses to this. That, of course, is what builds a good morale and authority.
>
> I think that a person who governs or a leader does not need the trappings of power, what he or she needs is moral authority, is moral power.
>
> ... Ethics and an honourable behaviour are invaluable. That is the most powerful force anyone can have.[62]

That this is no artifice for the benefit of a sympathetic foreign audience is best evidenced by its presence as a theme in his speeches to domestic audiences. In 1978, on the twenty-fifth anniversary of the Moncada uprising, an event of cardinal significance in the revolutionary calendar, as it were, Castro made the same point to his Cuban audience as he was to make in Riverside church, New York, almost a quarter of a century later:

> Our strength is not in lies or demagoguery but in sincerity, truth and consciousness. In addition the weapons are in the hands of the people and they use them to defend the revolution without torture, crime, death squads, missing persons, illegalities, or arbitrary acts such as occur every day in the countries in which imperialism keeps unjust oppressive, reactionary regimes in power. Even our most bitter enemies have begun to acknowledge this now – the fruits of our having planted seeds of principle and revolutionary ethics at the time of Moncada, seeds that flourished during the war of liberation and the subsequent development of the revolution. Rising above the mountains of imperialist slander, our historical reality stands firm and invincible.[63]

Castro has been very conscious of the critical importance of the moral factor as the very basis of defence of the revolution and its state. Being so utterly conscious of it makes it less likely that he would risk it being a contrivance and far more likely that it is invested with authenticity.

Other revolutions, especially those based on doctrines of Peoples' War, did emphasise the moral factor, but in a self-referential, axiomatic, circular argument: the revolution is morally strong because millions of people will fight to defend it, and millions of people will fight to defend it because it is a revolution, which by definition benefits them by ensuring a more just social order. Fidel Castro goes one better. The revolution is strong because the people will defend it, and they will defend it because it is morally strong. Moral strength is not taken to be an axiomatic attribute, but is the very reason that people will defend the revolution. The moral factor is seen as causative, as a condition of the strength of the revolution. This is a departure from or development of previous revolutionary thinking:

Technical means exist to neutralize a given weapon, but there are no technical means to neutralize a people in struggle. They didn't exist in Vietnam, which was an example, and they don't exist here. We are millions of people willing to defend the country and willing to defend the revolution. But why? Because there is moral strength. A revolution can only be defended with moral strength, with political strength, ideological strength and deep conviction.[64]

... weapons much more powerful than any produced through technology, namely: the weapons of morality, reason and ideas; with them no country is weak, but without them no nation is powerful. ... These are not weapons of mass destruction, but rather weapons of mass moral defence...[65]

Fidel repeatedly identified the avoidance of the erroneous, excessive use of violence as one of the wellsprings of the moral strength of the revolution, which strength was itself the best defence and guarantee of the revolution:

There is a set of principles that has ruled here and that can explain the strength of the Revolution, over the power of our adversaries and despite all the slander. One is the strict way in which, over these 26 years, we have abided by the principles that emerged and became sacred during the war: those of never killing a prisoner, never mistreating a prisoner ... a prisoner has never been beaten here ... So, the strength of our Revolution, which seems to be a miracle, is not a miracle; it's the result of a principled policy, followed consistently for the 26 and a half years of our Revolution.[66]

This identification of humaneness in the use of force and violence as 'sacred' and as the very secret of the strength of the revolution, and by extension the durability of the revolutionary state, is unique to Fidel's political thought.

In 1965, Castro summed up the most essential aspect of the balance of forces as he saw it: 'They know their material strength, but we know our moral force, and that is our power.'[67] Castro consistently referred to the moral factor as one of the main defences of Cuba. In a 1984 speech he listed three factors, military, economic and moral:

Our strength is no threat to anybody; but our strength does make a successful attack on our country virtually impossible. Our power is an element of containment. It is militarily defensive, not offensive. In the field of moral values, the example, the ideas... we represent, go beyond the borders of our small island and are more powerful than the most sophisticated strategic weapons....[68]

Castro's grand strategic doctrine, then, is a unique mix, not in its triple combination of military, economic and moral, but in the respective roles assigned to the military and the moral in which the military plays a defensive function, circumscribing or deterring an aggressor while the moral factor, constituted of ideas and example, functions in an offensive capacity.

That the concept of the revolution's true strength and defensive capacity residing in its moral worth is a central one to Castro is evidenced by its surfacing at perhaps the two most crucial testing points for that revolution: the Missile Crisis and, almost three decades later, the collapse of socialism: 'I recall the October crisis and a phrase that we used during that crisis: "we don't have strategic weapons, but we have moral weapons". These are the arms our people use to defend themselves.'[69]

Thus the strength and durability of the revolutionary state within its own borders, as well as its relative popularity in the regional and international theatres, have been sourced in these essentially moral factors, while the political, ideological and propaganda attacks against it by the US have been relatively unsuccessful, certainly in comparison with Eastern Europe, also because of their moral weakness. Castro's regime has not gone the way of the USSR or Eastern Europe primarily because it rests on a far stronger foundation of moral legitimacy (the sources of which have been indicated above).

The leaders of many significant Latin American countries, elected leaders running market economies, requiring trade, foreign investment and the goodwill of the USA, have run the risk of showing their friendship with Castro and Cuba. Being openly identified with Cuba, taking one's stand alongside it, is a risky, costly business. Cuba is controversial and will always remain so, however rational, knowledgeable, responsible and irrefutable the arguments of its leaders in international forums, for Cuba has the most powerful of all possible enemies: the mightiest power in human history.

By refusing to bend the knee and tug the forelock, by its proud and outspoken behaviour, by the guerrilla war of arguments and opinions it ceaselessly wages, by its continuing non-conformism and permanent rebelliousness, Cuba shows that there is another – and it would claim higher, more moral – way of being in the world; a way of being whereby a fairly small, poor country of the global South, with a relatively small population, can exist with self-esteem, honour and dignity, without a patron and ally and in the shadow of great hostility.

The idea that Cuba's achievement is essentially moral, and the parallelism between that achievement and that of early Christianity, is urged by a contemporary Cuban philosopher and historian, Juan Antonio Blanco, a former dissident who runs a non-governmental institute for the study of politics and ethics, the Felix Varela Centre:

Yes, we are part of a historical movement of the ethic of being against the ethic of having. We are part of a movement that believes that human happiness does not reside in our unlimited capacity to consume but in our unlimited capacity to give solidarity to our fellow human beings. We are part of a tradition that believes that people have a mission to accomplish on earth, which is not the search for individual success but the search for the humanity we carry within us. In this way our existence forms part of a continuous historical thread and the way to immortality is to be part of this historic mission.

According to capitalist thinkers, we are crazy people swimming against the tide of history. Socialism will inevitably fall everywhere and the Cuban revolutionary mission is therefore an anachronism – an anachronism that corresponds to a romantic, modern era that is being overtaken by a post-modern era. We can answer that the true Christians, not those of the Inquisition but those who have been fighting for a particular ethical code, have also been swimming against the tide of history of some 2000 years!

It's not about winning; it's about taking a moral stand...[70]

Independent research bears out that far from being a narcissistic fantasy, the quintessentially moral nature of Cuba's image and appeal resonates beyond its shores. Writing on the leaders of the Chilean left, Katherine Hite confirms that:

Cuba drove home to the Chilean left a heightened sense of the 'moral imperative' of revolutionary struggle... much of the imagery surrounding the Cuban struggle, conceived in 'epic' terms as the ultimate self-deliverance or sacrifice on behalf of the revolution, appealed to the deeply rooted Catholic sentiments that were so much a part of the Latin American culture. Cuba symbolised the weakness of capitalism on moral as well as social or distribution grounds. The idea of Cuba as a moral imperative consistently surfaced in interviews with leaders of the Chilean left, from the Catholic to the secular left....

Isabel Allende, daughter of the cousin of slain Chilean president Salvador Allende, testifies that 'We felt it was a moral imperative to defend Cuba.'[71]

The understanding of Cuba's stance in essentially ethical terms and as morally superior; the fact that an ethical evaluation is part of Cuba's self-image and self-consciousness is an aspect of the efficacy and power of the moral dimension in the political achievement of its leader, Fidel Castro.

In the twilight of his life it is possible to see in stark relief the central motifs of Castro's thought: a belief in the power of ideas, and the central idea of the correct use of violence, while upholding the right to use violent means of struggle against injustice and oppression. Castro displays a belief that ideas can compensate for the asymmetry in military and economic power, a conviction that correct ideas allied with the readiness to resist, to fight and die, can triumph over the greatest odds.

Just ideas have greater power than all the reactionary forces put together... ideas are and always will be the most important weapon of all... There is no weapon more powerful than a profound conviction and clear idea of what must be done. It is with these kinds of weapons, which do not require enormous sums of money, but only the capacity to create and transmit just ideas and values, that our people will be increasingly armed. The world will be conquered by ideas, not by force...[72]

Castro's assumption of a firm stance of moral and ethical superiority comes equipped with 'an arsenal of arguments' (as he puts it). These include the relatively restrained use of violence as compared to its massive use, especially by the USA, in war; the more equitable social opportunities and better social indicators in comparison to the other Latin American countries and in some cases even the

USA itself; the lesser magnitude of violence in everyday law and order; the conditions in Cuban prisons where some prisoners are even allowed to wear their own clothes; the generosity of Cuba to foreign students; Cuba's handling of the drug issue; Cuba's strong deterrents to hijackers in comparison to the US encouragement; the US sponsorship or protection of terrorism; the US role in destabilising electoral democracies not to its liking; US support for dictatorships with bloody records; Cuba's military resistance to apartheid; and Cuba's generous civic assistance overseas.

Castro sees himself and Revolutionary Cuba as 'men that would never sell or yield or be corrupted', unlike those Latin American leaders beloved by the United States. As for the issue of democracy, his counter-attack is multi-pronged. One axis of attack is the listing of elected democratic leaders who were deposed with US backing, or whose dictatorial successors were embraced by the US. A second thrust was to indict the democratic leaders as being sham democrats who had sold out to the rich, domestic and foreign, the military and the United States. What were common to both types of regimes was the neglect of social development and indeed a worsening of the social situation, chiefly its inequities. Thus Castro strove to assume the moral high ground using all three issues.

AUTONOMY AS MORAL FACTOR

The fall of the Cuban Revolution was deemed imminent soon after the collapse of the mighty Soviet superpower in 1991. It is over a decade and a half since then and Cuba is still standing defiant.

A wellspring of Castro's notion of moral superiority has been the independence of the Cuban Revolution. It was not a revolution that was made by a Communist party or one that owed its ideology and affiliation to Europe (such as Trotskyism). It is a revolution that stood firm even when the USSR withdrew its rockets, under US pressure. It was revolution that had existed without wilting, 90 miles from history's mightiest power. It was a revolution that had prepared to defend itself militarily from a US invasion knowing that its ally the Soviet Union was too far away to come to its aid. Therefore it was a revolution that could spiritually survive the fall of European/ Soviet socialism.

Castro has often said Cuba did not ask for anyone's permission to make its revolution; Cuba did not consult anyone as to how and when to make its revolution; Cuba did not make a single one of its strategic decisions at the dictates of the Soviet Union. We may identify this as one of the sources of its moral strength. Therefore its will to resist and defend its revolution and its socialist option has not been weakened by the collapse of the USSR – indeed it has been strengthened by the knowledge that its situation is singular, unique; it is alone, the last incarnation of an age and an ideal.

Castro turns Cuba's status as sole survivor after the fall of socialism into evidence of moral superiority. Cuba survived despite the loss of the great assistance it obtained from the USSR – assistance that Castro always acknowledged before and after the fall – precisely because it was not a puppet. It survived because it was independent. Thus he fells, at one stroke, the decades-long US argument that its opposition to Cuba was not because of its revolution but its status as satellite of the USSR. Castro thus inverts the logic of the embargo in an argumentative counter-encirclement: now that the Soviet Union is no more, and the USA has won the Cold War, why maintain the blockade? Is it not precisely because of the type of social changes that Cuba has made, changes beneficial to the vast majority of people and bringing prestige to Cuba as a nation?

Castro uses Cuba's status as sole survivor as a counterpoint to the status of the USA as sole superpower, depicting Cuba as the repository of humanity's hopes for a fairer and more just social order different from capitalism and older class societies. The Cuban people are thus vested with a universal duty to protect the standard of socialism. Castro considers Cuba's survival in the face of overwhelming odds a grand moral task. As noted earlier, Defence Minister Raul Castro likened the situation of Cuba to that of the three hundred Spartans who defended to the last man the pass at Thermopylae against the immeasurably superior force of the Persian emperor.

Castro garners further moral capital by implying that the survival of Cuban socialism is evidence of the correctness of the distinct ideas that he and Che Guevara put forward, ideas critical of the trajectories of the USSR and Eastern Europe. Cuba's survival is also attributed to the militant qualities and traditions of its people, traditions deriving from the long history of anti-colonial struggles and the thoughts of José Marti. It is the Cuban Revolution and its socialist system that has enabled it to survive and perform in a manner that has carved it a distinctive niche in the world. Thus socialism is linked to Cuban patriotism and the collective ego of the Cuban people. Capitalism's appeal to the individual ego is combated by appealing to the collective ego, almost a notion of a chosen people, albeit not in an overtly religious sense.

PATRIOTISM, NATIONALISM AND INTERNATIONALISM

Castro's ideological move only partly justifies those analysts who attribute the survival of Cuban socialism to nationalism, because the collapse of socialism was preceded and paralleled by the collapse of the nationalist-statist project in the Third World. It is not so much, or not only, that Cuban socialism is a form of Cuban nationalism, but that Castro has successfully interpreted Cuban nationalism as being served by and buttressed by Cuba's Revolution and socialism.

However, while doing this he simultaneously sees himself as and asserts that Cuban nationalism is internationalist, indeed that he is primarily an internationalist and secondarily a patriot:

Nationalism is not our essential idea, although we do love our homeland deeply. We consider ourselves internationalists and internationalism is not contrary to the love for the homeland.[73]

But we do not defend national interests, we're not very nationalistic. We're patriots but we're not very nationalistic, and we're staunchly faithful to our political principles. On many occasions we've sacrificed our national interests for the sake of the principles of our revolution and our internationalist principles. The United States doesn't understand that, it's too difficult for them. They're somewhat used to thinking that national interests must prevail over any other interests. But we've said that our homeland is not just Cuba, our homeland is also humanity.[74]

This is not simply a posture for external consumption, outside the ranks so to speak. Castro initially articulated it on the sixth anniversary of no less passionately patriotic a public occasion than the victory at the Bay of Pigs. Concluding his oration he said:

We internationalist revolutionaries will always say: we love our country, we love the welfare of our people, we love the riches that we create with our own hands, but humanity comes before our country![75]

This synthesis of nationalism and internationalism, with the main accent on the latter, is a constant over decades in Castro's thinking, under very different historical conditions.

While Stalin, faced with the gravest danger to the Russian Revolution in the form of the Nazi invasion, shifted to an appeal to Russian patriotism, Castro, when faced with the collapse of socialism in the USSR and the USSR itself, couched the challenge to the Cuban people in internationalist terms – which in turn revealed just how deeply ingrained the internationalist values were in Revolutionary Cuban consciousness.

We are now asking the country to carry out an extraordinary internationalist mission: saving the revolution in Cuba. Saving socialism in Cuba. And that will be the greatest internationalist service that our people can render humanity... revolutionary ideas haven't become obsolete or anything like that – they're going through difficult times but they will return with added strength. And they will return sooner if there is more injustice in the world, more exploitation, more hunger, and greater chaos in the world. Revolutionary ideas will return and it's up to us, the standard bearers of those ideas, to raise them high up, for that's the mission history has assigned to us. And as I said, we have the intelligence, the moral virtue, the courage and the heroism to fulfil this mission.[76]

Armando Hart, secretary of the Central Committee of the Cuban Communist party, and Cuba's Minister of Culture, provided a suggestive definition and explanation of the triangular socialism/internationalism/patriotism linkage, in an essay on Che Guevara: 'The essence of socialism is internationalism, and Cuban cultural history shows an inescapable international vocation.'[77]

Speaking to fellow revolutionary, Sandinista commander Tomas Borge, who knew the Cuban Revolution and Castro's policies so intimately that he could not have been lied to, Castro reiterated this while going on to explain how his internationalism and Cuban patriotism are perfectly compatible:

I've always placed humankind above homeland. I am an internationalist first and foremost, without ceasing to be a patriot. But now, when our homeland embodies the highest virtues of a nation – the highest virtues of a noble, combative, heroic people – and of internationalism; when it is confronting the imperialists in an unprecedented unparallel gesture, when it has become the frontline in the defence of Latin America; and when it is what Marti wanted to make it on the eve of his death at dos Rios, a line of defence against the ' brutal and turbulent north' – now, when our homeland symbolizes all that, it is not only a source of pride, but, for me, a greater privilege than ever to be a Cuban.[78]

While the thaw in US relations with the USSR and China was used by Washington to depict Castro as an isolated anachronism refusing to enter the mainstream of the marketplace, the very fact of US hostility towards Cuba at a time (the late 1980s and early 1990s) when it had good relations with both the USSR and China was used by Fidel, in a judo-like move, to enhance the moral prestige of Socialist Cuba:

Of course it's an honour! Because for a country as small as Cuba, to have a giant like the United States obsessed with this small country, when now it doesn't consider itself the adversary of the USSR or the adversary of China, and still considers itself the adversary of Cuba, this must be regarded as an honour. ...We have the honour of being a great adversary of the United States, at least a staunch adversary, an adversary that doesn't surrender, an adversary that doesn't give in, and a very strong moral adversary... We cannot help feeling proud of it.[79]

Thus by two philosophical moves, morphing Cuban patriotism with universal ideas, and the universal cause of socialism with a larger tradition in human thought that is just, ethical and moral, Fidel Castro cements his claim to moral superiority. That then is the dialectical contradiction he seeks to use in defence of the Cuban Revolution: if the USA is the sole superpower, Cuba is the sole moral and ethical counter-power. But this counter-power not only knows, unlike Savonarola, how to defend itself weapons in hand, but could never and cannot be sold out by a higher or remote authority, unlike the utopian Jesuit mission in Paraguay.

The moral counter-offensive has been consistent through time. In the 1960s, Castro focused on racism in the United States, from the bombings of churches and the murder of civil rights workers in the Deep South, through to the Watts and Detroit rioting and the deployment of the National Guard in a military crackdown, contrasting it with the desegregation drive in Cuba. In 1968, at the height of the Vietnam War and with the assassination of Martin Luther King, Castro's opposition to the US reveals itself to be a fierce moral indictment, when in his introduction to Che Guevara's *Bolivian Diary* he continues to draw a distinction between the people and the 'system' of the USA, and accuses the latter of 'moral barbarism'.[80]

In the 1990s he pointedly asked how many capitalist countries could have withstood the economic devastation that Cuba did with the collapse of the USSR and the tightening of the US embargo, without cutting back on essential social services, especially in the fields of health and education. This was a powerful argument at a time when precisely such cutbacks were being effected in Latin America and also the former socialist societies. Castro turned this contrast into one between socialism as obtaining in Cuba and capitalism as a system. His point was that the logic of capitalism as a system meant that the burden of such hardship would be passed on to the people, the most vulnerable elements of society, but that Cuba was able to protect her education system, even in the face of such odds, precisely because of the superior virtues of socialism as a system.

What is important is that this sort of case was made in the 1930s during the Great Depression while the five-year plans were unfolding in the USSR, but Castro made this case at a time when capitalism as a system had triumphed globally over socialism. He chose not to respond to capitalism's triumph by cutting away from the world as North Korea did, and nor did he abandon the socialist economic system and ideology as did China and Vietnam. Instead he pioneered an original synthesis. Economic reforms, stabilisation measures and structural adjustments were undertaken, the architect of which was the young Vice Premier, now Vice President Carlos Lage.

Despite the crisis, Castro remained committed to providing social services. He prided himself in speeches for not closing a single school, day care centre, or hospital, and for not leaving a single person destitute....[81]

But other economic measures don't fit the pattern of encroaching capitalism. Food rationing, for example, continues to ensure that scarce goods such as milk go to the sectors that most need them: children are still guaranteed milk up to age seven. Health and education continue to be national priorities, and despite scarcities, indicators such as infant and child mortality and life expectancy continue to rival or surpass those of other wealthy industrialised countries, including the United States.[82]

Cuba did not resist globalisation but drew the important conceptual distinction, not yet made by the anti-globalisation protest movement, between the phenomenon and process of globalisation and neo-liberal globalisation. It sought to use inter-capitalist economic competition to reach out to Europe, Canada and even US agribusiness. It did all this while maintaining its social indicators, and waging the 'battle of ideas', asserting with this kind of argumentation the continuing superiority of socialism over capitalism as a system.

ETHICS OF AN EXCEPTIONAL REVOLUTION

Fidel Castro sought to derive moral capital not only by demarcating himself as against Batista, the USA and capitalist regimes, dictatorial and elected, in Latin America and elsewhere, but also as against fellow revolutionaries. This demarcation itself was unique in that it was twofold. On the one hand Castro projected the Cuban Revolution as more militant, purer and more intelligent: more militant in its commitment to armed struggle in the 1960s, more intransigent in relation to the United States. Purer, not as defined in a cultural sense or those of private mores (as in Khomeini's revolution) but in the non-accordance of priority to material over moral incentives. He also identified his revolution as being tougher and more intelligent, in neither being violently overthrown nor having taken the liberal reformist path of Eastern Europe and the USSR, which led to the downfall of socialism. 'Of course, there are two kinds of Communists; Communists who let them be killed easily and Communists like us who don't let themselves be killed easily!'[83]

On the other hand, he has drawn attention to the humane and relatively non-repressive character of the Cuban process, in explicit contrast to other revolutions, and he has done so at a time when the political and ideological polarisation of the New Cold War was at its height, and the collapse of the USSR was nowhere in the realm of the predictable.

Any resemblance to other strands of Marxism such as Trotskyism and Titoism are superficial and do not stand up to scrutiny. Trotskyism was unable to address successfully the question of state power and its protracted sustainability in a hostile environment. Titoism, while projecting itself as more humane than Stalinism, had a record of internal executions, and as importantly, abandoned a militant external policy for a more moderate one. Castro's was a unique synthesis, combining a greater militancy than the world communist mainstream with a greater humanitarianism and far lesser levels of internal violence.

Someday when serious and respected historians analyse these 25 years of the Revolution, they will see that it is perhaps the only Revolution that has never gone outside the law. We have laws that punish, even with severity because we have to defend ourselves. But they'll see that we weren't repressive, that we weren't criminals, that we weren't torturers, and there weren't missing persons in our country. There's not even one, not a single case of torture in our country! And the day that serious historians delve into the realities and carry out research, our Revolution's history will become known. And we'll have to see how many revolutions had the even-temperedness and the peacefulness of our Revolution in spite of having lived through 25 years of the imperialists' death threats.[84]

An important aspect of the battle of ideas was the continued activism in the global arena, not through the export of revolution as in the

1960s but through a two-pronged process of dialogue with elements and sectors in US society (including agribusiness), and regional and global conferences, developing a critical consciousness about neoliberalism and promoting solidarity, waiting for and feeding into the next waves of global youth protest and Latin American political change. That wave has manifestly arrived in Latin America.

Fidel Castro, the Jesuit-educated revolutionary, was thus attempting perhaps to play the role of Ignatius Loyola, spearheading the Counter-Reformation, but as in the case of the Jesuits with a new, sophisticated and impressive synthesis, combining zeal and moral strength with modernity, reason and intellectual appeal. The exemplary dedication of Cuba's soldiers in Africa until the end of the 1980s, and its doctors, teachers and even sports instructors in the Third World, including Latin America up until today, is reminiscent of and arguably inspired by that of the Christian missionaries, especially the Spanish Jesuits who taught Castro.

Castro's most dramatic moral claim, his claim to moral hegemony, is a suggestion of absolute historical uniqueness of the Cuban Revolution and, by implication, his guiding role and ideas. This uniqueness is identified by him as residing chiefly and precisely in the realm of the use of armed violence; of the 'right and wrong use of violence', the Kautilyan philosophical criterion identified above. While this is the central claim, it is interlinked with and forms a complex whole with ancillary others. It is noteworthy that Fidel makes this claim most explicitly in conversation with Tomas Borge, a leader of the other revolution (Nicaragua's) renowned for its absence of excessive violence, and a revolutionary commander known both for his long experience in armed struggle and his humanitarian gesture of pardoning his torturer.

Castro's claim is several-fold. Most strikingly he suggests that never in the entire history of warfare has an army behaved in as humane a fashion as the Cuban revolutionary guerrillas. He then asserts that this was not specific to the civil war but was consciously inculcated in the Cuban armed forces and manifested in their conduct during long overseas campaigns. He makes direct reference to justifications of and rejects the excessive use (abuse) of violence even under the pressure of combat and/or with the prospect of tangible military gain. He reiterates his claim of the absolute exceptionality of the Cuban Revolution ('never in human history'), using the Bay of Pigs invasion as an example.

He then brings in the practice of non-military solidarity by Cuba, in the form of doctors and teachers, in many parts of the world, throwing down a moral gauntlet: which country has done either, let alone both – practising restraint and humanitarianism in its violence and warfare, and such generosity in its extension of human solidarity?[85]

Tellingly, and in another example of Castro's combination of ethical and strategic criteria, indeed his claim that good ethics make good strategy, he asserts that the secret of victory has been an ethical policy:

.... [The Cuban Revolution] it may well be the only revolutionary process in the world – and I know history – that never used violence against a prisoner, against a detainee. ... There was not a single case of a prisoner who was tortured, neither after the triumph of the revolution nor in our war of liberation – not even when anyone could have used the pretext of needing to obtain military information so as to save his own troops or win a battle. Not a single case. There were hundreds of prisoners, and then thousands, before the war ended. You could look up the names of all of them; and not even one of those hundreds and thousands of prisoners was humiliated or even insulted. Early always, we set those prisoners free. That helped us win the war, because it gave us great prestige, great authority in the eyes of the enemy soldiers. They trusted us. In the beginning none of them surrendered; but in the end they surrendered en masse.... Therefore I can state something that I don't know if any other revolutionary process in the world can declare: not even once has there been a case of a prisoner being tortured or murdered in our country. And of course, there has not been, in the history of the revolution, any cases of prisoners disappearing.

Our soldiers took all of those habits and norms that guided our conduct in the mountains with them when they went to Angola, Ethiopia or wherever else they were, and these norms governed our conduct in the cooperation that we gave the revolutionary movement. Never can it honestly be said that a Cuban soldier on an internationalist mission murdered or tortured a prisoner. Our soldiers never did that.[86]

This is an ensemble of arguments that also involve rejection of excessive violence in the maintenance of stability and order within revolutionary society, and a conscious rejection of the cult of the personality in post-revolutionary society:

In Cuba, in more than 30 years of the revolution, there have never been any official pictures. ... the pictures of me that people have in their homes are taken from magazines and posters for national meetings. ... but there isn't any official picture in Cuba; that was prohibited in the first few months after the triumph of the revolution. Another thing: we absolutely forbade naming schools, institutions and other installations after living people; they can be named only after people who are dead. Lastly, we don't allow statues, busts or other things like that to be put up in honour of living people. No streets, or schools – nothing – may be named after living revolutionaries, nor may there be any statues or busts of living revolutionaries.[87]

This is confirmed by Brian Latell:

At his insistence a law was enacted prohibiting the installation of statues of any leaders in public places, or the naming of streets, parks or towns after them. There would be no cult of personality, as in Stalin's Soviet Union or Mao's China.[88]

While the entire set of claims marks the Cuban Revolution from other socialist revolutions, the latter aspects of internal repression and cult of personality were absent from the American Revolution of 1776. However, the American Revolution is something of a misnomer, insofar as it was a war of independence – and as Kevin Phillips has demonstrated, a civil war between loyalist and anti-loyalist forces divided in good part along confessional lines[89] – rather than a social upheaval. Excessive internal violence was a hallmark of the great bourgeois revolution, that of France, and therefore Castro's claims go beyond superiority within the family of twentieth-century *socialist* revolutions to *revolutions as such*. His assertion about the behaviour of the Cuban revolutionary army, during the civil war and overseas, is of course unique and thus lays claim to a moral superiority surpassing that of the armed forces of even the most democratic-bourgeois states, including his chief antagonist, the USA.

Part IV

Reflections and Conclusion

Introduction

The study of a thinker has validity independent of the fate of his thought in the real world. The study of a political leader is valid independently of the institutional continuity of his ideas.

What, then, is Fidel Castro's real achievement in history, politics and political ideas? What is the importance of the Castroist or *Fidelista* synthesis? The concluding part of this study attempts to sum up the answer to these questions.

6
The Achievement of Synthesis

This chapter attempts to demonstrate that Castro's unique deployment of the moral and ethical factor in the matter of political violence enables a resolution of a debate that is not only relevant to the contemporary world but also sheds new light on a perennial problem of political philosophy. I return to the Camus–Sartre polemic introduced earlier in this study, then locate Castro within the terms of the exchange and argue that Castro's stance suggests a resolution of that debate on violence and morality. This chapter also examines Castro's Christian formation as one of the roots of his specific ethics and morality. It reconstructs the synthesis of values that he achieves and focuses on his notion of heroism, which combines the realistic and the romantic.

What is Fidel's (or the *Fidelista*) synthesis?

Though F. Scott Fitzgerald's slightly expanded version is the better known, it is Blaise Pascal who said that the mark of genius is the ability to hold two opposite ideas in the mind at the same time. Castro's stand is remarkable in political philosophy because it is profoundly dialectical, holding in equipoise two seemingly opposing ideas: the moral and ethical right to use weapons against oppression, and the injunction not to do so in a manner that is terrorist, that is, unethical. Though theologians and theoreticians of just war have striven to do so before and after him, Castro is unique in that he is perhaps the only top political leader, the only wielder of political power (and a determined one, in prolonged conditions of adversity), to do so.

CASTRO AND THE CAMUS–SARTRE DEBATE

In his *Pride & Solace: The Functions and Limits of Political Theory'*,[1] Norman Jacobson accords Albert Camus a status (deriving from *The Rebel*) equal to that of Hannah Arendt and George Orwell; a prominent member of a subset of political theorists Jacobson discusses as annexure to the greats – Machiavelli, Hobbes and Rousseau. In its early years the victorious Cuban Revolution was famously embraced by Sartre, and yet in retrospect it would seem that Fidel Castro also bore resemblance to the ideal portrayed by Albert Camus in *The Rebel*, the work that led to the bitter polemic in 1952 between Sartre and Camus, resulting in the public and private break between them. In truth, Castro was the synthesis of their opposed positions, a synthesis that these gifted intellectuals could not conceive of. In his revaluation of the debate, Ronald Aronson concludes with the desirability and possibility of a synthesis of Sartre's and Camus' positions on politics, emancipationist violence and morality.[2] Yet it remains an ideal type, and he makes no mention of any political personality. Fidel Castro attempted to incarnate such a possibility.

Camus chose the rebel over the revolutionary, the rebellion over the revolution, and in this he would have found no confirmation in Castro. But he also – and far more subtly – indicated the way in which a revolution could avoid its seeming destiny of culmination in tyranny. This pathway to redemption was for the revolution always to recall its roots in rebellion and to observe 'measure' and limits.[3] Camus commended rebellion because it was limited, unlike revolution; he commended rebellion as the limit itself.

Camus was right in his identification of the problem of the preservation of humane values – of morality – within violent rebellion and revolution. He was demonstrably in error, however, when he opted for revolt and rebellion, in contradistinction to revolution, as the solution to the problem. The very example of the Algerian FLN, whose use of terrorism against civilians was unacceptable to Camus, negates his own point. The FLN did not have the perspective of a socialist, let alone socialist revolution, but the more limited one of national liberation. It was a revolt, a rebellion against colonial oppression. And yet it resorted to the kind of terrorist attacks, which may or may not have been justifiable in that they were directed against armed settlers, but were clearly unacceptable to Camus himself. Furthermore, the anti-Nazi French Resistance, which had limited objectives and in which Camus was a celebrated participant, resorted to deadly vengeance on an extensive scale against collaborators, following Liberation.

Sartre charged that Camus, in opting for the stand of morality, had turned his back on practice and stood aside from history. Sartre held that a writer or intellectual must live and work within history, with and upon the concrete choices that the history of his or her time presents him or her. History, implies Sartre, usually offers only two choices, the violence of the oppressor and the violence of the oppressed. It is impossible to remain neutral or posit a third (nonexistent) choice. Sartre himself opted to defend, or not to publicly criticise, the violence of the oppressed – including the violent system issuing from a revolution, the USSR. Camus, refused this option, and in doing so, alleged Sartre, acted in 'bad faith' and therefore lacked authenticity. Camus similarly felt that Sartre's silence about the massive violation of human rights and freedoms in the USSR was an illustration of bad faith on his part. In his obituary for Camus, Sartre made an even subtler but more pointed critique, implying that Camus had placed himself in an impossible situation: '... because morality, taken on its own, at the same time demands rebellion and condemns it'.[4]

Mao Ze Dong was one revolutionary who fitted the first half of Camus' bill, in that he never forgot the revolution's origins in rebellion and always attempted to recall the revolution to its spiritual roots; but, as the horrors of the Cultural Revolution were to reveal, he had no notion of limits, of 'measure'.

In Castro, revolutionary political practice, the making of History from a class perspective, has been shown to be compatible with a principled stance in politics – something that neither Sartre nor Camus seemed to have thought possible. Fidel justified and practised the violence of the oppressed. He also refused to be equidistant between the USA and USSR. In that he was closer to Sartre. Yet he did not regard all actions of violence by the oppressed as desirable or justifiable. In this he was closer to Camus.

Fidel Castro recalled the revolutionary state to its roots in rebellion by the mode of internationalist engagement whereby successive generations of Cubans rediscovered the rigours and idealism of their guerrilla 'fathers' who landed in the rebel yacht *Granma* on 2 December 1956. Unlike Mao, however, he also observed limits in the exercise of violence. Dostoevsky and Nietzsche notwithstanding, for Castro, not everything was permitted. In this he represents not only a contrast to Bin Laden but also a departure from Lenin, Trotsky and Stalin. Ironically, it was Trotsky, who in his 'Marxism and Terrorism' and 'Our Morality and Theirs', replying to the Social Democrats of the Second International (primarily Kautsky and the Mensheviks), provided explicit theoretical justification for mass terror unconstrained by moral scruples.

POWER AND VIRTUE

Fidel Castro's moral-ethical code, especially its dimension of discrimination and restraint in the use of violence, is notable owing to a cluster of factors. The history of Cuba was filled with violence, conquest and several wars for independence. The Cuba in which Castro grew up and practised politics was a violent one. There had been a revolution in 1933 and upheavals in the 1940s. The university milieu was fraught with violence, with groups of former political militants degenerating into armed gangs enjoying state patronage. While fighting the revolution and at the moment of assuming power, he had as competitors several armed organisations. Then there was Castro's own temperament, which was a militant, combative, even violent one. 'Castro was never a believer in non-violence. Both by instinct and by conviction he favoured hitting back.'[5] 'Almost everything about the man seemed to make him ideally suited to lead such a movement; his penchant for politics, his affinity for the outdoor life and, most importantly, his passion for action, *violent* action.'[6]

Finally, and most remarkably, is the fact that Castro was a man of war, a man who without any formal military training participated in violent expeditions, assaulted a large army barracks, was imprisoned, released and then returned to the country to launch a guerrilla war, supported armed revolution in Latin America, sent Cuban volunteers to fight on other continents, commanded the defence of Cuba against the US-supported Bay of Pigs invasion, involved Cuba in two major wars in Africa (Angola and Ethiopia/Somalia), personally immersed himself in the strategy and tactics of major, decisive campaigns in Angola, and repeatedly entertained the possibility of and planned for a military confrontation with the United States, the world's mightiest military power.

Castro's leadership avoided the Scylla and Charybdis of politics: total lack of scruple as regards means on the one hand, and lack of purposiveness on the other, in gaining, wielding and retaining state power. Examples of the first abound, from the aftermath of the French Revolution through that of the Russian, and the Cultural Revolution in China. The Nicaraguan Revolution and the Zapatistas in Mexico provide examples of the latter. The FSLN, humane revolutionaries who hoped to pioneer a model that combined direct and indirect democracy (as envisaged by Rosa Luxemburg), lost state power in 1990.[7] The Soviet Communists under Gorbachev provide the classic example of this outcome. The Zapatistas deliberately eschewed the classic focus of politics, the assumption of state power, and limited themselves to opening up an autonomous space at the periphery.

Fidel Castro remained relentlessly focused on the dispossession of 'the enemy' from state power, and unlike the Sandinistas (in 1990) and Gorbachev in their different ways, would not gamble with the revolution's hold on state power.

As he prepared to speak, he removed his pistol from its holder and placed it on the table. The gesture was clear... His words 'within the Revolution, everything; against the Revolution, nothing' thereafter became the hallmark.... The Revolution had rights, he explained, and its first right was to exist.[8]

Castro himself is explicit about the realist dimension of his thinking and action:

But we are also realists – if you are not a realist you may lose the battle, you need to be aware of the problems. In other words, you have to be optimistic but, at the same time, realistic and you must believe in human beings, despite the fact that the human being hasn't yet given much proof of being sufficiently wise.[9]

Despite his realist determination Castro has not practised a doctrine of 'by any means necessary' and has maintained a sense of proportionality between (often coercive, sometimes violent) means and (revolutionary) ends.

A characteristic of revolutionary struggles is the loss of innocence. With the loss of innocence comes the loss of self-control and selectivity in the use of violence. However idealistic they are at the outset, the shock of repression induces a metamorphosis in revolutionary movements. The lesson that is learned from initial failure followed by repression, torture and extrajudicial execution is that the movement was not harsh enough. The behaviour of the oppressor causes a mirroring in that of the rebellion. It is compounded by the impulse of vengeance.

The Cuban Revolution under Fidel Castro avoided this process of brutalisation. The horrific torture and arbitrary executions of the July 26 Movement after Moncada did not result in a geographic progression in the ruthlessness of the Castro forces. The indiscriminate repression conducted by the Batista forces after the Granma landing and throughout the war did not result in corresponding conduct on the part of the Rebel Army. At no point in the struggle was there a moral equivalence between the regime and that of the revolutionary army. In a 1985 speech to Latin American trade unionists, Castro revealed that this was a deeply held personal value and conviction:

I exclude torturers, murderers, but I don't exclude any man in advance, even if he had been my adversary. Because I feel deep contempt for those who murder prisoners, for those who kill, but I do not feel any contempt for the men who fight openly on the battlefields.[10]

Many revolutionary vanguards, which remain restrained and selective in the struggle for power, lose that restraint in the struggle to retain power, when faced with internal and external foes. In the Cuban case, there were executions in the post-revolutionary period with a hostile estimate of 5,000–7,000.[11] However, there was no unleashing of plebeian passions on the defeated enemy, there was no mass terror and no collective punishment of whole social categories in the name of patriotic or class struggle.

Liberation struggles and revolutions tend to follow identifiable pathways and fall into predictable patterns. They often fail, are defeated or aborted by compromise or military putsch, owing to a lack of the necessary combination of political will, organisational skill and strategic clarity. Sometimes they win, but are overthrown by foreign intervention allied with domestic counterrevolution. Sometimes they succeed only in their initial objectives, only part way: overthrowing the immediate oppressor, the foreign occupier or local tyranny, but leaving the structures of oppression and exploitation untouched, and the promise of social liberation unfulfilled.

This almost inevitably generates a second wave of struggle from below, either against the perceived betrayal, the rolling back of the revolution, or for the fulfilment of its original aims and/or latent promise. This 'second wave' usually takes the form of the slogan that political liberation should be followed by economic and social liberation.

Sometimes revolutions move uninterruptedly into a more radical phase, going beyond the usually stated objectives, either driven by social demands or the exigencies of the post-revolutionary moment, such as foreign invasion and domestic counterrevolution. This radicalisation then generates a backlash and a new or renewed social conservatism. This in turn triggers the 'second wave from below', which is crushed and results in greater political tyranny.

Cuba under Castro defied these patterns in both its internal and external dynamics. It contained the qualities necessary to unite broad forces yet proceed uninterruptedly from political liberation towards more radical objectives of social justice and equity.

A pattern reveals itself in the relationships between a revolution and the world outside. Revolutions attempt to export themselves only to fail and adjust to the existing state system, limiting themselves to state-to-state relations, or to succeed and become new, annexationist empires. A third variant is the revolution that never had, or forgets, its sense of a universal mission and remains stuck within its national shell.

The Cuban Revolution remained defiant and resolute in the face of US hostility, arguably the most unequal contest in modern history, and yet observed at all times the distinction between the US government and the American people. It was sufficiently determined in its own defence not to be undermined or overthrown, and yet did not impose cultural closure or a reign of terror. It allied itself with the Soviet bloc while retaining the quintessential independence that permitted it to sustain itself psychologically, materially and strategically following the collapse of the USSR. It surmounted its isolation neither by surrender to a hostile world order nor by closing in on itself to ward off contamination. It was nationally rooted but not circumscribed, and practised an internationalism that manifested itself variously, successively and at times in combination, as solidarity with liberation movements and statesmanlike global stances; as martial and humanitarian constructive presences. It shed its blood in causes far beyond its strategic environment, often when its own national security was not involved, and at the cost of enhancing its military vulnerability – and did so without seeking or retaining a single economic asset or permanent base in those theatres of engagement.

Symptomatically, it commemorated the anniversaries of the Warsaw Ghetto uprising and observed the cultural holidays of its infinitesimal Jewish minority, while sending a tank unit to stand shoulder to shoulder with the Syrians from 1973 to 1975, facing the victorious Israeli Defence Forces in the Golan Heights. Thus it observed the distinction, so often obliterated, between anti-Zionism and anti-Semitism.

These qualities of head and heart formed a unique combination and cannot be understood apart from the guiding ideas and ideology, the political thought, of the leader and strategist of the Cuban Revolution, Fidel Castro.

MORALITY AND POLITICS: DUALITY OR TRINITY?

In Chapter 10 of his *After Marxism*,[12] entitled 'We should be talking about right and wrong', political philosopher Ronald Aronson argues that Marxism is dead and that a radical project must be born that liberates the disguised moral kernel aspect of Marxism and places it explicitly at the centre.[13] His epitaph for Marxism is followed by suggestions for a post-Marxist moral project of emancipation. I have argued that Fidel Castro's Marxism has been marked precisely by an explicitly moral-ethical aspect.

Aronson draws attention to the warm and cold streams in Marxism: passion and cold intellect. He recognises that, at its best, Marxism's strength was in uniting the two. The history of socialism (and revolutions in general) shows, however, that this was not enough. Lenin represented the unity of reason and passion, as did his pre-socialist role model, the Jacobins. Yet that combination was insufficient to guard against moral horrors such as collective punishment after 1917, and contained enough ambivalence to make way for Stalinism. I would argue that a binary combination, head and heart, is insufficient. What is required is a triad or trinity: reason and passion mediated by conscience; head, heart and soul.[14]

Morality has a bad name in politics. It lends itself to two alternative outcomes: either a fuzzy, 'feel-good' theory, allied to ethics, allergic to clear analysis and purposiveness, which makes for effective political intervention, or a moralising fanaticism. Fidel Castro and Cuba show that morality can be explicitly introduced as a touchstone of politics, without succumbing to either.

COMMUNISM AND CHRISTIANITY?

Sheldon B. Liss observes of Castro: 'He believes in a moral imperative in politics…'[15] This study suggests that the moral and ethical dimension stems from a unique synthesis of Marxism and Christianity, which Armando Hart has designated the 'two most important historic wellsprings of man's thinking and emotions'.

In the wake of the Nicaraguan Revolution and against the backdrop of the revolutionary upsurge in Central America, Fidel Castro gave expression to ideas of a Marxist–Christian convergence, which, he speculated significantly, would reinvigorate both traditions, Marxism and Christianity:

In Chile once, and also in Jamaica, we spoke of the strategic alliance between Christians and Marxist-Leninists…. If we bear in mind that Christianity was, in the beginning, the religion of the poor, that in the days of the Roman Empire it was the religion of the slaves, because it was based on profound human precepts, there is no doubt that the revolutionary movement, the socialist movement, the communist movement, the Marxist-Leninist movement, would benefit a great deal from honest leaders of the Christian church and other religions returning to the Christian spirit of the days of the Roman slaves. What's more, Christianity would also benefit, along with socialism and communism.

And some religious leaders in Nicaragua asked us why strategic alliance, why only strategic alliance; why not speak of unity between Marxist-Leninists and Christians?

I don't know what the imperialists think of this. But I'm absolutely convinced the formula is highly explosive.[16]

For Castro, Communism and Christianity, the two sources of his moral convictions, are on a continuum: 'If there ever was a name that the reactionaries hated more than "Communist", it was "Christian" in another time.'[17] For him the model of communist conduct is provided by ministering Catholic nuns: 'We are not talking only about respect... I once said at the National Assembly that the nuns who run asylums are models of communism. I referred to their attitude, spirit, generosity and charity.'[18]

The most explicit and complete, if succinct, disclosure by Castro of his moral-ethical formation and code is framed by the contexts of Angola and allegations of the involvement of Cuba in drug smuggling. It is noteworthy that the statement itself is made *four years prior* to the episode of Arnaldo Ochoa.

Of all the Caribbean countries, Cuba is the one that has the largest number of drug traffickers in jail... we've really become the police of the Caribbean and we often wonder why, since the United States doesn't pay us for this service... I assure you we've had plenty of offers. You know how brazen these underworld characters are. We would practically have solved our foreign exchange problems, but we're not interested in that kind of money... *I don't know whether it has to do with morals or the fact that I studied the catechism or studied all about Christian morality in Christian schools, but to me it is a question of Christian morality and Marxist-Leninist morality, and that's what we go by.*[19]

A decade before liberation theology made its appearance in Latin America with the Medellin Conference of Bishops, Fidel Castro had begun to publicly reinterpret Christianity in radical terms. Doubtless it was a response to a situation that he found himself in. On the one hand, the Cuban Church had taken a stand against his revolution and its reforms. Castro knew of the counterrevolutionary role played by the Catholic Church during the Spanish Republic. On the other hand, 90 per cent of the Cuban people were Christians, practising Catholicism or a syncretic belief system called Santeria.

Castro chose not to proceed along the route taken by the French, Russian and Chinese Revolutions or the Republicans in Spain during the Civil War. In those revolutions not only was the religious hierarchy and institutions attacked sometimes physically and even bloodily, the revolutions persecuted common people for their beliefs. Castro took a firm stand against the attacks by the official church on his revolution. At the same time, he never broke diplomatic relations with the Vatican. Most importantly, he embarked on a flanking manoeuvre: initially keeping his party atheistic (and, in the mid-1980s, reversing that policy), while working with the Christian beliefs of his citizens, reinterpreting them to justify a revolution. More, he indicated that making the revolution or at the least supporting the radical reforms was very much in keeping with Christ's message, while opposing them was not, and therefore being a good Christian meant being a good revolutionary.

In practice, the implementation of the agrarian reform law became less a matter of the letter of the law than of 'moral conviction'.... It was only for genuine revolutionaries, for those willing to say 'leave all that you have and follow me'. In an even more explicit comparison with the first Christians, he told a Catholic Congress that Christ's teachings had met a lot of opposition. 'They did not prosper in high society, but germinated in the hearts of the humble people of Palestine.'[20]

It is impossible to avoid the conclusion that while Christians were a strategic partner for Castro, Christianity was much more, and that it was a wellspring of his worldview, a source of the moral and ethical dimension of his political thought. As he disclosed to the *Washington Post* in a 1985 interview, 'I had attended religious schools from the first grade up to my last senior high school year. I had, moreover, lived the whole experience of religion, of the church, of religious work...'[21]

The key seems to be the deep inspiration from and degree of identification with the figure of Jesus Christ, as distinct from the Church. The history of the Catholic and Protestant churches is interwoven with that of massacres, tortures and crimes, which is why many historians have seen the parallels between the Inquisitorial practices of Communism and those of the Church. Had Castro's identification been mainly with the Church, he too may have had an added layer of self-justificatory zeal, for shedding the blood of unarmed opponents. However, since Christ seems to have been a role model, this constituted a moral safeguard within *conscienzia*, a combination of conscience and consciousness. This becomes clear when examining several instances of Castro's invocation of Christ.

Castro himself must have felt a profound kinship with Christ; in a pre-Easter speech in March [1959] he intoned: 'because there are those who say they are Christians and are racist. And they are capable of crucifying one like Christ because one tells the truth to an insensitive and indolent society. Because Jesus Christ – and I don't want to compare myself even remotely, I don't want to compare myself in the least – because what I say is, why did they crucify Jesus Christ? It is good that we should speak of this during this Holy Week. They crucified Christ for something. And it was simply because He defended the truth. Because He was a reformer within that society, because within that society He was a whip against all that Pharisaism and all that hypocrisy. Because for Christ there was no difference of race, and He treated the poor the same as He treated the rich, and the black the same as the white. That society, to which He told the truth, did not want to forgive His preachings, and they ended up simply crucifying Him because He told them the truth.'

   Antonio Nunez Jimenez says that later in 1959, in a 'secret speech' before officials of the new Agrarian Reform Institute, Castro said, 'The Revolution… ceased to be that romantic thing to become that in which there is only room for those who are suffering the metamorphosis of conversion into revolutionaries, and are in accordance with that precept of Christ when He said: "Leave all that you have and follow me." This is the reality.' In a televised speech in December delivered in defence of the revolution, Castro said he made a point of attending a Roman Catholic congress in Havana because '… When Christ's preachings are practiced, it will be possible to say that a revolution is occurring in the world…. Because I studied in a religious school, I remember many teachings of Christ, and I remember He was implacable with Pharisees…. Nobody forgets that Christ was persecuted; and let nobody forget that he was crucified. And that his preachings and ideas were very much fought. And that these preachings did not prosper in high society, but germinated in the hearts of the humble of Palestine…' Twenty-five years later, Fidel Castro continued to invoke Christ as his role model, and Christianity as the philosophical basis of the Cuban socialist revolution.[22]

The most explicit and intimate explanatory revelation comes from Fidel Castro himself:

Jesus Christ was one of the most familiar names to me, practically ever since I can remember – at home, at school, and throughout my childhood and adolescence. Since then, in my revolutionary life – even though, as I told you, I never really acquired religious faith – all my efforts, my attention, and my life have been devoted to the development of a political faith, which I have reached through my own convictions... I never saw any contradiction in the political and revolutionary sphere between the ideas that I upheld and the idea of that symbol, that extraordinary figure that had been so familiar to me ever since I could remember.[23]

Nobel Prize-winning author Gabriel Garcia Marquez, counted by Fidel Castro as a personal friend, recounts[24] a later and more dramatic disclosure in an unusual setting:

On one occasion, before a bipartisan group of Congressmen and even a Pentagon official, he gave a very realistic account of how his Galician ancestors and his Jesuit teachers infused some moral principles in him which had proved very useful in the formation of his personality. And he concluded: 'I am a Christian.' It hit the table like a bombshell.[25]

In his 1998 CNN/BBC interview Castro makes repeated reference to one person who was reflecting on the contemporary global situation and whose observations and slogans he obviously approves in the main, and that is Pope John Paul II. The late pope is the only such personality of the day to whom Castro makes such a complimentary reference, with the clear implication that, apart from Castro himself, this was the one man who was thinking deeply about globalisation and whose thinking ran parallel with his own. He even finds some consonance between Karl Marx's notion of proletarian internationalism and Pope John Paul II's slogan of 'the globalisation of solidarity'.[26]

Castro returns to his roots, his knowledge of Christianity, in dealing with the collapse of socialism and its future prospects. He does not equate the whole of the socialist tradition with Marxism. He dives into the history of ideas and finds two sources of solace, the second being the persistence and revival of the ideas of the French *philosophes* and the French Revolution despite the defeat both of that revolution and its Napoleonic successor. The source of inspiration he mentions first, however, is the history of Christianity:

You mentioned Marxism and socialism, and I don't want to make comparisons but other things come to my mind now. It also seemed that Christianity would be buried in the Roman catacombs. When the Romans occupied Jerusalem and scattered the Jews and the first Christians, nobody would have bet that, one day, the ideas of Christianity would survive over Rome's pagan ideas and would spread through a large part of the world to become a religion with over one billion followers.[27]

Faced with the calamitous collapse of socialism and Marxism, and orienting himself in the new age while mobilising and motivating others, Castro's almost instinctive reference to the history of Christianity as a source of solace, inspiration and example is an indicator of how powerful its influence on him has been and how important an ingredient it is in his thinking.

As we have seen, Castro's references to Christianity are not only in conversation with religious personalities or Western audiences. Even a meeting with militant Latin American women produces evidence of Christianity as a point of reference with regard to ethics and morality:

Can we resign ourselves to that future? Is that a Catholic, Christian or Marxist concept? ...You don't have to be Communist or socialist; you only have to be Christian, to have a basic sense of ethics, to say, 'That's not right. That goes against the most basic moral principles, against the most basic ethical principles.' And a Christian could say, 'That goes against the most basic Christian principles.'[28]

Most telling here are the assumptions of an organic commonality or continuum ('Catholic, Christian or Marxist concept') and the overlap and interchangeability of a Christian and socialist ethic.

That same year, 1985, Castro told a Latin American trade unionist audience at a conference on debt moratorium: 'I have a lot more respect for the cross than for the sword.'[29] Given that it was made in a context of criticising colonialism and the role that Christianity played in sanctifying it, and given also that Castro has been identified with the doctrine of armed struggle – the rifle, or metaphorically, 'the sword' – it is a remarkably revealing assertion.

FIDEL AND THE JESUIT STANCE

While Marxism prided itself on inheriting and superseding previous constellations of ideas and moving history into the realm of science, emphasising rupture and leap rather than continuity, Fidel Castro explicitly and consciously wove a different tapestry in which Marxism was a thick strand, but not perhaps the guiding thread.

He quite consciously linked a whole field of ideas, excavating it to unearth older forms of ideologies motivated by the notion of justice.

The commonalities of that stock and tradition of ideas were their ethical-moral character and stress on social justice, the two going hand in hand and co-dependent on, even co-derivative from each other. The invocation of religion, chiefly but not only Christianity, the notion of a common ethical charter to be derived from these religions, in short a sophisticated version of notions of good and bad, while not original in and of itself, and certainly part of the early Utopias, is an original contribution of Castro's to Marxist and Communist thought.

It has to emerge from the sum of the more revolutionary thinking and the sum of the best ethical and humanistic ideas of more than one religion, I would say of every authentic religion...We have to add the ethical and human sense of many ideas dating back to the beginning of the history of mankind; the ideas of Christ, to socialist ideas, scientifically founded, so just and deeply human. These are the ideas of Karl Marx, the ideas of Engels, the ideas of Lenin, the ideas of Marti, those of European Encyclopaedists that preceded the French revolution and the ideas of the heroes of the independence of this hemisphere.[30]

This quotation is notable because it was not made at a meeting of religious personalities whom Castro was trying to woo, but at a meeting of economists to discuss globalisation. It is as part of a tradition in human thought that he sees or seeks to locate Marx, Engels (the separate mention of him by Castro is notable) and, more interestingly, the supremely tough-minded Lenin. In doing so, Castro cuts across the usual divide of Utopian and scientific, of ideology and science.

HEROISM AND SYNTHESIS OF VALUES

Fidel Castro's argument is that the means are as important as the ends, and that emancipatory ends, for him the most honourable ideals in history, require honourable means. His survival demonstrates that the correct choice of means, the 'good' use of violence, is eminently functional in the service of the acquisition and retention of power. His notion of heroism combines the honourable use of often violent means in the service of honourable ends.

While successful in the traditional concerns of politics, the acquisition and retention of power, Castro has, seemingly paradoxically, rejected the idea that success is the criterion of validity, of correctness. Underscoring the element of chance, luck, contingency and indeterminacy, he argues that the Cuban revolutionaries were acutely vulnerable at several points of his struggle and could have been wiped out, but that such defeat would not have meant they were wrong, that their ideas and political line was wrong. For him the proof of the pudding was not in the eating. By this he emphasises the importance of volition and choice, of the subjective factor, of will, but does so in a sense rather different from that of Lenin.

For Lenin, volition is allied to the most advanced scientific ideas, but for Castro in the final analysis, it is the heroic stance *with its new synthesis of values*, that is determinant. Noteworthy is his celebration of Don Quixote, a figure in literature that was used by Marx and Engels precisely for the opposite purpose. For Marx, Cervantes' Don Quixote proved that chivalry is not compatible with every mode of production – an observation that illustrated the divergence between their scientism and what they described as 'utopian socialism'. A search of the Castro Speech Database reveals at least two hundred speeches with references to the Man from La Mancha. Fidel goes as far as to liken Cuba's military and humanitarian globalism to the spirit of Don Quixote: 'We have been around the world like pilgrims, like missionaries, like Don Quixote; not only our soldiers have been there, but also our doctors, teachers and engineers.'[31] Based on Fidel's recollections in personal conversation with him, George Galloway traces the identification with Don Quixote back to the influence of the Jesuits and as coexisting in a fusion of virtues:

St. Thomas Aquinas, whom the Jesuits followed, taught the importance of harmony between idealism and reason. The Jesuits added the ideal of the Spanish *caballero*, of Don Quixote, with his qualities of modesty, tenacity and self-sacrifice. The essentially pre-capitalist moral values of Don Quixote are poorly understood in the Anglo-Saxon world, but in Hispanic cultures Don Quixote is a great hero as he has always been to Fidel.[32]

It is noteworthy that the very first book published in Cuba after Castro's victory was Cervantes' great novel. As Cuba's Minister of Culture Abel Prieto relates:

The first book that was published after the Revolution, when the national printing house was established in 1960 under the direction of the famous Cuban writer Alejo Carpentier, was not a Marxist textbook or some speech by Lenin… it was Don Quixote de la Mancha. A book that Fidel loves very much. The most important novel of all time. It was printed on newspaper presses, which had been nationalised by the revolution. An edition of 100,000 copies was printed on newsprint. A crazy number at that time. A very beautiful craziness. Including the engravings by Gustave Dore. There were four volumes in all, costing just 25 cents for the complete set, one peso at the time. They were sold on newspaper stands, alongside the regular newspapers. This is very instructive – Fidel never sees things just on a local level.[33]

For Fidel, every revolutionary must have a little bit of Don Quixote, must be a little mad, but not with the lunacy of extremism that he excoriated in Pol Pot, Bernard Coard (murderer of Maurice Bishop of Grenada) and Osama Bin Laden. Che Guevara's self-identification with Don Quixote is of course the stuff of legend. His farewell letter to his parents refers to himself as hitting the road once again with his shield on his arm and the ribs of Rosinante between his heels.

The *Fidelista* synthesis brings together values and modes of behaviour of quite distinct epochs and experiences, and Castro commends a type of personal conduct as a general morality, ethic and code of virtue. Castro's New Man carries over aspects of the old:

Because it would be very sad if, with the revolution, there wasn't even the recollection of what certain men in bourgeois society did out of bourgeois or feudal chivalry.... And I say this with the certainty that the people understand it and share it, with the certainty that every mother and every father would like their son to be a chivalrous proletarian...[34]

The yoking together of feudal or bourgeois chivalry and proletarian revolutionary spirit, or of the two character types, chivalrous feudal-bourgeois and revolutionary proletarian, to form a new synthesis, proletarian chivalry, and a new model, the 'chivalrous proletarian', is unique. Congruent with Castro's ethics of violence, and a *Fidelista* ideal type, it helps explain the conduct in war of the Cuban armed forces.

Castro crosses a barrier and combines two alternating foci of attention: that of the state and that of heroic behaviour; the latter is almost always an attribute in literature and philosophy, of the individual. Castro thus posits the notion, albeit implicitly rather than explicitly, of a heroic state and society. He combines the stress on the heroic individual, exemplified by Che Guevara, with that of a heroic state, that of Revolutionary Cuba performing altruistic internationalist missions, and a heroic society surviving against tremendous odds on the doorstep of its enemy, history's mightiest power.

In the twentieth century at least two states wore heroic-idealistic garb, episodically: the USA under Kennedy and Israel until and including the 1967 war. However, US foreign policy even in the days of Kennedy (the Bay of Pigs, Vietnam) and the annexationist character of Israel's victories rendered the heroic stance unsustainable. In the role of David, a role for Cuba that was projected by its nationalist hero and martyr Jose Marti ('and mine is the sling of David') Fidel Castro and Cuba seem to have more credible claim and a greater measure of success.

Often, men and women will rebel, violently, arms in hand. The nature of their circumstances and of the enemy will push or pull them into armed resistance, rebellion or revolution. The excitement, intensity and collective spirit of engagement, the romance and solidarities of rebellion, will be another motivator. The questions are: which values will sustain the struggle, which codes of conduct will govern it throughout? In moral terms will the rebels remain superior to the enemy they fight? Will the resort to armed violence, the power to inflict pain and death, to impact drastically perhaps irrevocably on the lives of others, cause moral corruption?

The decision to run the risks involved in armed activism gives the participants in such political practice the sense of belonging to a moral aristocracy, an aristocracy of risk and sacrifice. 'No task is more honorable, noble, or stimulating than the task of being a revolutionary. However it is also the most difficult...'[35] This sense of belonging to a moral aristocracy, a spiritual elite with a way of being that is superior, usually breeds a moral arrogance that is then reinforced by a sense of natural justice commingled with vengeance for the tortures and killings perpetrated by the enemy. The next stage is an absence of restraint in the use of violence, resting on the notion that the inherent justice of the cause and injustice of the enemy sanctifies any kind of violence. Terrorism is the consequence of this moral pathway and process.

Fidel Castro and the Cuban revolutionary ideology are marked by a conscious resistance to this temptation and a deliberate choice to take another path, though manifestly not one of pacifism.

7
The Contemporary Relevance of Castro

This chapter poses the issue of the relevance of Fidel Castro's ideas and practice in today's world – a historical context considerably different from that in which they arose. It contrasts Castro's doctrine of resistance and liberation with contemporary fanaticism and terrorism. It contains an outline of Castro's unique strategic variant of asymmetric warfare. I argue that his ideas and example are relevant and will continue to be, wherever there is oppression and exploitation, because they constitute an ethic of resistance and rebellion, a moral and strategic compass for all those who resist oppression and struggle for liberation. I further argue that Fidel Castro's ideas are relevant not only for rebellion but also for rulership, in that he demonstrates the possibility of effective yet ethical use of violence. The chapter concludes that Castro suggests an answer to an abiding problem of politics, that of power and morality, while presenting a different way of being, a new existential model. The argument is in the spirit of an intervention in the current global ideological setting, and posits a possibility of a transcendence of prevailing polarisations.

FIDELISMO OR FUNDAMENTALISM?

While in strategic terms the global picture is bipolar (between the sole superpower and terrorism of Islamic provenance), it is not necessarily so at a philosophical and ideological level. In this domain the game is not zero-sum, but triangular. Between unipolar hegemonism (with its ideological variants of neo-conservatism/neo liberalism and liberal 'humanitarian' interventionism *à la* Kosovo), and the forms of terrorism that challenge that hegemony, lies a third zone. In this zone are those alienated, albeit unequally, by both the fanaticism of terrorism and the arrogance of neo-conservative 'market fundamentalism'; those who oppose both 9/11 and the Iraq War. The alienated are the offspring of reason and modernity: social democracy, reform communism, residual Marxism, social or communitarian liberalism and the moderate liberal and progressive currents of all religions.

Anti-war US Democrats, Western European social democrats, Eastern and Southern European ex-Communists who are 'reform communists' or 'new social democrats', the African ex-Marxist ex-guerrillas who are 'new 'or 'emergent democrats', the dramatically revived Latin American left originating in the São Paulo and Porto Allegro forums but now wielding governmental power in a majority of South American states, the anti-globalisation and anti-Iraq War global movements, the Non-Aligned Movement and Fidel Castro's Cuba. These are some of the diverse trends and tendencies of a potential broad Third Zone.

The moral critique of the dominant polarisation of the post-Cold War world has been made by Wole Soyinka in his Reith Lectures. Soyinka, playwright, poet, former political prisoner and Nobel Prize winner for literature, indicts both states and liberation movements for their crimes against civilians. His, however, is neither a pacifistic condemnation of violence nor a broad-brush critique of all states and all movements at all times.

Particularly trenchant is his critique of movements claiming to stand for liberation, which, however, make no distinction between the enemy and the innocent, going on to target and victimise even children. Soyinka draws a distinction between such movements, exemplified by the Chechen separatists and the Algerian GIA, and the earlier conduct of the Vietnamese and the ANC in their liberation struggles. He similarly distinguishes between, on the one hand, the US war against al Qaeda and the Taliban in Afghanistan, and the Algerian military crackdown on the Islamic insurgents, both of which he justifies (the former more comfortably and unambiguously than the latter), and on the other, the US invasion of Iraq, which he roundly condemns.

Soyinka therefore makes the ethical and moral critique and demarcates, albeit implicitly and faintly, the contours of a moral third position that recognises the category of innocents and their immunity even while acknowledging the necessity for the deployment of violence by states and resistance movements. Certain norms must be universally recognised and certain zones must be ethically inviolable, not only by states but, as indicated by 9/11, perhaps even more pressingly in the contemporary period by resistance and liberation struggles.[1]

Though he does not say this himself, Soyinka's can be interpreted as a plea for a doctrine of just war that encompasses both states and anti-state movements. This position runs the risk of seeming Utopian and idealistic insofar as it does not point to the possibility of concrete incarnation except in the specific cases of the Vietnamese liberation war, the ANC and the US counter-strike in Afghanistan. He does not recognise any sustained real-world example of the morality he suggests. That Fidel Castro's ideas and practice on violence constitute the most consistent sustained attempt at such a moral-ethical stand in the real world, and is therefore an example and model of conduct – a practicable, sustainable doctrine, realistic and realisable – has been the central contention of the present study.

The anti-imperialism or opposition to unipolar hegemonism that is a major facet of Fidel Castro's political thought is at variance with the crude anti-Americanism and anti-Westernism of the most prominent currents of resistance worldwide. Even in his most intransigently militant phase, Castro drew distinctions not only between the people and government of the United States, but between the United States as a nation and its imperialist structures. He rejected any destructive impulses towards the United States as such.

The imperialist press has attempted to distort some of the ideas expressed in Che's splendid message to the peoples of the world, opining that this message proposes the destruction of the United States. Nothing could be further from the truth. The message clearly expresses the idea that revolutionary strategy aims at the destruction, not of the United States, but at the destruction of the imperialist domination of the United States of America. Let the imperialist not attempt to confuse the people of the United States, the nation of the United States – which is not composed of imperialists only – with the imperialists themselves. And what is perfectly clear in the message of Major Ernesto Guevara is the proposition that revolutionary strategy be directed towards the destruction of imperialist domination.[2]

Castro explains that his Marxism does not permit a chauvinistic attitude towards the US in which the American people would be regarded with hostility. Indeed, that Marxism prescribes a division of the American people into exploiters and exploited, oppressed and oppressors, thereby precluding any animus towards them as a whole. The acknowledged influence upon Castro of Hemingway's writings, his admiration for US leaders such as Lincoln and Franklin Roosevelt, his nuanced attitude even to foes such as John F. Kennedy and Henry Kissinger, his constant interaction with dissident trends in US society, his dialogue with mainstream US institutions ranging from the corporate sector to the cinema, his openness to access by the US media, mark the gulf between Castro's anti-imperialism and crude anti-Americanism, with its bloodiest expression being the attacks of 9/11.[3]

Castro's is in marked contrast to 'cultural nationalist' anti-imperialism, which is anti-Western and anti-modern. The Iranian Revolution of 1979 is the most prominent example of the latter, though the ideology of al Qaeda and other similar organisations are cases in point. This brand of anti-imperialism is not solely Islamic in provenance: most countries of the global South display some variety of it, prior to the Bolshevik Revolution of 1917 and subsequent to the collapse of socialism in 1991. This nationalist anti-imperialism is marked by ethnic majoritarianism and therefore the inability to deal sensitively with internal nationalities and ethno-religious questions.

The anti-imperialism of Lenin was of a different variety, cutting across and indeed going against nationalism, asserting transnational class solidarity and stimulating anti-systemic forces with the overriding purpose of using the moment of crisis to overthrow the system. The Bolshevik stand during World War I right up to the founding of the Communist International in 1919 were the zenith of this type of anti-imperialism. It had no trace of cultural nationalism, and was conscious of its own cultural backwardness. Though after 1920 and the failure of revolutions to sustain themselves in Europe, Lenin did assert that the centre of gravity of world revolution had shifted eastwards, at no time did Leninism base itself on a notion of the cultural superiority of the East over the West. Marxist anti-imperialism was anti-Western only in the politico-strategic sense. It considered itself the inheritor and continuator of that which was best in Western thought and it contested Western imperialism with the tools of Western thought. Far from being anti-modern, it represented an 'alternative modernity', as Fred Halliday designates it.[4] The Russian Revolution after Lenin gave rise to a different brand of anti-imperialism, that of Stalin. It was nationalist insofar as it was statist. Since Russia alone had sustained a revolution, since the revolution was 'made flesh' only in Russia, the defence of the revolution implied the defence of the Soviet state, which was for the most part Russian. However, this statist-nationalist or patriotic anti-imperialism was not cultural, still less religio-cultural.

It must be noted that varieties of anti-imperialism were not limited to Marxism and cultural nativism. The global East and South also saw forms of anti-imperialism that were non-Marxist, which, while being nationalist or patriotic, were not anti-Western, anti-modern or traditionalist. The main examples would be José Marti in Cuba, Sun Yat Sen in China and Nehru in India. These anti-imperialist nationalisms were in a sense Westernising and modernising ideologies, fighting against the backwardness of their own societies, albeit drawing on dissident traditions of the West. Marti's patriotism had a continental sweep and went even further, invoking a humanistic universalism.

Castro echoed the anti-imperialist internationalism of Lenin and the early Comintern in that he projected his revolutionary ideas and cadres across borders. But he also wove in the statist nationalism of Stalin, insofar as the defence of the Cuban Revolution and the revolutionary state was given emphasis. Castro's anti-imperialism based itself on that of José Marti but proceeded, as in most subject areas, to cross-cut existing trends and forge a new synthesis. Castro's anti-imperialism has a moral and cultural dimension, but not in the sense of the Iranian mullahs and other Islamic extremist ideologues who view Western society as decadent and their culture as both self-sufficient and inherently superior.

His anti-imperialism had a strong cultural component, but it was not a blanket condemnation of Western culture as a whole. Castro's moral critique of imperialism is not based on a rejection of Western personal behaviour, but builds bridges with elements and figures within Western culture and society. In fact Castro's outreach and utilisation of progressive and dissident trends in Western culture has given him the kind of supportive constituency in Western societies that a purely rejectionist anti-Westernism of the Islamic sort forfeits.

This brand of anti-imperialism is broad, inclusionary and multi-faceted. From Marti and Simon Bolivar Castro has inherited a continental, Latin American vision, but this he combines with a Tricontinentalism or Third Worldism (which found the most dramatic incarnation in the internationalist missions in Africa). Castro's anti-imperialism was not purely Third Worldist or equidistant; it wove in solidarity with the socialist state system. Most interestingly, it reached deep into Western society, identifying with youth movements and making an indelible impression on the consciousness of successive generations of Western youth. This it was able to do because of its nuanced dialectical critique of the West and identification with certain aspects and trends of Western history and culture.

The moral and cultural dimensions of Castro's anti-imperialism did not take the form of protectionist puritanism, as in the case of many Third World nationalisms. He denounced the West *in moral terms that were universal*: injustice, oppression, poverty, inequality. He also projected the Cuban Revolution and Cuban socialism as morally superior in terms that were not culturally circumscribed but could be subscribed to by all humanity: for example, in the provision of free universal health care and education. (Cuba has more doctors serving abroad than does the World Health Organisation.) In the domain of culture, Cuba's praxis takes the forms of indigenous and contemporary popular music and dance, which do not seek to shut out Western music but can compete with it, while drawing from and contributing to it.

The overall argument about Castro and Cuba is that the Cuban experiment owes its sustainability in the face of unparalleled odds to *the assertion of the moral within the project of alternative modernity*. The figure of Che Guevara shows the imaginative power and continued cultural valency in universal terms of the combination of the values of reason/modernity and morality.

Marx said that the anatomy of man is the key to the anatomy of the ape, meaning that in terms of methodology and epistemology, the study of the highest level of evolution enables us to understand its lower forms. Thus the ideas and practice of Fidel Castro warrant examination so as to derive a 'typology of morals' within the traditions of 'violent politics' (Hobsbawm) or 'politico-military' endeavour. The present study argues that the apprehension of his guiding values is a necessary prelude to the 'revaluation of values' (Nietzsche) within the current upsurge of terrorism, simplistic anti-globalisation (as distinct from anti-neo-liberal globalisation) and vulgar anti-Americanism.

Both the Marxist and Leninist interventions in progressive thought proceeded by way of critique and rupture with the dominant ideas and practices of existing radicalism. Marx and Engels carved out their theoretical space through the critique and rejection of utopianism and anarchism on the left and the nationalism and vulgar egalitarianism of Lassalle on the other flank of the movement ('The Critique of the Gotha Programme'). The Russian Marxist movement under Plekhanov cut its teeth on the critique of populist terrorism (Narodnism). This point of departure was more pronounced with Lenin's intervention. The Leninist space was demarcated as against populist terrorism, on the one hand, and dilution and conformist capitulation (Eduard Bernstein), on the other.

Today's new wave of radicalism has avoided major theoretical and philosophical and political challenges. There has been no intellectual settling of accounts with the collapse of socialism. There has been no critique of and sundering with the contemporary equivalents of vulgar egalitarianism and populist terrorism.

FIDELISMO, MORAL ASYMMETRY AND TERRORISM

Among the ideas of justice, independence and liberation, which are the common stock of emancipationist ideology, is one that is original to Fidel Castro: the moral-ethical gulf between revolutionary armed struggle and terrorism. He rejects terrorism in both its meanings: in the classic, surgical and even heroic sense (of the Narodniks) as the assassination of heinous individuals, and the contemporary targeting of non-combatant civilians in a cause deeply felt to be just. Castro has remarked that he could well have deployed the group that joined him in the Moncada uprising for an assassination attempt on Batista instead, but chose not to do so. This marks him out from even the moral and ethical Russian terrorists that Camus celebrates in *The Rebel* and depicts in his dramatic works.

The discussion and debate on terrorism polarises between two main approaches. One response, deeply wedded to the status quo, condemns terrorism out of hand with no reference to its context and causative factors. This approach makes no attempt to understand the phenomenon. A variant of this approach goes so far as to condemn all forms of anti-establishment violence as terrorism. The other seeks to set terrorism in its context but in doing so tends either to condone it, or exculpate it as the product of deep injustice and the response of the weak against the oppressor. State terrorism is seen as the root cause of and therefore morally worse at all times and places than anti-state terrorism.

Students, both critical and sympathetic, of the phenomenon of terrorism, and of course its practitioners, view it as asymmetric warfare, the war of the weak against the strong. However, the bitter irony involved in terrorism (and war crimes) is that it rests precisely on the notion of symmetry, not asymmetry. While asymmetrical in strengths, the terrorist insists on symmetry in the practice of violence: the enemy abducts, kills family members of militants, bombs civilians; therefore the liberation or resistance fighter has every right to do so, and indeed an obligation. The terrorist form of asymmetric warfare, supposedly resting on a doctrine of moral superiority (the martyr is morally superior to the enemy and the victim) actually rests on the deeper foundation of behavioural, moral and ethical symmetry. This is explicit in the statements of Osama Bin Laden as well as those of suicide bombers the world over.

For how long will fear, massacres, destruction, exile, orphanhood and widowhood be our lot, while security, stability, and joy remain your domain alone? It is high time that equality be established to this effect.... As you kill, so will you be killed, and as you bomb so will you likewise be bombed.[5]

When I asked them if they had any qualms about killing innocent civilians, they would immediately respond, 'The Israelis kill our children and our women. This is war and innocent people get hurt.'.... Another Islamist military leader said 'If our wives and children are not safe from Israeli tanks and rockets, theirs will not be safe from our human bombs.'[6]

Robert A. Pape's path-breaking research on suicide bombers[7] argues that they are not religious fanatics motivated by irrationalism, but are striving to attain a rational goal, namely the eviction of an occupier in the context of asymmetric warfare. Pape concludes that suicide terrorism is the tactic of choice in asymmetric warfare waged in a context marked by the confluence of three factors: a perceived military occupation of land thought to be theirs by national or ethnic community, the occupier being a democratic state, and the existence of a religious difference between the occupier and the occupied.

This argument, while it cuts through much prejudice and propaganda (Pape correctly emphasises that the most number of suicide bombings have been by the non-Islamic, secular Tamil Tigers), begs a vital question. Why is it that in earlier liberation wars, with no less markedly asymmetric a balance of forces, liberation movements eschewed suicide bombings, and more emphatically, suicide terrorism, that is, the targeting of civilians by suicide missions? Vietnam fitted all three criteria of occupation, a democratic occupier and a religious difference, and yet suicide terrorism was conspicuously absent.

Pape's argument could be reinforced by the following modification. Terrorism in general and suicide terrorism in particular is more in evidence when the occupation is not only military, as it was in Vietnam, but involves a civic component, that is, settlers, and is a settler-colonial situation. Even in such a context, though, there are significant exceptions such as the armed liberation struggles in the Portuguese colonies of Africa – Angola, Mozambique and Guinea Bissau – in which national liberation struggles were waged of such an enlightened nature, devoid of terrorism, that they impacted on the Portuguese armed forces, radicalising young officers and catalysing a revolution within the colonial 'mother country', Portugal itself. Part of the explanation for their conduct and the eschewing of terrorism resides in the character of the leaderships concerned – Frelimo's Samora Machel, the MPLA's Agostinho Neto and, above all, the PAIGC's Amilcar Cabral, but note must be made of the sustained Cuban input: the prolonged involvement of Cuban forces as trainers, advisors and fellow fighters in these liberation struggles.[8]

Pape's study does not observe a distinction between the use of suicide bombing as a tactic, and the use of suicide bombing against soft, that is, non-combatant targets. This results in twin errors: either all suicide attacks are seen as terrorism, or none are, and they are all seen as implicitly legitimate resistance to occupation. However, Pape's own case studies and empirical data show a considerable difference between the suicide attacks of the Lebanese resistance movement (chiefly Hezbollah, but also by many leftist and Christian elements), which were almost exclusively directed at military targets (US, French, Israeli, South Lebanese Army), and organisations such as Hamas and the Tamil Tigers, which have directed suicide bombers against civilian targets as well. The former use of suicide attacks could not be classified as terrorist while the latter could.

Today's terrorism, waged as a form of asymmetric warfare, works counterproductively in the vital arena of world opinion: it forfeits a 'moral surplus' in favour of the liberation fighter, bridges the moral gap and establishes an equivalence between the two sides, translates itself into the perception of moral symmetry between the liberation fighters and the oppressive government in the global perception, and at times actually tilts the moral asymmetry between the liberation fighters and the oppressive government in favour of the status quo or regime.

From the American War of Independence to the Vietnam War, leaders of liberation struggles eschewed such tactics. In the case of Vietnam, the choice of tactics paid off handsomely, with significant sympathy for the Vietnamese cause being generated in the West and in the USA in particular. Contemporary suicide terrorism, such as that of Hamas and Islamic Jihad, forfeits such support in the rear of the enemy, as well as in the international arena, precisely because of the targeting of civilians. If the armed Intifada (including suicide bombers) limited itself to attacks on the Israeli armed forces and armed settlers, and the Iraqi resistance eschewed the targeting of either foreign journalists or religious rivals, they would have garnered far greater sympathy. These movements ignore or are unable to answer the question of why historically successful liberation struggles did not target civilians while certain others do. Pape's study too fails to raise the question.

The Castro doctrine of armed struggle, by contrast, is based upon the conscious cultivation of a moral asymmetry between the enemy and the liberation fighter, a moral superiority that is cultivated not by abstinence from violence as in the case of Gandhi, nor by the low-intensity, tactical and largely symbolic use of violence as in the case of Mandela's ANC, but by willed restraint in the conduct, methods and targeting.

There were 3000 soldiers there who had been fighting against us in harsh battles a few days before; but they respected us, they respected us as adversaries who knew how to fight, and never murdered a prisoner, never mistreated a prisoner, who never left an enemy soldier wounded in combat, who cured them, who saved many lives; that made us gain prestige and respect among the enemy.[9]

While it is on the one hand a doctrine of absolute or total war in that it seeks, as did the Jacobins and Napoleon, to mobilise the whole people, it is also a doctrine of limited war in terms of targeting, one that welds together asymmetric and just war; an asymmetric war that is total, fought with weapons of ethics and morality. Castro's asymmetric war maintains an asymmetry of terrain. In it, the guerrilla always seeks to occupy the moral mountain range.

Fidel's contemporary relevance is most clearly evidenced in what was a defining moment in contemporary history: 9/11, the attacks on the Twin Towers and the Pentagon. Castro's response to the 9/11 attacks, expressed in his speeches of 22 and 29 September 2001, constitutes a unique 'third perspective'. It contains an understanding of the deep, causative roots of terrorism and the culpability of the powerful and privileged in its emergence. However, none of these factors stand in the way of a resolute denunciation of terrorism; a denunciation that pre-empts the argument that there are any extenuating circumstances for its adoption and practice. The moral-ethical criterion operates as an autonomous factor, which is absolute and unconditional. Castro's country and its revolution are themselves the victims of US policy that has often taken the form of state-sponsored terrorism. He is therefore acutely aware of the hypocrisy of the US denunciation of terrorism. He warns against a militaristic response to terrorism and argues for deep-going structural changes to eliminate its causes. Castro's is therefore an unambiguous and uncompromising moral denunciation of terrorism, not relative to or qualified by the socio-economic or political causes, of which he is nonetheless aware and goes on to address:

No one can deny that terrorism is today a dangerous and ethically indefensible phenomenon, which should be eradicated regardless of its deep origins, the economic and political factors that brought it to life and those responsible for it.[10]

Terrorist actions in the United States, and anywhere else in the world, inflict terrible damage on the peoples fighting for a cause that they objectively consider to be fair. Terror has always been an instrument of the worst enemies of Mankind, bent on suppressing and crushing the peoples' struggle for freedom. It can never be the instrument of a truly noble and just cause.

All throughout history, almost every action intended to attain national independence, including that of the American people, was carried out with the use of weapons and nobody ever questioned, or would question, that right. But, the deliberate use of weapons to kill innocent people must be definitely condemned and eradicated for it is as unworthy and inhuman as it is repulsive, the same as the historic terrorism perpetrated by the oppressing states.[11]

Despite the protracted and armed enmity of the United States, Castro is utterly unambiguous in his denunciation, and does not attempt to surf the tide of anti-Americanism. Nor does he attempt to ingratiate himself with the sole superpower and dominant opinion in the First World. In the same breath as his denunciation of al Qaeda's attack, he reiterates the right to use arms in the struggle for a just cause such as national independence (and refers to the American War of Independence as an example). Most pertinently he makes a clear link between means and ends, arguing, with all his experience and prestige as a revolutionary and liberation leader, that no truly just cause can wield the weapon of terrorism, implying that any struggle that does so damages itself by sacrificing its moral legitimacy.

CONCLUSION

What, then, of the self-image and ideological motivation of the elderly Fidel Castro? In private conversation with Sir Leycester Coltman, the Westerner who was closest to him after Herbert Matthews, Castro musingly disclosed his credo:

Very few people will remember me. Who remembers the dust, unless he was a saint like the apostle James? ... No glory lasts over two thousand years, except that of Christ, Julius Caesar and Charlemagne, or a few persons from antiquity...

I don't worry about history. I ask myself: What is my duty? What should I do? I am not bothered what people will say about me. What has been said already is enough, some good things and some bad things. In the end people have to acknowledge that we have been steadfast, defended our beliefs, our independence, wanted to do justice, and were rebellious.[12]

Carl Schmitt's critique is that romanticism in politics introduces aesthetic criteria, and in doing so weakens its capacity for decision and demonstrates a propensity for defeat.[13] Castro's synthesis of the traditions of realism, reason and romanticism not merely avoids but demonstrates an aversion to such 'Hamletesque' political behaviour. Castro has shown a vocation for (Schmittian) 'decisionism'. He struggled to win and to defend the gains of victory. He has succeeded in doing so using criteria other than or supplementary to those of realism, of power; and introduced precisely aesthetic criteria and values especially in the notion of the heroic. Common to realism and romanticism is the centrality of the phenomenon of struggle, of great contestation. In the realist tradition this is couched in terms of power, its acquisition and retention. In the romantic tradition, the aesthetic of heroism is defined in terms of struggle and stance. Romanticism often relies on 'irrational criteria', while the Castroist synthesis combines reason's reliance on science and logical argumentation, and above all on the labour of convincing, explanation and persuasion.

Schmitt notoriously asserted that every field of human endeavour is structured by a duality (morality, for example, by good and evil) and identified that which defines the political as the friend/enemy distinction, a distinction he said applied to war as well. He took pains to locate the friend/enemy distinction as belonging exclusively to the realm of the state, and differentiated it from the personal realm. In the personal realm (in keeping with Christian ethics) one could or should forgive one's enemy – one's private foe or rival – but this was impossible in the public domain. Conceptually unsurpassable as this definition is, it is dangerously unsatisfactory in its ascription of the enemy as (the) one whose very alienness makes his existence incompatible with one's own.[14] This sub-definition makes the heart of politics, the friend/enemy distinction, the heart of moral darkness, justifying genocide, ethnic cleansing and terrorism; hence the gas chambers, Hiroshima and 9/11.

Operating on the friend/enemy distinction requires a set of parameters or a regulatory framework, which was understood a millennium before Carl Schmitt, by the great Indian sage Kautilya, also known as Chanakya, the author of the *Arthashasthra,* who said that philosophy teaches, above all, the good and bad use of force.[15] In the twentieth century the thinker who most explicitly combined the friend/enemy distinction with a set of policy parameters was Mao Ze Dong. However, in the post-revolutionary period, Mao virtually threw overboard his own philosophical and policy criteria.[16]

From colonialism to fascism, capitalism has displayed its barbaric side. From the firebombing of Dresden to Hiroshima and Nagasaki, Western liberal democracy has shown a propensity to retaliate massively, riding roughshod over the issue of the proportionality of means and ends. From the taking of families hostage in Lenin's Russia, through the Great Purges under Stalin, socialism has shown itself oblivious to the problem. From the Great Terror after the French Revolution to Year Zero under Pol Pot, the emancipationist project has been blighted by a moral 'dark side'.[17]

In the age of modernity, Fidel Castro and the Cuban Revolution appear the sole, sustained exception. The relevance of Castro's achievement and contribution and his political ideas could be contested on the grounds that they belong to an age that has disappeared, the age of socialism and revolution. However, the work of Nietzsche most strongly demonstrates the philosophical and intellectual validity of such excavation.

Kaufmann and Hollingdale draw attention to Karl Jaspers' assertion that 'Caesar with Christ's soul' is a terse definition of none other than Nietzsche's Overman. According to Jaspers, it is an attempt

to bring together again into a higher unity what Nietzsche has first separated and opposed to each other... Nietzsche imagines ... the synthesis of the ultimate opposition... the very heart of Nietzsche's vision of the Overman. Being capable of both sympathy and hardness... not using claws though having them.[18]

Fidel Castro is offered in this study as composite example of such a synthesis. The relevance of the study is enhanced by the fact that the alternative values are incarnated and practised in two antithetical states of being, as armed rebel and as ruler, thus constituting an all-encompassing ethic and morality.

As Vincent Descombes reprovingly identifies in *The Barometer of Modern Reason*:

... modern philosophy gives birth to a social theory that can only understand politics as defined by the legitimate and illegitimate use of violence and the categories of enemy and friend.[19]

Fidel Castro's doctrine of struggle, while founded upon the friend/ enemy distinction, rejects the notion that violence without ethical restraints against the enemy is legitimate, sets out clear criteria for the good/legitimate and bad/illegitimate use of violence, and constitutes a code as regards the use and abuse of violence. It is vital in that it thereby addresses and attempts to resolve nothing less than the defining issues of politics and modern politico-moral philosophy.

A Personal Postscript

This study was born of a prolonged, intense personal experience and is intended as an intervention in a particular global conjuncture.

It was Franz Fanon's former secretary, Eqbal Ahmed,[1] a member with Abbie Hoffman of the famous Chicago Seven, who used the term 'moral hegemony' to sum up Fidel Castro to me in a conversation in Penang, Malaysia in 1984. I reported the episode at the time in the *Lanka Guardian* (a journal edited by my father Mervyn de Silva, an appreciative obituary of whom appeared alongside that of Eqbal Ahmed in the respected Indian journal *Seminar* in 1999).

Eqbal Ahmed told me that when Che Guevara disappeared from Cuba, and there was much speculation including in fickle radical circles in the West, that he had left owing to a split with Castro or, worse, been disposed of by the latter, Eqbal had posed the question to a Pentagon official during a research visit to the Defence Department. The official had dismissed the rumours. When Eqbal asked him what the evidence was for his derisive dismissal, he had replied, 'well, Fidel says that's not what happened and Fidel doesn't lie'. Referring to this testimonial from the mouth of a sworn enemy of Castro, Eqbal Ahmed exclaimed, 'Now that's moral hegemony!'

I was first taken into custody by Sri Lanka's political police (then known as the Intelligence Services Division) and questioned about armed revolutionary activism in 1976 when I had just left high school and was awaiting university entrance. Years later, I was on the run, having dropped out of a Fulbright scholarship and doctoral studies in New York with Immanuel Wallerstein, James Petras *et al.*, and become a revolutionary activist. I was indicted together with 22 others in the High Courts of Colombo, on 14 counts under the Prevention of Terrorism Act and the Emergency. The charges began with conspiracy to overthrow the state through violence, and included many involving arms, explosives, weapons training and armed actions. I was the first accused in the case. I was never apprehended, and, after three years underground, was amnestied on 2 December 1988 under the Indo-Sri Lanka peace accord of the previous year.

Like Ron Kovacs, who was 'born on the fourth of July', I had been struggling to be born when the *Granma*, carrying Fidel, Che, Raul and others, landed on the shores of Cuba on 2 December 1956. I was born in Sri Lanka near dawn the next day.

Fidel Castro's injunctions, 'the duty of every revolutionary is to make the revolution' and 'Be like Che!', were part of the motivation for my choices. I turned 30 while underground, and some of the strength to survive the rigours of that experience was renewed by reading Fidel's speech on the thirtieth anniversary of the *Granma* landing.

My experience, however, turned out to be harrowingly different. Having been prepared to be tortured or killed by the capitalist state (Che's attitude 'wherever death may surprise us let it be welcome' was a watchword), my generation of Sinhala and Tamil internationalist revolutionaries and radicals, those whose consciousness, solidarities and practice transcended their ethno-national and religious identities, was to suffer most of its deaths at the hands of other 'liberation movements', which soon overran us. These were the JVP (Janatha Vimukthi Peramuna – People's Liberation Front) in the Sinhala areas and the LTTE (Tamil Tigers) in the north and east of Sri Lanka. This was not a uniquely Sri Lankan phenomenon. Pol Pot's Khmer Rouge, the anti-imperialist Islamic revolutionaries who decimated the Iranian Fedayeen-e-Khalq, Bernard Coard's group that murdered Maurice Bishop of Grenada, and Peru's Sendero Luminoso all constituted examples of what I would call 'neo-barbarism' within the anti-systemic space. Preliminary reflections on this new phenomenon went into a series of articles and a book written after I surfaced from underground.[2] My retrospective look at the Cold War from the distinctive perspective of the global South led me to conclude that this phenomenon and the resultant loss of the moral high ground had much to do with the defeat of socialism.

Fidel Castro figured throughout this experience of political, intellectual and personal tumult, and in several ways. He was an exception to this practice and resultant collective historical outcome. He was an antipode to the kind of political behaviour and outlook I experienced with the JVP and LTTE, and observed in Pol Pot-type radical movements. He was an exception to the practice of internecine bloodletting that one could trace in almost all social revolutions, going back to the great French Revolution of 1789.

I understood that my abhorrence of the behaviour of the LTTE, JVP and other such movements rested on a model and criteria derived from the ideas and practice of Fidel Castro and Che Guevara. Fidel and Che formed a model of heroism that not only inspired me but also constituted a standard of right and wrong by which I measured others. Over time I realised (also by rereading and rediscovering Che's explicit acknowledgments) that without Fidel, there would have been no Che, only Ernesto Guevara. Fidel, then, was the fount of these values.

The events of 9/11 crystallised these perceptions. Rejecting terrorism, defined as *the witting targeting of non-combatant civilians*, I emphasise the importance of another way of being a rebel, even an armed rebel and liberation fighter: that of Fidel and Che. I reject terrorism because it runs contrary to my notion of the hero, and because those who struggle against the system must be demonstrably superior in their ethics, morality and behaviour to the enemy. Those who practise terrorism, from the LTTE's Prabhakaran to Osama Bin Laden and Ayman al-Zawahiri, fail this moral test. The practice of terrorism also makes it easier for the dominant elite to demonise and weaken the struggle, while the maintenance of moral superiority actually assists the struggle, as was the case in Vietnam. Imagine the moral strength of the struggle of the Palestinians and the Lebanese resistance, if instead of attacks on Israeli civilians, they were focused exclusively on the army of occupation and armed settler-colonisers!

Having faced quasi-fascist 'national socialist' movements and realised that there was a fate worse than state, so to speak, my experiences as a Minister in the North-East Provincial Council, alongside the Indian peacekeeping forces, and functioning (while Director, Conflict Studies at the Institute of Policy Studies, Colombo) as a political analyst/advisor to the populist President Premadasa, gave me a perspective from the other side: alongside or within the state, albeit during radically reformist interludes. Dealing with the JVP and LTTE as armed enemies, and years later, watching the horrors of military counterterrorism unfold from Iraq through Lebanon to Sri Lanka, it was clear that Castro once again provided a counter-example. During a protracted counter-insurgency in Angola, involving a total of 300,000 troops over twelve years, the Cuban armed forces did not face even an allegation from the USA or South Africa of a single atrocity!

Fidel is both a wellspring of my critique and an example that another way, not pacific but radical and militant, yet ethical, is possible.

An only child, in the aftermath of the personal crisis of the loss of my parents – relatively suddenly and within 18 months of each other – I discovered Nietzsche. His idea of a *typology of morals* seems relevant to me as applied to armed movements and states. There are those who practise the 'right use of violence' and remain on the moral high ground, and those who do not. Fidel Castro is almost a paradigm of one morality and a control experiment to identify others.

The present resistance to globalisation seems to emanate from quarters that are opposed to the values of modernity and reason, and whose consciousness is characterised by parochial and primordial values, which no one outside their cultural and civilisational coordinates can share. Fidel Castro, on the contrary, represents a resistance and rebellion that shares and emanates from the traditions of reason, modernity and universalism.

Mao summed up the essence of Marxism as 'it is right to rebel!' Marxism apart, this is a motivation to be recognised and applauded, but what happens when the rebel becomes a fanatic, as or even more intolerant than the oppressor he strives to overthrow? Does one remain silent because such movements fight against the main enemy, or are such movements also an enemy and (at times and in places) even the main enemy? These are among the implications of the debate between Camus and Sartre, which has been recently rediscovered and which I consider the most relevant philosophical debate of the last half of the last century. Fidel Castro, as I understand him, provides an answer.

I had started out willing to sacrifice my life in support of the underdog, welcoming every armed rebellion against the state and status quo, and had ended up, as my (ex) revolutionary friends were slain by fellow liberationists – a collective Abel slain by a collective Cain – understanding that underdogs can go rabid, and that it is imperative to have your underdog inoculated! I have tried in this study to derive a 'vaccine' from Fidel's ideas and example. It is in that sense an intervention in the ideological conjuncture constituted by unipolar hegemony, neo-liberalism/neo-conservatism and Christian fundamentalism, on the one hand, and fanaticism and terrorism, most prominently but not exclusively of Islamic provenance, on the other.

Is it possible to be tough, hard, a warrior who wins, but also eschews cruelty? Nietzsche upholds as model a synthesis: a Caesar with the soul of Christ, which others have interpreted as 'having claws but not using them'. Fidel Castro seems to me to be the approximation of such a synthesis. Through this study I have tried to distil his distinctive ideas, values and example, which I hope will be an inspiration, helping change consciousness and make the world a better place.

Notes to the Text

PART I, INTRODUCTION

1. Joseph Contreras, 'Latin America: Castro's Comeback', *Newsweek*, 20 March 2006, p. 26.
2. Jorge Castaneda, 'Latin America's Turn to the Left', *Foreign Affairs* (Council on Foreign Relations, New York), May/June 2006.
3. Colin McMahon and Hugh Dellios, 'Region shifts to the left', *Chicago Tribune*, 8 August 2006.
4. *The Routledge Dictionary of Twentieth Century Political Thinkers*, eds Robert Benewick and Philip Green, Routledge, New York, 1991.
5. Leo Strauss, *What is Political Philosophy?*, The Free Press, New York, 1959.
6. Ulises Estrada, *Tania: Undercover with Che Guevara in Bolivia*, Ocean Press, Melbourne, 2005, p. 18.
7. Isaiah Berlin, 'The Originality of Machiavelli', in *Against the Current: Essays in the History of Ideas*, Viking, New York, 1980.
8. *Ethical Writings of Cicero: De Officiis (On Moral Duties); De Senectute (On Old Age); De Amicitia (On Friendship), and Scipio's Dream*, trans. Andrew P. Peabody, Little, Brown, and Co., Boston, 1887.
9. Quentin Skinner, *Machiavelli*, Oxford University Press, Oxford, 1981, pp. 21–73; Mark Hulliung, *Citizen Machiavelli*, Princeton University Press, Princeton, 1983; Martin Fleisher, ed., *Machiavelli and the Nature of Political Thought*, Atheneum, New York, 1972.
10. Strauss, *What is Political Philosophy?* and *Studies in Platonic Political Philosophy*, University of Chicago Press, Chicago, 1983.
11. Friedrich Nietzsche, *The Will to Power*, trans. Walter Kaufmann and R. Hollingdale, Vintage, New York, 1968, Book IV, No. 983, p. 513.
12. Ernesto Che Guevara, 'Cuba: Historical Exception or Vanguard in the Anticolonial Struggle?', 9 April 1961, in *The Che Reader*, Ocean Press, Melbourne, 2005.
13. Carl Schmitt, *Political Theology*, MIT Press, Cambridge, MA, 1985, p. 15.
14. Sheldon B. Liss, *Fidel! Castro's Political and Social Thought*, Latin American Perspectives Series No. 13, Westview Press, Boulder, CO, 1994.
15. Marta Harnecker, *Fidel Castro's Political Strategy from Moncada to Victory*, Pathfinder Press, New York, 1987.
16. Theodore Draper, *Castroism: Theory and Practice*, Praeger, New York, 1965.
17. Loree Wilkerson, *Fidel Castro's Political Programme: From Reformism to Marxism-Leninism*, University of Florida Press, Gainesville, 1965.
18. Donald E. Rice, *The Rhetorical Uses of the Authorizing Figure: Fidel Castro and José Marti*, Praeger, New York, 1992.
19. Che Guevara, 'Cuba: Historical Exception?'

20. Ibid.
21. Regis Debray, *Strategy for Revolution: Essays on Latin America*, Monthly Review Press, New York, 1970; *Revolution in the Revolution?*, Pelican Latin American Library, Penguin Books, Harmondsworth, 1967.
22. Che Guevara, 'Tactics and Strategy of the Latin American Revolution' (1962), *Tricontinental*, Havana, 1970.
23. Frei Betto, *Fidel and Religion: Fidel Castro in Conversation with Frei Betto*, Ocean Press, Melbourne, 1990, pp. 3–5.

CHAPTER 1, 'THE ETHICS OF VIOLENCE'

1. Kautilya, *The Arthashastra*, Penguin, New Delhi, 1992, p. 106.
2. Gail M. Presbey, 'Fanon on the Role of Violence in Liberation: A Comparison with Gandhi and Mandela', in *Fanon: A Critical Reader*, eds Lewis R. Gordon, T. Denean Sharpley-Whiting and Renee T. White, Blackwell, Cambridge, MA, 1996, pp. 283–96.
3. Mandela describes a careful selection process for a method of violence that would take the least lives. Carefully chosen sites for sabotage would cripple the economy and make a point; but lives would not be taken because of special concern for the healing process, since avoiding direct loss of lives 'offered the best hope for future race relations'. Ibid., pp. 289–90.
4. Dietrich Bonhoeffer, *Ethics*, Touchstone Edition, Simon & Schuster Inc., New York, 1995.
5. Mao Ze Dong, 'On the Reissue of the Three Main Rules of Discipline and the Eight Points for Attention – Instruction of the General Headquarters of the Chinese People's Liberation Army (10 October 1947)', in *Selected Military Writings of Mao Zedong*, Foreign Languages Press Edition, Beijing, 1968, pp. 343–4.
6. Mao Ze Dong, *Four Essays on Philosophy*, Foreign Languages Press Edition, Beijing, 1968.
7. Michael Walzer, *Just and Unjust Wars*, Basic Books, New York, 1977; James Turner Johnson, *Just War Tradition and The Restraint of War*, Princeton University Press, Princeton, 1981; Oliver O'Donovan, *The Just War Revisited*, Cambridge University Press, Cambridge, 2003; Daniel S. Zupan, *War, Morality and Autonomy*, Ashgate, Aldershot, 2004; Jean Bethke Elshtain, ed., *Just War Theory*, New York University Press, New York, 1992.
8. James Turner Johnson, *Morality and Contemporary Warfare*, Yale University Press, New Haven and London, 1999.
9. James Turner Johnson, *Just War Tradition and The Restraint of War*, Princeton University Press, Princeton, 1981.
10. Michael Ignatieff, *The Lesser Evil: Political Ethics in an Age of Terror*, Edinburgh University Press, Edinburgh, 2004.
11. 'The Second Declaration of Havana', 4 February 1962, in James Nelson Goodsell, *Fidel Castro's Personal Revolution in Cuba: 1959–1973*, New York, Knopf, 1975, pp. 264–8.

12. Jon P. Gunnemann, *The Moral Meaning of Revolution*, Yale University Press, London, 1979, pp. 4–8.
13. Walzer, *Just and Unjust Wars*, Chapters 11–14, pp. 176–232.
14. Ignatieff, *The Lesser Evil*; Mao, *Selected Military Writings*, pp. 343–4; Mao, *Four Essays on Philosophy*.
15. Antonio Gramsci, 'Some Theoretical and Practical Aspects of Economism', in *The Modern Prince*, http://www.marxists.org/archive/gramsci/editions/s pn/modern_prince/ch07.htm. See also 'Fourteen Major Issues or Dimensions or Meanings of Hegemony', *Hegemony*, in *Gramsci's Original Prison Notebooks*; Carl Cuneo's *Notes on the Concept of Hegemony in Gramsci*, http://socserv2.mcmaster.ca/soc/courses/soc2r3/gramsci/gramheg.htm; and Christine Buci-Glucksmann, *Gramsci and the State*, Lawrence & Wishart, London, 1980.
16. Paul Hollander, 'Clinging to Faith', *The National Interest*, No. 83, Spring 2006, pp. 107–14.
17. See Hannah Arendt, 'Reflections on Violence', *New York Review of Books*, 27 February 1969; also William Ash, *Morals and Politics: The Ethics of Revolution*, Routledge, London, 1977.
18. Marx to Engels, 14 December 1867, in Marx–Engels, *Ireland and the Irish Question*, Progress Publishers, Moscow, 1978, p. 159.
19. Engels to Marx, 19 December 1867. Ibid., p 159.
20. Engels to Marx (in London), *Marx and Engels Correspondence*, International Publishers, 1968, and http://www.marxists.org/archive/marx/works/1870/letters/70_09_04.htm
21. Marx to Kugelmann (London), 12 April 1871, in *Marx–Engels Selected Correspondence*, Progress Publishers, Moscow, 1975, p. 247.
22. V. I. Lenin, *The Proletarian Revolution and the Renegade Kautsky*, Progress Publishers, Moscow, 1974.
23. Saverio Merlino, *Formes et essences du socialisme*, with Preface by G. Sorel, Paris, V. Giard and E. Briere, 1898, p. xlii. cited in Jack Roth, *The Cult of Violence: Sorel and the Sorelians*, University of California Press, Berkeley, Los Angeles and London, 1980, p. 14.
24. Roth, *Cult of Violence*.
25. Nabanita Roy, *Jean Paul Sartre on Literature, Freedom and Commitment*, Allied Publishers, New Delhi, 1997; Ronald E. Santoni, *Sartre on Violence: Curiously Ambivalent*, Pennsylvania State University Press, University Park, PA, 2003; Ronald Aronson, *Camus & Sartre*, University of Chicago Press, Chicago, 2004.
26. Raymond Aron, *History and the Dialectic of Violence*, Basil Blackwell, Oxford, 1975.
27. Cedric Robinson, 'Frantz Fanon', in Robert Benwick and Philip Green, eds, *The Routledge Dictionary of Twentieth Century Political Thinkers*, Routledge, London, 1992, p. 65.
28. Aron, *History and the Dialectic of Violence*.
29. The following works are a sample of the literature in the field: Roth, *Cult of Violence*; Santoni, *Sartre on Violence*; G. Bree, *Camus and Sartre: Crisis and Commitment*, Calder & Boyars, London, 1972; Aron, *History and the Dialectic of Violence*; Gordon et al., eds, *Fanon: A Critical Reader*; Lewis R. Gordon, *Fanon and the Crisis of European Man*, Routledge, New

York, 1995; R. D. Laing and D. G. Cooper, *Reason & Violence*, Tavistock, London, 1971.

30. Albert Camus, *The Just Assassins*, in *Caligula and 3 Other Plays*, trans. Stuart Gilbert, New York, Vintage Books, 1958, pp. 257–60. In his critical study of Sartre, Ronald E. Santoni considers this representative of Camus' position. Santoni, *Sartre on Violence*, p, 112.

31. David Sprintzen, 'Albert Camus', in *The Routledge Dictionary of Twentieth Century Political Thinkers*, pp. 38–40.

CHAPTER 2, 'COMPARATIVE HISTORICAL PERSPECTIVE'

1. Norberto Bobbio, 'The Upturned Utopia', in Robin Blackburn, ed., *After The Fall: The Failure of Communism and the Future of Socialism*, Verso, London, 1991.

2. Richard Fagen, 'Continuities in Cuban Revolutionary Politics', in Philip Brenner et al., eds, *The Cuba Reader*, Grove Press, New York, 1989, pp. 51–62.

3. Fidel Castro, speech given to Cuban residents in Moscow at the Lomonosov University, 7 April 1977, in *Fidel Castro Speeches: Cuba's Internationalist Foreign Policy*, Pathfinder Press, New York, 1981, p. 37. He reiterated this to the Cuban nation on the twenty-fifth anniversary of the Moncada uprising: 'Internationalism and its ideals of solidarity and fraternity among peoples form the beautiful essence of Marxism-Leninism.' Ibid., p. 53.

4. Zbigniew Brzezinski, 'The Cold War and its Aftermath', *Foreign Affairs*, 1992, vol. 71, no. 4, p. 40.

5. Ibid., p. 41.

6. Ibid., p. 46.

7. Elizabeth Gerle, 'From Anti Nuclearism to a Détente in the 1980s', in Mary Kaldor et al., eds, *The New Détente*, Verso, London, 1989, p. 369.

8. 'How close we could look into a bright future if two, three, or many Vietnams, flourish throughout the world with their share of deaths and their immense tragedies, their everyday heroism and their repeated blows against imperialism, impelled to disperse its forces under the sudden attack and the increasing hatred of all peoples of the world!', in John Gerassi, ed., *Venceremos! The Speeches and Writing of Che Guevara*, Clarion, New York, 1968, p. 423.

9. 'Speech at the Plaza de la Revolucion', Havana, 26 July 1972, in *Cuba's International Relations*, ed. H. Michael Erisman, Westview, Boulder, CO, 1985.

10. Fred Halliday, *The Making of the Second Cold War*, Verso, London, 1983, p. 92.

11. Eric Hobsbawm, *Age of Extremes*, Penguin, London, 1994, p. 459.

12.

Country	Event	Date
1. Ethiopia	Deposition Haile Selassie	12 Sept. 1974
2. Cambodia	Khmer Rouge take Phnom Penh	17 April 1975
3. Vietnam	NLF take Saigon	30 April 1975

4. Laos	Pathet Lao take over state	9 May 1975
5. Guinea Bissau	Independence from Portugal	9 Sept. 1974
6. Mozambique	"	25 June 1975
7. Cape Verde	"	5 July 1975
8. Sao Tome	"	12 July 1975
9. Angola	"	11 Nov. 1975
10. Afghanistan	PDPA military coup	27 April 1978
11. Iran	Khomeini's government installed	11 Feb. 1979
12. Grenada	New Jewel Movement to power	13 March 1979
13. Nicaragua	FSLN take Managua	19 July 1979
14. Zimbabwe	Independence from Britain	27 April 1980

Source: Fred Halliday, *The Making of the Second Cold War*, Verso, London, 1983, p. 92.

13. For an introduction to the nature of the pre-revolutionary Portuguese regime, its political economy, the April 1974 Revolution and its dynamics, see Paul M. Sweezy, 'Class Struggles in Portugal', *Monthly Review* (New York), vol. 27, nos 4/5, September/October 1975, and Nicos Poulantzas, *The Crisis of the Dictatorships: Portugal, Spain, Greece*, New Left Books, London, 1976.

14. Zbigniew Brzezinski, *The Grand Failure: The Birth and Death of Communism in the Twentieth Century*, Charles Scribner's Sons, New York, 1989.

15. Sweezy, 'Class Struggles in Portugal', October 1975, p. 2.

16. Michael Harsgor, 'Portugal in Revolution', *The Washington Papers*, no. 32, a SAGE Policy Paper written under the auspices of the Centre for Strategic and International Studies (CSIS), Washington, DC and London, 1976. Dr Harsgor lived in Portugal for extended periods as a Gulbenkian Fellow, is author of *Naissance d'un nouveau Portugal* and Professor of Western European History at Tel Aviv University.

17. Ibid., p. 25.

18. Ibid., pp. 25–6.

19. Ibid., p. 34.

20. Ibid., pp. 36–7.

21. Nicos Poulantzas, *Crisis of Dictatorships*, New Left Books, London, 1976, p. 137.

22. Ibid., p. 141.

23. Harsgor, 'Portugal in Revolution', p. 38.

24. Ibid., p. 47.

25. Poulantzas, *Crisis of Dictatorships*, p. 141.

26. Ibid., p. 83.

27. Sweezy, 'Class Struggles in Portugal', September 1975, p. 3.

28. For an account of the setting of the Ethiopian Revolution, see Addis Hiwat, *Ethiopia: From Autocracy to Revolution*, Occasional Publication No. 1, Review of African Political Economy, London, 1975; Fred Halliday and Maxine Molyneux, *The Ethiopian Revolution*, Verso, London, 1982; Basil Davidson et al., eds, *Behind the War in Eritrea*, Spokesman Books, Nottingham, 1980.

29. Hiwat, *Ethiopia*, Chapter 5, 'The Decline and Fall of The Feudal Autocracy 1960–1974', p. 92; Chapter 6, 'Military Rule and Which Way Ethiopia', p. 110.

30. Meison, consisting of Marxist intellectuals, grew up under the Dergue umbrella and gave qualified support to the regime. It was bloodlessly crushed when it showed signs of autonomy. Its leaders were smuggled to safety courtesy of the Cuban ambassador – which created tension between the Dergue and Cuba. The Waz League, consisting mainly of revolutionary students returning from the US, was eliminated by executions. A protracted civil war ('Red Terror', actually a 'red-on-red' terror) between the Dergue and the trade union/student-based EPRP (an urban underground organisation) was won by the Dergue. The struggle for Eritrean independence was waged by the conservative Eritrean Liberation Front (ELF) and the stronger, Marxist-oriented Eritrean Peoples' Liberation Front (EPLF) founded in 1970 by Tigrina-speaking left-wing Christian intellectuals led by Isaias Aferwerki. EPLF engaged in a classic peoples' war. Gerard Chaliand characterised the EPLF as 'by far the most impressive revolutionary movement produced in Africa in the last two decades'. The war between the Dergue and the EPLF was a full-blown mid-intensity war. Ethiopia's ally Cuba refused to allow its troops to fight against the Eritreans.
31. Until 1985, the TPLF declared itself Marxist-Leninist (pro-Stalin). The Tigreans and the Oromos merged into the EPRDF (led by Meles Zenawi) and defeated the Dergue.
32. Somalia was officially designated a state of 'socialist orientation' by Soviet ideologues, and, in 1976, President Siad Barre addressed the 25th Congress of the CPSU. Soon Somalia and Ethiopia were embroiled in a conventional war. The USSR and the Cubans, having to choose between the two, opted for the larger, 'more authentically revolutionary' Ethiopia, which was carrying out the most thoroughgoing land reform in Black Africa.
33. For deep background on Kampuchea and the rise of the Khmer Rouge, see Craig Etcheson, *The Rise and Demise of Democratic Kampuchea*, Westview, Boulder, CO, 1984; Ben Kiernan, *How Pol Pot Came To Power*, Verso, London, 1985; Michael Vickery, 'Cambodia', in Douglas Allen and NgoVinh Long, eds, *Coming To Terms*, Westview, Boulder, CO, 1991, pp. 89–128.
34. China launched an attack on Vietnam in February 1979.
35. Burchett, a radical journalist who reported on world and Asian events for 40 years, covering the Geneva talks of 1954, and later living in Kampuchea, was co-author of Prince Sihanouk's book, *My War With the CIA*. Burchett has written a compelling insider's account of the subject, *The China–Cambodia–Vietnam Triangle*, Zed Press, London, 1981.
36. Burchett, *China–Cambodia–Vietnam*, p. 4.
37. Malcom Yapp, 'Colossus or Humbug? The Soviet Union and its Southern Neighbours', in *The Soviet Union & the Third World*, eds E. J. Feuchtwanger and Peter Nailor, St Martin's Press, New York, 1981, pp. 137–63; Raja Anwar, *The Tragedy of Afghanistan*, Verso, London, 1989.
38. Raja Anwar, *The Tragedy of Vietnam*, Verso, London, 1988.
39. On the Grenadan Revolution, see Fitzroy Ambursley, 'Grenada – The New Jewel Revolution', in Fitzroy Ambursley and Robin Cohen, eds, *Crisis in*

the Caribbean, Heinemann, London, 1983, pp. 191–222; Maurice Bishop, Selected Speeches 1979–1981, Casa de Las Americas, Havana, 1981.

40. Chris Searle, 'Maurice Bishop on Destabilisation: An Interview', Race & Class (London), vol. 25, no. 3, Winter 1984, pp. 1–15.

41. Fidel Castro, War and Crisis in the Americas, Pathfinder Press, New York, 1985, p. 8.

42. Ibid., p. 7.

43. Fidel Castro, In Defence of Socialism, ed. Mary Alice Waters, Pathfinder Press, New York, 1989, p. 7.

44. Bizhan Jazani, Capitalism & Revolution in Iran, Zed Press, London, 1980; Fred Halliday, Iran: Dictatorship & Development, Penguin, New York, 1979; John D. Stempel, Inside the Iranian Revolution, Indiana University Press, Bloomington, 1981.

45. Val Moghadam and Ali Ashtiani, 'The Left and Revolution in Iran', Race & Class, vol. 33, no.1, July–September 1991, pp. 86–93.

46. Ervand Abrahamian, Iran: Between Two Revolutions, Princeton University Press, Princeton, 1982.

47. Moghadam and Ashtiani, 'The Left and Revolution in Iran', p. 87.

48. Val Moghadam, 'The Left and Revolution in Iran', in Hooshang Amirhahmadi and Manoucher Parvin, eds, Post-Revolutionary Iran, Westview, Boulder, CO, 1988, p. 35.

49. Robert Armstrong and Janet Shenk, El Salvador: The Face of Revolution, South End Press, Boston, 1982; James Chase, Endless Wars, Vintage Books, New York, 1984; James Dunkerley, The Long War, Junction Books, London, 1982; Tommie Sue Montgomery, Revolution in El Salvador: Evolution & Origins, Westview, Boulder, CO, 1982.

50. Fidel Castro, An interview for NBC with Maria Shriver, 24 February 1988, Editoria Politica, La Habana.

51. Benjamin Schwarz, 'American Counterinsurgency Doctrine and El Salvador', RAND Corporation/National Defense Research Institute, Santa Monica, CA, 1992, pp. 2–3, quoted in Jorge Castaneda, Utopia Unarmed: The Latin American Left After the Cold War, Vintage Books, New York, 1994.

52. John Rettie and Richard Gott, 'El Salvador's Leading Guerrilla Commits Suicide', Guardian/Washington Post Weekly, 1 May 1983, p. 9.

53. Ibid.

54. Clifford Krauss, 'Revolution in Central America?', Foreign Affairs, vol. 65, no. 3, 1987, p. 565.

55. Castaneda, Utopia Unarmed, p. 352.

56. James LeMoyne, 'El Salvador's Forgotten War', Foreign Affairs, vol. 68, no. 3, Summer 1989, p. 106.

57. Sheldon B. Liss, Radical Thought in Central America, Westview Press, Boulder, CO, 1991, p. 81.

58. Castaneda, Utopia Unarmed, p. 98.

59. Ibid., p. 101.

60. Ibid., p. 102.

61. Ibid., p. 99.

62. Ibid.

63. LeMoyne, 'El Salvador's Forgotten War', p. 106.

64. ' ... the guerrillas sent their best surviving cadre after early 1981 to Cuba and Vietnam for advanced military training according to several former rebels. They say virtually all top military commanders have had at least some training abroad. Miguel Castellanos, a senior guerrilla commander who deserted in 1985 only to be shot dead as a "traitor" by assassins last February, described his training in Vietnam in 1983. He was in the third group of rebels to go to Vietnam, he told me. His graduation exercise was to stage a mock assault on the former American embassy in what had been Saigon, mastering the Vietcong techniques.... The army captured rebel commander Nidia Diaz in 1985 and found that her personal diary contained plans to send more than 30 rebels to Vietnam and other communist countries such as Bulgaria, East Germany and the Soviet Union for training.... Castro, the Cuban ambassador to Nicaragua and senior Sandinista officials helped plan the rebels' 1981 offensive, according to four former senior Sandinista officials, one of whom says he sat in on the planning. The guerrillas' first major attacks to destroy the country's main bridges and the Salvadoran Air force base were planned and trained for in Cuba. General Rafael del Pino Diaz, the deputy commander of the Cuban air force who defected in 1987, says he personally watched Cuban Special Operations officers training the Salvadoran rebel unit that attacked the air base in 1982 after being re-infiltrated via Nicaragua...'. LeMoyne, ibid.
65. Rettie, 'El Salvador's Leading Guerrilla Commits Suicide'.
66. Castaneda, *Utopia Unarmed*, p. 353.
67. Ibid., p. 131.
68. Ibid., p. 354.
69. Ibid., p. 352.
70. Ibid., p. 354.
71. Liss, *Radical Thought in Central America*, p. 81.
72. Rettie, 'El Salvador's Leading Guerrilla Commits Suicide'.
73. Castaneda, *Utopia Unarmed*, p. 356.
74. Ibid., p. 355.
75. Krauss, 'Revolution in Central America?', p. 572.
76. Edward Boorstein, *Allende's Chile*, International Publishers, New York, 1977; Ian Roxborough et al., *Chile: The State &Revolution*, Macmillan, London, 1977.
77. Personal recollections – DJ.
78. Pamela Constable and Arturo Valenzuela, 'Is Chile Next?', *Foreign Policy*, no. 63, Summer 1986, pp. 58–76.
79. Fidel Castro, *War and Crisis in the Americas*, Pathfinder Press, New York, 1985, p. 221.
80. Pamela Constable and Arturo Valenzuela, 'Letter on Chile', *Foreign Policy*, no. 65, Winter 1986–87, p. 178.
81. Carmelo Furci, *The Chilean Communist Party and the Road to Socialism*, Zed Press, London, 1984.
82. Engels referred to the 'law of negation of negation' as 'an extremely general, and for this reason extremely far-reaching and important, law of development of nature, history and thought; a law which holds good ... in history and in philosophy... The law of negation of the negation which

is unconsciously operative in nature and history and in our heads… was first clearly formulated by Hegel.' *Anti-Duhring*, Foreign Languages Press, Beijing, 1976, pp. 179–82.

83. Interview with Fidel Castro by Tomas Borge for *El Nuevo Diario* (Managua), 3 June 1992.

84. Fidel Castro, speech at the concluding plenary session of the Sixth Congress of the Union of Young Communists (UJC), Havana, 4 April 1992.

85. Fidel Castro, *Cold War: Warnings for a Unipolar World*, Ocean Press, Melbourne, 2003, pp. 20–75.

86. Closing speech to the First Party Congress, 22 December 1975, in *Fidel Castro Speeches: Cuba's Internationalist Foreign Policy 1975–80*, ed. M. Tabor, Pathfinder Press, New York, 1981, p. 76.

CHAPTER 3, 'EVOLUTION OF CASTRO'S ETHICS OF LIBERATION'

1. Fidel Castro, statements made in Quito, *Granma*, 16 August 1988.
2. Fidel Castro, *My Early Years*, Ocean Press, Melbourne, 1998, pp. 69–71.
3. Ibid., p. 57.
4. Ibid., pp. 69–71.
5. Ibid., p. 63.
6. Ibid., pp. 69–71.
7. Thomas M. Leonard, *Fidel Castro: A Biography*, Greenwood Press, London, 2004, p. 8.
8. Castro, *My Early Years*, p. 68.
9. Ibid., p. 69.
10. Ibid., p. 77.
11. Ibid., pp. 69–71.
12. Ibid., p. 71.
13. Fidel Castro, *Cold War: Warnings for a Unipolar World*, Ocean Press, Melbourne, 2003, pp. 3–4.
14. Castro, *My Early Years*, p. 79.
15. Ibid., p. 90.
16. Ibid.
17. Ibid., pp. 84–5.
18. Ibid., p. 87.
19. Ibid., p. 121.
20. Brian Latell, *After Fidel*, Palgrave Macmillan, New York, 2002, p. 108.
21. Ibid., p. 104.
22. Ibid., p. 105.
23. Ibid., p. 108.
24. Castro, *My Early Years*, p. 118.
25. Ibid.
26. Ibid., pp. 125–6. My italics.
27. 'Proclamation on Batista's seizure of Power', 13 March 1952, in Ronaldo Bonachea and Nelson P. Valdes, eds, *Revolutionary Struggle 1947–1958: The Selected Works of Fidel Castro*, MIT Press, Cambridge, MA, 1972, p. 147.
28. Ibid.

29. 'Brief to the Court of Appeals', 24 March 1952. Ibid., p. 152.
30. 'Critical Assessment of the Orthodoxo Party', 16 August 1952. Ibid., pp. 152–3.
31. Ibid., p 153.
32. 'This Movement Will Triumph', 26 July 1953. Ibid., p. 159.
33. 'History Will Absolve Me', Appendix in Marta Harnecker, *Fidel Castro's Political Strategy: From Moncada to Victory*, Pathfinder Press, New York, 1987, pp. 75–152.
34. Ibid.
35. Volker Skierka, *Fidel Castro: A Biography*, Polity Press, Malden, MA, 2004, p. 35.
36. Ibid., p. 62.
37. 'History Will Absolve Me', Harnecker, *Fidel Castro's Political Strategy*, pp. 75–152.
38. Ibid.
39. Ibid.
40. Ibid.
41. Ibid.
42. Ibid.
43. Letter, 11 April 1954, in Mario Mencia, *The Fertile Prison: Fidel Castro in Batista's Jails*, Ocean Press, Melbourne, 1993.
44. '… the thought that these things can take place in Cuba with absolute impunity, in the midst of horrifying indifference on the part of the press. The more you learn about the moral degradation from which the republic is suffering, the harder it is to stomach… Still, when I think about it I come to the conclusion that this national crisis was inevitable and necessary and that the greater the crisis, the greater the hope that we can conceive of a different future.' Letter to Melba and Haydee, 18 June 1954. Ibid., pp. 81–2.
45. 'The regime has issued us a moral challenge declaring that there will be amnesty if the prisoners and exiles retreat from their stance, if there is a tacit or expressed commitment to respect the government.' Ibid.
46. '… we can be deprived of these and all other rights by force, but no one can ever make us agree to regain them by unworthy compromise'. Ibid.
47. Ibid., p. 168.
48. Harnecker, *Fidel Castro's Political Strategy*, pp. 41–2.
49. Mario Mencia, 'The Mexico Charter', *Bohemia*, 24 September 1976, pp. 87–8. In Harnecker, *Fidel Castro's Political Strategy*, p. 47.
50. Haydee Santamaria, *Moncada*, Lyle Stuart Inc, Secaucus, NJ, 1980, pp. 38–9.
51. Lionel Martin, *The Early Fidel*, Lyle Stuart Inc., Secaucus, NJ, 1978, p. 159.
52. 'Chiaviano, you lie!', 29 May 1955. In Bonachea and Valdes, *Revolutionary Struggle*, p. 244.
53. Ibid., p. 249.
54. 'Manifesto No. 1 to the People of Cuba', 8 August 1955. Ibid., p. 263.
55. 'To the description he makes of us as criminals full of hatred, I reply with the words of the prosecution at the Urgency Court of Santiago de

Cuba, published in the section En Cuba, in the same issue of Bohemia where the unfortunate letter appeared (page 63, column 2, paragraph 2). It reads... "Chaviano,, you lie!'" 29 May 1955. Ibid., p 245.

56. Latell, *After Fidel*, p. 19.
57. Ibid., p. 173.
58. *Bohemia*, 25 May 1955. In Harnecker, *Fidel Castro's Political Strategy*, p. 27.
59. *Bohemia*, 1 April 1956. Ibid., p. 14.
60. Martin, *The Early Fidel*, p.160.
61. 'Against Crime and Terror', 11 June 1955. In Bonachea and Valdes, *Revolutionary Struggle*, p. 253.
62. 'Speech at Flagler Theatre', 20 November 1955. Ibid., p. 284.
63. 'Manifesto No. 2 to the People of Cuba', 10 December 1955. Ibid., p. 289.
64. Leycester Coltman, *The Real Fidel Castro*, Yale University Press, New Haven, 2003, p. 109.
65. Ibid.
66. Ibid., p. 121.
67. 'Report on the Offensive: Part 2', 19 August 1958. In Bonachea and Valdes, *Revolutionary Struggle*, pp. 408–15.
68. Skierka, *Fidel Castro: A Biography*, p. 54.
69. Ibid., p. 53.
70. Letter to the Cuban Liberation Junta, 14 December 1957. In Bonachea and Valdes, *Revolutionary Struggle*, p. 358.
71. Enrique Meneses, *Fidel Castro*, Faber & Faber, London, 1966, p. 55.
72. Dicky Chapelle, *How Castro Won*, in *The Guerrilla – and How to Fight Him*: *Selections from the* Marine Corps Gazette, ed. T. N. Greene, New York, 1965, p. 223, quoted in Walzer, *Just and Unjust Wars*.
73. 'Letter to Major Jose Quevedo', 9 June 1958. In Bonachea and Valdes, *Revolutionary Struggle*, p. 380.
74. 'Report on the Offensive: Part 2', 19 August 1958. Ibid., pp. 408–15.
75. 'Thus on July 24, 253 prisoners were returned at Las Vegas. The liberation documents were signed by John P. Jequier and J. Schoenhozer, delegates of the International Red Cross Committee who came from Geneva, Switzerland. On the tenth and thirteenth of August, 169 prisoners were returned at Sao Grande. The liberation document was signed by Dr. Alberto C. Llanet, lieutenant colonel of the Cuban Red Cross. There could be no exchange of prisoners because throughout the offensive the dictatorship did not take one rebel prisoner. We did not demand any conditions whatsoever, as otherwise our liberation of the prisoners would cease to have the moral and political meaning which that act entails. We only accepted the medicine which the International Red Cross sent when we returned the second group of prisoners because we interpreted it as a generous and spontaneous gesture of that institution, partly compensating for the medicine we invested in curing enemy wounded...' 'Report on the Offensive: Part 2', 19 August 1958. Ibid.
76. Orders to the Rebel Army, 13 November 1958. Ibid., p. 437.
77. Julia Sweig, *Inside the Cuban Revolution: Fidel Castro and the Urban Underground*, Harvard University Press, Cambridge, MA and London, 2002.

78. Speech in New York, 15 August 1955. In Bonachea and Valdes, *Revolutionary Struggle*, p. 283.
79. 'To the Rebels of Las Villas', 2 February 1958. Ibid., p. 368.
80. '… The battle for Cuba's future "was a power struggle", the now deceased Commandante Manuel Pineiro acknowledged to me, as much within the opposition as against the Batista dictatorship itself.' Sweig, *Inside the Cuban Revolution*, Introduction, pp. 9–10.
81. John Dorschner and Roberto Fabricio, *The Winds of December*, Coward, McCann & Geoghegan, New York, 1979.
82. Coltman, *The Real Fidel Castro*, p. 144.
83. Wilfred Burchett, *Memoirs of a Rebel Journalist: The Autobiography of Wilfred Burchett*, eds George Burchett and Nick Shimmin, UNSW Press, Sydney, 2006.

CHAPTER 4, 'DEFENDING THE REVOLUTIONARY REGIME'

1. Quoted by Peter G. Bourne, *Castro: A Biography of Fidel Castro*, New York, 1986. In Volker Skierka, *Fidel Castro: A Biography*, Polity Press, Malden, MA, 2004, p. 70.
2. 'The media were overflowing with reports about the victims of the former regime. Unimaginable instruments and practices of torture were described, together with tragedies of horrifying dimensions. Mothers and wives of the killed and missing marched through the streets demanding vengeance.' Skierka, *Fidel Castro: A Biography*.
3. Ibid.
4. Thomas G. Paterson, *Contesting Castro: The United States and the Triumph of the Cuban Revolution*, Oxford, 1994. Quoted in Skierka, *Fidel Castro: A Biography*, p. 65.
5. Phil W. Bonsal, *Cuba, Castro and the United States*, University of Pittsburgh Press, Pittsburgh, 1971, p. 36.
6. Skierka, *Fidel Castro: A Biography*, p. 86.
7. Tad Szulc: *Fidel: A Critical Portrait*, William Morrow, New York, 1986, p. 483.
8. Samuel Farber, *The Origins of the Cuban Revolution Reconsidered*, University of North Carolina Press, Chapel Hill, 2006, pp. 96–7.
9. *Fidel Castro Speaks to the Children*, Fair Play for Cuba Committee, New York, 1959, p. 21.
10. Szulc, *Fidel*, p. 51.
11. Coltman, *The Real Fidel Castro*, p. 185.
12. Ibid.
13. Szulc, *Fidel*, pp. 554–7.
14. Ibid., p. 556.
15. John Kane, *The Politics of Moral Capital*, Cambridge University Press, Cambridge, 2001.
16. Latell, *After Fidel*, p. 109.
17. Victor Dreke, *From the Escambray to the Congo*, Pathfinder Press, New York, 2002.
18. Ibid., pp. 111–14.

19. Ulises Estrada, *Tania: Undercover with Che Guevara in Bolivia*, Ocean Press, Melbourne, 2005, pp. 37, 41.
20. Dreke, *From the Escambray to the Congo*, p. 137.
21. Ibid.
22. Ibid., p. 28.
23. 'Relative to Cuba's population, the overseas armies represented a larger deployment than that of the United States at the peak of the Vietnam war. Cuba's sizeable military deployment in Angola endured for the same length as the US wartime commitment in Vietnam.' Jorge Dominguez, 'Cuba since 1959', chapter in *The Cambridge History of Latin America*, vol. VII, ed. Leslie Bethell, Cambridge University Press, Cambridge, 1990, p. 506.
24. Author's interview with Roelf Meyer, former South African Minister of Defence and De Klerk's chief negotiator with the ANC, conducted in Colombo, Sri Lanka, 2004. Meyer said that the only allegations of bad conduct against the Cuban forces in Angola that he recalls 'were to do with the game reserves, and that did not involve any human beings'.
25. *The Australian*, 29 May 2006.
26. Dominguez, 'Cuba since 1959', p. 464.
27. Gabriel Garcia Marquez, 'Operation Carlota', *New Left Review* (London), no. 101–102, February–April 1977.
28. *Che Guevara Reader: Writings on Guerrilla Strategy, Politics and Revolution*, ed. David Deutschmann, Ocean Press, Melbourne, 2003.
29. Bibliography of Che's writings, in Jon Lee Anderson, *Che Guevara: A Revolutionary Life*, Grove/Atlantic, New York, 1997.
30. Preface by Camilo Guevara, *The Bolivian Diary*, Ocean Press, Melbourne, 2006, p. 7.
31. H. Michael Erisman, *Cuba's Foreign Relations in a Post Soviet World*, University Press of Florida, Gainesville, 2000, p. 81.
32. Ibid., p. 223.
33. Dominguez, 'Cuba since 1959', pp. 507–8.
34. Fidel Castro, CNN TV interview, 13 September 1998; Laurence Chang and Peter Kornblugh, *The Cuban Missile Crisis 1962: A National Security Archive Documents Reader*, National Security Archive, Washington, DC, 1992, p. 346. In Skierka, *Fidel Castro: A Biography*.
35. Fidel Castro, *Cold War: Warnings for a Unipolar World,* Ocean Press, Melbourne, 2003, p. 19.
36. Castro's secret speech of January 1968. In James G. Blight and Philip Brenner, *Sad and Luminous Days: Cuba's Struggle with the Superpowers after the Missile Crisis*, Rowman and Littlefield Publishers Inc., Oxford, 2002, p. 21.
37. Skierka, *Fidel Castro: A Biography*, p. 130; Chang and Kornblugh, *The Cuban Missile Crisis 1962*, p. 350.
38. Skierka, *Fidel Castro: A Biography*, p. 131, quoting Mark J. White, *Missiles in Cuba*, Ivan R. Dee Publishers, Chicago, 1997, p. 49.
39. Castro, *Cold War: Warnings for a Unipolar World*, p. 28.
40. Ibid., p. 25.
41. Ibid.
42. Ibid., p. 40.

43. Coltman, *The Real Fidel Castro*, p. 218.
44. Ibid., pp. 242–3.
45. Skierka, *Fidel Castro: A Biography*, p. 209, quoting Carlos Moore, *Castro, the Blacks and Africa*, University of California Press, Los Angeles, 1988, p. 328.
46. Piero Gleijeses, *Conflicting Missions: Havana, Washington and Africa*, University of North Carolina Press, Chapel Hill, 2003.
47. Ibid., p. 210, quoting Balfour, *Castro*, p. 135.
48. Nelson Mandela and Fidel Castro, *How Far We Slaves Have Come!*, Pathfinder Press, New York, 1991, pp. 9–10.
49. 'Fidel Castro personally kept a tight grip on operations. For nearly a year starting November 1987, he devoted 80% of his time by his own account, to the war in Angola, taking an interest in the smallest tactical deployments, and even in the rations and hours of sleep allowed to his troops. He saw Cuito Cuanavale as his Stalingrad, the rock on which the military machine of the South Africans would be broken, paving the way for the fall of the apartheid regime... In January 1988 Ochoa was summoned back to Havana for face to face consultations with the Castro brothers on the defence of Cuito Cuanavale. When Ochoa returned to Luanda he continued to receive a flow of detailed written instructions from Castro. In February 1988, 35,000 UNITA and 9,000 South African troops, supported by tanks, artillery and aircraft, launched their expected attack on Cuito Cuanavale.... Finally they were forced to retreat. Left to him, Castro would have held out for total victory. But he could not do so without Soviet support.' Coltman, *The Real Fidel Castro*, pp. 257–8.
50. Fidel Castro, *Speeches at Three Congresses*, Editora Politica, La Habana, 1982, pp. 101–5.
51. Coltman, *The Real Fidel Castro*, p. 275.
52. Ibid., p. 320.

PART III, INTRODUCTION

1. Isaac Deutscher, 'Violence and Non-Violence', in *Marxism, Wars & Revolutions*, Verso, London, 1984, p. 262.
2. Christine Buci-Glucksmann, *Gramsci and the State*, Lawrence &Wishart, London, 1980.

CHAPTER 5, 'THE MORAL HIGH GROUND'

1. Jean-Paul Sartre, 'Merleau-Ponty', in *Situations*, Braziller, New York, 1965.
2. Raymond Aron, *History and the Dialectics of Violence*, Harper & Row, New York, 1975, p. 91.
3. Donald E. Rice, *The Rhetorical Uses of the Authorizing Figure: Fidel Castro and Jose Marti*, Praeger, New York, 1992, p. 102.
4. Lionel Martin, *The Early Fidel*, Lyle Stuart, Secaucus, NJ, 1978.
5. Speech commemorating the *Granma* landing, 2 December 1961, in Jack Barnes, *Selected Speeches of Fidel Castro*, Pathfinder Press, New York,

pp. 11–40; 'Fidel Castro in 1968 explained to me that he had become a Marxist from the very time that he read the Communist Manifesto in his student days, and a Leninist from the period when he read Lenin while in prison on the Isle of Pines in 1954.' Saul Landau, 'Cuba and Its Critics', *Monthly Review*, May 1987.

6. Fidel Castro, *To Pay Tribute to the Empire or to Pay Tribute to the Homeland*, Editora Politica, La Habana, 1985, p. 31.

7. Ignacio Ramonet's compilation of his conversations with Fidel Castro over two and a half years, referred to in the English-language media as 'Hundred Hours with Fidel'. Published in Spain as *Fidel Castro: biographia a dos voces* and in Cuba as *Cien Horas con Fidel*, Havana, April 2006. The quotation is from George Galloway, *Fidel Castro Handbook*, MQ Publications, London, 2006, p. 67.

8. Latell, *After Fidel*.

9. Ibid., p. 125.

10. Ibid., p. 149.

11. Ulises Estrada, *Tania: Undercover with Che Guevara in Bolivia*, Ocean Press, Melbourne, 2005, p. 15.

12. Castro Speech Database, http://www.lanic.utexas.edu/la/cb/cuba/castro.html

13. Fidel Castro, 'A Revolution Can be Born Only From Culture and Ideas', in *On Imperialist Globalization*, Zed Books, London, 1999, pp. 57–8.

14. V. I. Lenin/Slavoj Zizek, *Revolution at the Gates, Zizek on Lenin: The 1917 Writings*, Verso, London, 2004.

15. Castro, in Harnecker. *Fidel Castro's Political Strategy*, p. 40.

16. Giuseppe Fiori, *Antonio Gramsci – Life of a Revolutionary*, NLB, London, 1970.

17. Chapter 3, subheading: The Absence of Internecine Violence.

18. Buci-Glucksmann, *Gramsci and the State*.

19. Latell, *After Fidel*, p. 118.

20. Ben Corbett, *This is Cuba: An Outlaw Culture Survives*, Westview Press, Cambridge, MA, 2004, pp. 267–8.

21. Coltman, *The Real Fidel Castro*, p. 231.

22. Borge and Castro, *Face to Face with Fidel Castro: A Conversation with Tomas Borge*, Ocean Press, Melbourne, 1993, pp. 74–5.

23. Fidel Castro, NBC interview, 24 February 1988, Editorial Political, La Habana, 1988, p. 59.

24. 'No serious organization has ever accused Cuba... of carrying out "disappearances", engaging in extrajudicial executions, or even performing physical torture on detainees. The same cannot be said of the United States in its five-year-old "war on terror". Of these three types of crimes, not a single case exists in Cuba.' Ignacio Ramonet, 'Castro's Enviable Record', in 'Was Fidel Good for Cuba?', *Foreign Policy*, vol. 86, no. 1, January-February 2007.

25. Wayne S. Smith, *Closest of Enemies: A Personal and Diplomatic Account of United States and Cuban Relations Since 1957*, W. W. Norton & Co., New York, 1988, Chapter 8; Barry Skar, 'The Cuban Exodus of 1980: The Context', in Brenner, Rich et al., eds, *The Cuba Reader*.

26. Alma Guillermoprieto, *Looking For History*, Random House, New York, 2001, p. 134.
27. Coltman, *The Real Fidel Castro*, p. 298.
28. Quoted in ibid., p. 299.
29. Borge and Castro, *Face to Face with Fidel Castro*, p. 13.
30. Skierka, *Fidel Castro: A Biography*, p. 149.
31. Borge and Castro, *Face to Face with Fidel Castro*, p. 83.
32. Speech at Closing Session of Economy 98 International Event, 3 July 1998.
33. Fidel Castro, *Che: A Memoir*, Ocean Press, Melbourne, 1994, p. 33.
34. Fidel Castro, *Cuba at the Crossroads*, Ocean Press, Melbourne, 1996, pp. 147–8.
35. Fidel Castro, 'War and Crisis in the Americas', in *Speeches 1984–85*, Pathfinder Press, New York, 1985, p. 205.
36. 'Other nations of the world summon my modest efforts of assistance. I can do that which is denied you due to your responsibility as the head of Cuba, and the time has come for us to part... I carry to new battlefronts the faith that you taught me, the revolutionary spirit of my people, the feeling of fulfilling the most sacred of duties: to fight against imperialism wherever it may be. This is a source of strength, and more than heals the deepest of wounds.' Che Guevara, http://www.marxists.org/archive/guevara/1965/04/01.htm
37. http://www.marxists.org/archive/guevara/1967/04/16.htm
38. 'There was also the consideration of whether there was any benefit in maintaining doubts about the news. Regardless of the circumstances, however – even if we felt it beneficial in any way to maintain doubts about it – such a consideration would not have kept us from telling the truth. As a matter of fact, we do not believe such a course of action would be in any way beneficial. ... Even if keeping it in doubt could have been beneficial in any way, the revolution has never used lies of any kind as its weapons. We could not do so under any circumstances. Not only do revolutionaries abroad place their trust in our telling the truth, but so do our own people. They have always been sure they have never been lied to...' Castro, *Che: A Memoir*, p. 39.
39. Frei Betto, *Fidel & Religion*, Ocean Press, Melbourne, 1990, p. 265.
40. Memorial rally, 18 October 1967, in Castro, *Che: A memoir*, pp. 76–8.
41. Introduction to the 1968 edition of *Bolivian Diary*. In ibid., p. 95.
42. Speech in Chile, 1971. In ibid., p.109.
43. Ibid., pp. 64–5.
44. Speech in Santa Clara, 17 October 1997.
45. Speech, 26 July 1989, Editora Politica, La Habana.
46. Borge and Castro, *Face to Face with Fidel Castro*, pp. 33–47.
47. Castro, *The Cold War*, pp. 65–6.
48. *Fidel Castro Speeches: Cuba's Internationalist Foreign Policy 1975–80*, Pathfinder Press, New York, 1981, p. 31.
49. 14 September 1978, in ibid, p. 134.
50. Ibid., p. 303.
51. Fernando Claudin, *The Communist Movement: From Comintern to Cominform*, Parts 1 and 2, Monthly Review Press, New York, 1976.

52. Gianni Mina, *An Encounter with Fidel*, Ocean Press, Melbourne, 1991, p. 85.

53. Robert M. Levine, *Secret Missions to Cuba*, Palgrave Macmillan, New York, 2001, p. 213.

54. Latell, *After Fidel*, p. 169.

55. Ibid., p. 109.

56. Ibid., p. 152.

57. Mandela and Castro, *How Far We Slaves Have Come!*, pp. 32–3, 54.

58. Latell, *After Fidel*, pp. 34–6.

59. Ibid., p. 194.

60. Ibid., pp. 44–5.

61. 'Fidel's public health care system was recommended as a "model for the world" by the World Health Organisation in 1989 and … in literacy Cuba leads not only Latin America but the United States as well.' Stephanie Elizondo Griest, *Around the Bloc*, Villard, New York, 2004, p. 335.

62. AfroCubaWeb, http://www2.ceniai.inf.cu/gobierno/discursos/2000/ing/f080900i.html

63. *Fidel Castro Speeches*, p. 46.

64. Fidel Castro, *Talks with US and French Journalists*, July–August 1983, Editorial Politica, La Habana, p. 57.

65. Statement issued on 10 May 2002 by Fidel Castro in response to allegations by the US government that Cuba was developing biological weapons. http://www.greenleft.org.au/back/2002/493/493p17.htm

66. Fidel Castro, *To Pay Tribute to the Empire or to Pay Tribute to the Homeland*, Editora Politica, La Habana, 1985, pp. 33–4.

67. Fidel Castro, *Apply Theory to the Particular Conditions of Each Country*, Republic of Cuba, Ministry of Foreign Relations, Department of Information, p. 22.

68. Fidel Castro, *This Must Be an Economic War of All the People*, speech, 28 December 1984, Editora Politica, La Habana, 1985, p. 62.

69. *Socialism: The Science of Example*, 26 July 1989, Editora Politica, La Habana, p. 27.

70. Juan Antonio Blanco, 'Cuba: Crisis, Ethics and Viability', interview by Medea Benjamin, in Susan Jonas and Edward J. McCaughan, *Latin America Faces the Twenty-first Century*, Westview Press, Boulder, CO, 1994.

71. Katherine Hite, *When The Romance Ended: Leaders of the Chilean Left 1968–1998*, Columbia University Press, New York, 2000, pp. 36, 73.

72. Speech on the 45th Anniversary of the Landing of the *Granma* Expedition and the Birth of the Cuban Revolutionary Armed Forces, 2 December 2001.

73. Economy 98 speech, 3 July 1998.

74. Castro, *Talks with US and French Journalists*, pp. 34–5.

75. Martin Kenner and James Petras, eds, *Fidel Castro Speaks*, Grove Press, New York, 1969, p. 159.

76. Fidel Castro, Speech on the 30th Anniversary of the CDRs, 28 September 1990. In Gianni Mina, *An Encounter with Fidel*, Ocean Press, Melbourne, 1991, p. 263.

77. Armando Hart Davalos, 'Reflections on the Lessons of Che', Centro de Estudios sobre America, ed., *The Cuban Revolution into the 1990s: Cuban Perspectives*, Westview Press, Boulder, CO, 1992, pp. 81–4.

78. Borge and Castro, *Face to Face with Fidel Castro*, p. 178.
79. Castro, Interview given to Maria Shriver, NBC, 24 February 1988, Editora Politica, La Habana , pp. 33–4.
80. Castro, *Che: A Memoir*, p. 92.
81. 'Communist Solidarity to Communist Solitary'. Susan Eckstein in *The Cuba Reader*, eds Chomsky, Carr and Smorkaloff, Duke University Press, Durham, NC and London, 2003, p. 610.
82. 'Periodo Especial and Future of Revolution'. In ibid., p. 596.
83. Castro, *Socialism: The Science of Example*, p. 23.
84. *Talks with US and French Journalists*, p. 55.
85. 'Cuban medical aid affects millions of Third World people annually through direct provision of medical care, and thousands annually through medical education and training programmes both in Cuba and abroad... medical aid may be a more effective foreign policy instrument than other, more traditional ones. ... The large number of international health workers sent by Cuba compared with those sent by the United States not only signifies Cuba's emphasis on civilian aid as a foreign policy tool but also makes Cuba appear to provide more humanitarian aid than the United States.' Julie Feinsilver, *Healing the Masses: Cuban Health Politics at Home and Abroad*, Berkeley: University of California Press, 1993, pp.157–8, in *The Cuba Reader*, pp. 590–4. '... Since 1977 Cuba's overseas sports programme has been greatly expanded... In 1990, there were four hundred foreign students from thirty-three countries on scholarships. Also in that year there were a thousand technicians working overseas, and thirty-nine countries received technical aid. Hence, despite US pressures to reduce Cuba's international influence in the 1980s, Cuba was assisting numerous countries in sports as well as in health and education.' Paula Pettavino and Geralyn Pye, in *The Cuba Reader*, p. 479.
86. Borge, Castro, *Face to Face with Fidel Castro*, pp. 176–7.
87. Ibid.
88. Latell, *After Fidel*, p. 146.
89. Kevin Phillips, *The Cousins' Wars: Religion, Politics, and the Triumph of Anglo-America*, Basic Books, New York, 1999.

CHAPTER 6, 'THE ACHIEVEMENT OF SYTHESIS'

1. Norman Jacobson, *Pride & Solace: The Functions and Limits of Political Theory*, Methuen, New York, 1978.
2. Ronald Aronson, *Camus & Sartre*, University of Chicago Press, Chicago, 2004.
3. Albert Camus, 'Moderation and Excess', 'Thoughts at the Meridian', Chapter 5, *The Rebel*. In Albert Camus, *Selected Political Writings*, ed. Jonathan H. King, Methuen & Co., London, 1981, pp. 17–18.
4. Jean-Paul Sartre, 'Albert Camus', in *Situations* IV, Paris, 1964.
5. Ibid., p. 24.
6. John Dorschner and Roberto Fabricio, *The Winds of December*, Coward, McCann & Geoghegan, New York, 1979, p. 31. Italics in the original.

7. Katherine Hoyt, *The Many Faces of Sandinista Democracy*, Athens, Ohio University Press, 1997.

8. Thomas M. Leonard, *Fidel Castro: A Biography*, Greenwood Press, London, 2004, p. 77.

9. Fidel Castro, *Cold War: Warnings for a Unipolar World*, Ocean Press, Melbourne, 2003, p. 75.

10. Fidel Castro, *To Pay Tribute to the Empire or Pay Tribute to the Homeland*, Editora Politica, La Habana, 1985, p. 24.

11. Carlos Montaner, 'Cubans are Poor and Enslaved', in 'Was Fidel Good For Cuba?, A Debate Between Carlos Montaner and Ignacio Ramonet', *Foreign Policy*, vol. 86, no. 1, January–February 2007, pp. 59–64.

12. Ronald Aronson, *After Marxism*, The Guilford Press, New York, 1995, pp. 231–55.

13. The subheadings of the chapter summarise his argument: Morality in the Centre?, Marxism's Ambivalence Towards Morality, The Contemporary Crisis of Morality, Moral Bases for Radical Change: Immanent Critique, Moral Bases for Radical Change: Judging Societies by Their Possibilities, Moral Bases for Radical Change: The History of Freedom, Universal Rights, Difference, Connecting Difference and Universality, An Adequate Moral Basis?

14. A similar view has been expressed by Alexandre Trudeau, who as the son of Pierre Trudeau has known Castro almost all his life. 'For Fidel, revolution is really a work of reason. In his view, revolution, when rigorously adopted, cannot fail to lead humanity towards ever greater justice, towards an ever more perfect social order. Reason, revolution and virtue are becoming more and more distant and abstract concepts.' 'The Last Days of the Patriarch', *Toronto Star*, Sunday, 13 August 2006.

15. Liss, *Fidel! Castro's Political and Social Thought*, p. 38.

16. *Fidel Castro Speeches*, pp. 320–1.

17. Skierka, *Fidel Castro: A Biography*, p. 336, citing Frei Betto, *Fidel & Religion: Conversations with Frei Betto*, Melbourne, Ocean Press, 1990, pp. 271ff.

18. Castro, *War and Crisis in the Americas*, p. 104.

19. Ibid., p. 142. My emphasis.

20. Coltman, *The Real Fidel Castro*, p. 160.

21. Castro, *War and Crisis in the Americas*, p. 112.

22. Szulc, *Fidel: A Critical Portrait*, pp. 470–1.

23. Castro, in Frei Betto, *Fidel & Religion*, p. 227.

24. Gabriel Garcia Marquez, Introduction, 'Fidel – The Craft of the Word', in Gianni Mina, *An Encounter with Fidel*, Melbourne, Ocean Press, 1991.

25. Ibid., p. 21.

26. Castro, *Cold War*, pp. 66–74.

27. Ibid., pp. 67–8.

28. Fidel Castro, closing speech at *Meeting on the Status of Latin American and Caribbean Women*, 7 July 1985, undated pamphlet, p. 25.

29. Castro, *To Pay Tribute to the Empire*, p. 11.

30. Speech delivered at Economy 98 International Event, 3 July 1998.

31. Castro, *Cold War*, pp. 73–4.

32. George Galloway, *Fidel Castro Handbook*, MQ Publications, London, 2006, p. 29.
33. Ibid., p. 222.
34. *Women and the Cuban Revolution*, ed. Elizabeth Stone, Pathfinder Press, New York, 1981, p. 69.
35. Fidel Castro, *War and Crisis in the Americas*, Pathfinder Press, New York, 1985, p. 106.

CHAPTER 7, 'THE CONTEMPORARY RELEVANCE OF CASTRO'

1. Wole Soyinka, *Climate of Fear*, Random House, New York, 2005.
2. Martin Kenner and James Petras, eds, *Fidel Castro Speaks*, Grove Press, New York, 1969, p. 156.
3. Frank Mankiewicz and Kirby Jones, *With Fidel: A Portrait of Castro and Cuba*, Playboy Press, Chicago, 1975, p. 156.
4. Fred Halliday, *Revolution and World Politics: The Rise and Fall of the Sixth Great Power*, Palgrave Macmillan, Basingstoke, 1999.
5. David R. Sands and Bill Gertz, 'US Says Tape Shows Bin Laden Alive', *Washington Times*, 13 November 2002.
6. Nasra Hassan, 'Letter from Gaza: An Arsenal of Believers', *The New Yorker*, 19 November 2001, pp. 36–41.
7. Robert Pape, *Dying To Win: The Strategic Logic of Suicide Terrorism*, Random House, New York, 2005.
8. Piero Gleijeses, *Conflicting Missions: Havana, Washington, and Africa*, University of North Carolina Press, Chapel Hill, 2003.
9. Castro, *To Pay Tribute to the Empire*, p. 23.
10. Speech given by Fidel Castro, 22 September 2001, Havana, in http://www.raceandhistory.com/
11. Castro, speech at Ciego de Avila, 29 September 2001, http://archives.lists.indymedia.org/imc-dc-print/2001-September/001523.html
12. Coltman, *The Real Fidel Castro*, pp. 321–2.
13. Carl Schmitt, *Political Romanticism*, MIT Press, Cambridge, MA, 1986.
14. Carl Schmitt, *The Concept of the Political*, University of Chicago Press, Chicago, 1995; *The Theory of the Partisan*, Michigan State University Press, East Lansing, 2004.
15. Kautilya, *The Arthashasthra*, Penguin, New Delhi, 1992, p. 106.
16. Frantz Schurmann and Orville Schell, eds, *China Readings 3: Communist China*, Penguin, Harmondsworth, 1968; Mark Selden, ed., *The People's Republic of China*, Monthly Review Press, New York, 1979; Wilfred Burchett, *The China–Cambodia–Vietnam Triangle*, Zed Books, London, 1981.
17. Ronald Aronson, *The Dialectics of Disaster*, Verso, London, 1984.
18. Walter Kaufman and R. Hollingdale, Introduction to Fiedrich Nietzsche, *The Will to Power*, Vintage, New York, 1968; Karl Jaspers, *Nietzsche: An Introduction to the Understanding of his Philosophical Activity*, Johns Hopkins University Press, Baltimore, MD, 1998.
19. Vincent Descombes, *The Barometer of Modern Reason*, Oxford University Press, Oxford, 1993, p. 160.

A PERSONAL POSTSCRIPT

1   Eqbal Ahmed, *The Selected Writings of Eqbal Ahmed*, eds Carollee Bengelsdorf, Margaret Cerullo and Yogesh Chandrani, Columbia University Press, New York, 2006.
2. Dayan Jayatilleka, *Sri Lanka –The Travails of a Democracy: Unfinished War, Protracted Crisis*, Vikas, New Delhi, 1995.

Select Bibliography

Aronson, Ronald 1984 *Dialectics of Disaster* London: Verso Books.

—— 1995 *After Marxism* New York: The Guilford Press.

—— 2004 *Camus & Sartre* Chicago: University of Chicago Press.

Benwick, Robert and Green, Philip (eds) 1992 *The Routledge Dictionary of Twentieth Century Political Thinkers* London: Routledge.

Betto, Frei 1990 *Fidel & Religion: Conversations with Frei Betto* Melbourne: Ocean Press.

Blight, James and Brenner, Philip 2002 *Sad and Luminous Days: Cuba's Struggle with the Superpowers after the Missile Crisis* Oxford: Rowman and Littlefield Publishers Inc.

Bonachea, Ronaldo and Valdes, Nelson P. 1972 *Revolutionary Struggle 1947–1957: The Selected Works of Fidel Castro* Cambridge, MA: MIT Press.

Borge, Tomas 1992 *Face to Face with Fidel Castro: A Conversation* Melbourne: Ocean Press.

Bourne, Peter 1987 *Castro: A Biography of Fidel Castro* London: Macmillan.

Brenner, Phil, Rich, Donna et al. 1989 *The Cuba Reader* New York: Grove Press.

Camus, Albert 1991 *The Rebel* New York: Vintage International.

Castaneda, Jorge 1994 *Utopia Unarmed: The Latin American Left After the Cold War* New York: Vintage Books.

Castro, Fidel 1961 *History Will Absolve Me* New York: Lyle Stuart.

—— 1963 *Fidel Castro: This is our Line!* Havana: Ministry of Foreign Relations.

—— 1967 *Speech on 14th Anniversary of the Attack on the Moncada* Havana: Discursos, Instituto del Libro.

—— 1968 *A New Stage in the Advance of Cuban Socialism* New York: Merit Publishers.

—— 1981 *Fidel Castro Speeches: Cuba's Internationalist Foreign Policy 1975–80* New York: Pathfinder Press.

—— 1983 *Talks with US and French Journalists* La Habana: Editora Politica.

—— 1984 *War, Racism and Economic Injustice* Morant bay Jamaica: Maroon Publishing House.

—— 1985 *War and Crisis in the Americas* New York: Pathfinder Press.

—— 1986 *Nothing Can Stop the Course of History* New York: Pathfinder Press.

—— 1988 *The Extraordinary Feat of the Cuban Revolution* La Habana: Editora Politica.

—— 1989 *The Right to Dignity: Fidel Castro and the Non-Aligned Movement* Melbourne: Ocean Press.

—— 1989 *Socialism: The Science of Example* La Habana: Editorial Politica.

—— 1990 *US Hands off Middle East: Cuba Speaks Out at the United Nations* New York: Pathfinder Press.

—— 1992 *Can Cuba Survive?* Melbourne: Ocean Press.

—— 1993 *Tomorrow is Too Late* Melbourne: Ocean Press.

—— 1994 *Che: A Memoir* Melbourne: Ocean Press.

—— 1996 *Cuba at the Crossroads* Melbourne: Ocean Press.

—— 1998 *Fidel – My Early Years* Melbourne: Ocean Press.

—— 1998 *An Interview for NBC* La Habana: Editora Politica.

—— 2000 *Neoliberal Globalisation and the Third World* Chippendale NSW: Resistance Books.

—— 2003 *Cold War: Warnings for a Unipolar World* Melbourne: Ocean Press.

Coltman, Leycester 2003 *The Real Fidel Castro* New Haven: Yale University Press.

Debray, Regis 1973 *Strategy for Revolution* Harmondsworth: Penguin/ Pelican.

Dorschner, John and Fabricio, Roberto 1979 *The Winds of December* New York: Coward McCann & Geogehan.

Dreke, Victor 2002 *From the Escambray to the Congo* New York: Pathfinder Press.

Estrada, Ulises 2005 *Tania: Undercover with Che Guevara in Bolivia* Melbourne: Ocean Press.

Farber, Samuel 2006 *The Origins of the Cuban Revolution Reconsidered* Chapel Hill: University of North Carolina Press.

Galloway, George 2006 *Fidel Castro Handbook*, London: MQ Publications Ltd.

Gleijeses, Piero 2003 *Conflicting Missions: Havana, Washington, and Africa* Chapel Hill: University of North Carolina Press.

Gott, Richard 2004 *Cuba: A New History* New Haven and London: Yale University Press.

Guillermoprieto, Alma 2001 *Looking for History* New York: Random House.

Harnecker, Marta 1987 *Fidel Castro's Political Strategy: from Moncada to Victory* New York: Pathfinder Press.

Jacobson, Norman 1978 *The Functions and Limits of Political Theory* New York: Methuen.

Kane, John 2001 *The Politics of Moral Capital* Cambridge: Cambridge University Press.

Kenner, Martin and Petras, James (eds) 1969 *Fidel Castro Speaks* New York: Grove Press.

Latell, Brian 2002 *After Fidel* New York: Palgrave Macmillan.

Levine, Robert M. 2001 *Secret Missions to Cuba* New York: Palgrave Macmillan.

Liss, Sheldon B. 1994 *Fidel! Castro's Political and Social Thought* Boulder, CO: Westview Press.

Lockwood, Lee 1990 *Castro's Cuba, Cuba's Fidel* Boulder, CO: Westview Press.

Mandela, Nelson and Castro, Fidel 1991 *How Far We Slaves Have Come!* New York: Pathfinder Press.

Mankiewicz, Frank and Jones, Kirby 1975 *With Fidel: A Portrait of Castro and Cuba* Chicago: Playboy Press.

Marquez, Gabriel Garcia 1977 'Operation Carlota', *New Left Review* Feb.–April, Nos 101–102.

Martin, Lionel 1978 *The Early Fidel: Roots of Castro's Communism* Secaucus, NJ: L. Stuart.

Mencia, Mario 1993 *The Fertile Prison: Fidel Castro in Batista's Jails* Melbourne: Ocean Press.

Mina, Gianni 1991 *An Encounter with Fidel* Melbourne: Ocean Press.

Oltuski, Enrique 2002 *Vida Clandestina: My Life in the Cuban Revolution* San Francisco: John Wiley & Sons Ltd/Jossey Bass.

Pape, Robert 2005 *Dying To Win: The Strategic Logic of Suicide Terrorism* New York: Random House.

Quirk, Robert 1993 *Fidel Castro* New York: Norton.

Ramonet, Ignacio and Montaner, Carlos 2007 'Was Fidel Good For Cuba?', *Foreign Policy*, Jan.–Feb., pp. 56–64.

Rice, Donald E. 1992 *The Rhetorical Uses of the Authorizing Figure: Fidel Castro and Jose Marti* New York: Praeger.

Santamaria, Haydee 1980 *Moncada* Secaucus, NJ: Lyle Stuart Inc.

Santoni, Ronald E. 2003 *Sartre on Violence: Curiously Ambivalent* University Park: Pennsylvania State University Press.

Sartre, Jean-Paul 1961 *Sartre on Cuba* New York: Ballantine Books.

Skierka, Volker 2004 *Fidel Castro: A Biography* Malden, MA: Polity Press.

Smith, Wayne S. 1984 *Castro's Cuba: Soviet Partner or Non-Aligned?* Washington, DC: Woodrow Wilson Centre.

—— 1988 *Closest of Enemies: A Personal and Diplomatic Account of United States and Cuban Relations since 1957* New York: W.W. Norton & Co.

Stone, Elizabeth (ed.) 1981 *Women and the Cuban Revolution* New York: Pathfinder Press.

Sweig, Julia 2002 *Inside the Cuban Revolution: Fidel Castro and the Urban Underground* Cambridge, MA: Harvard University Press.

—— 2007 'Fidel's Final Victory', *Foreign Affairs*, Jan.–Feb.

Szulc, Tad 1986 *Fidel: A Critical Portrait* New York: William Morrow.

Taber, Michael 1981 *Fidel Castro Speeches* New York: Pathfinder Press.

Taber, Robert 1961 *M 26: Biography of a Revolution* New York: Lyle Stuart.

—— 1965 *The War of the Flea* New York: Lyle Stuart.

Villegas, Harry 1997 *At the Side of Che Guevara* New York: Pathfinder Press.

Waters, Mary Alice (ed.) 1989 *Fidel Castro: In Defence of Socialism* New York: Pathfinder Press.

Wilkerson, Loree A. R. 1965 *Fidel Castro's Political Programmes from Reformism to Marxism* Gainesville: University of Florida Press.

Index

Compiled by Sue Carlton